A history of the Isle of Man Fire Service

MANN
ABLAZE

Stan Basnett

Published by Lily Publications Ltd, PO Box 33, Ramsey, Isle of Man IM99 4LP
Tel: +44 (0) 1624 898446 Fax: +44 (0) 1624 898449 E-mail: sales@lilypublications.co.uk Website: www.lilypublications.co.uk

PREFACE

THE PREFACE to a book was something that I never used to read. Then, a little later, I would read it after I had completed the book.

Now it is the first thing I look at.

I hope that you find time to read my preface as it is really the only chance that the reader and writer have to get to know one another. Since the original version of this book was published I have been fortunate to have had a number of books published on various transport-related subjects and have held true to my views on the preface.

The desire to write a documentary on one of several subjects which interest me had been with me for a number of years. I had helped many friends with research and through my interest in photography had made more friends by providing illustrations for their books. The opportunity to fulfil at least part of my ambition came with the first edition of Mann Ablaze. Since then I have pretty well achieved all I set out to do.

Now the opportunity has presented itself for me to produce a second edition of Mann Ablaze and provide more illustrations drawing on Isle of Man Fire Service personnel who have been extremely helpful and supportive.

Why the Fire Service? Why the Isle of Man? The answer to the first question is very involved, but suffice to say that my interest started with a course in fire prevention as part of the Grand Prior badge with the St John Ambulance Brigade in my teens. Bert Kenna from the Douglas Fire Brigade was our instructor and it was he more than anyone who captured my interest. It stayed with me through my professional training to the point where at one time I wanted to become an insurance fire assessor. The answer to the second question is simple. As a Manxman I believe that any documentary of our way of life will broaden the foundation of our heritage.

While the book deals with the development of the Fire Service within the Island, it also parallels such development in many parts of rural England and I hope it will appeal to those outside the Island who are interested in the history of fire-fighting.

The development of the Service has quite properly, been founded on experience and I have tried to show how incidents which have occurred have led to legislation being passed in an effort to prevent their recurrence. In some instances, fires have highlighted the inadeqaucy of the equipment available and this in turn has led to the expansion of the Service and the continuous updating of equipment.

This is the theme of the book and to a large extent it is chronological, although I have tried to avoid it becoming too much of a list of facts and figures. It has also to some extent been something akin to a social history as a past way of life is revealed as we trace the development of fire-fighting through the years.

Throughout my research, two truths have come to the fore. Fire has nearly always been started by the careless use of the naked flame and death at fires is usually the result of suffocation through smoke inhalation.

Research is a most peculiar pastime, as I am sure anyone who has delved into archives will admit. While researching the history of the formation of the Douglas Brigade, I found that my great grandfather Claude Cannell, had been elected to the Town Commissioners in 1866, and this fact was confirmed by my mother. She shared an unusual Christian name with Claude Cannell's wife whose maiden name was McGhie. "Not by any chance the daughter of the brassfounder in Parade Street?", I asked.

"Yes, John McGhie," she affirmed, chastising me as if I should have known without asking!

So John McGhie, the mastermind behind the first fire engine owned by Douglas Town Council, was a distant relative; perhaps that is where my interest started. Who knows?

For this second edition of the book I have to mention the help given to me by all personnel that I have come in contact with but in particular Station Officer Alan Gawne of the IOM Fire & Rescue Service, Lindsay Armstrong, Rescue and Fire Services Manager and Watch Commander Nigel Rawlinson of the IOM Airport Fire and Rescue Service. For additional photographs and information I am indebted to former Deputy Chief Officer Bruce Kirkham, ADO Geoff Quayle and SubO Peter Killey; Leading Firefighters Justin McMullin, Roger Brown and Danny Dooley; and Firefighters Paul Rothwell, Trevor Moore and Brian Diehl. Several of those mentioned have corrected matters of fact together with Doug Drown of ROM-AN-AID. Finally to David Parsons for proof-reading the text, my wife Carol and my publisher Miles Cowsill - a big thank you.

Stan Basnett, Glenvine, Isle of Man

Title Page : A severe fire in 1980 gutted the former Howstrake Holiday Camp near Groudle. *(Author)*

CONTENTS

	Preface	2
1	The Beginnings	4
2	The Town Acts	10
3	The Local Government Act 1886	15
4	Defence of the Realm	25
5	War threatens	36
6	Towards one Service	45
7	Unity at last	56
8	The Service through the 1980s	66
9	Into the 21st century	73
10	Private Fire Brigades	88
	Appendices	101

Chapter 1 THE BEGINNINGS

THE **BEGINNINGS**
The arrival of the first fire engines on the Isle of Man

THE STORY of the Isle of Man Fire Service begins on Thursday, 20th October 1803, with the arrival of two fire engines by packet boat from Liverpool. They belonged to the Sun Fire Insurance Office and were immediately taken into the care of its Douglas agent, James Moore. However, any history of the Service must look at events in the preceding decades.

By 1707, legislation in England had placed a duty on the churchwardens of every parish to provide, maintain and repair a fire engine and other appliances. There was also a clear duty to provide fireplugs and a requirement for adjoining houses to have brick party-walls, but there was no such legislation on the Isle of Man.

Official records of the workings of the Manx Government were introduced by Sir John de Stanley soon after he obtained the patent of Henry IV which vested control of the Island in Stanley and his heirs. The Manx Statute Book commenced in 1417 and it will be referred to from time to time throughout the book as the formal obligation of protection of property from fire gradually evolves.

The High Bailiffs Act of 1777 introduced legislation which gave the Lieutenant Governor authority to appoint "...High Bailiffs for Castletown, Douglas, Peeltown and Ramsay (sic)...". The Act was intended to regulate the interior police of the Island and assist in the recovery of small debts. It also included a duty for the repair of streets and improvement of sanitary conditions in the various towns. The High Bailiffs were the administrators of the towns and they were soon to become involved in the problems associated with fighting

This photograph shows twelve of the thirteen men who made up the first fire brigade to be formed in Ramsey in 1887. Also depicted are examples of the type of equipment in use at that time, such as standpipes and the long copper branches or nozzles. Examples of this type of equipment from the Castletown Brigade are to be seen on display in the Manx National Museum at Douglas. *(IOMF&RS)*

outbreaks of fire.

In 1791 Sir Wadsworth Burke, the Attorney General, who lived at Newtown in Santon, wrote: "Till the commencement of the present century, the people appear to have been extremely illiterate and ignorant, incapable of forming, or comprehending an abstract scheme of civil government". It is against this contemporary description of the people of the Island that we start to see how they began to protect life and property from fire.

The fear of fire spreading was the prime consideration at this time; the saving of life was of secondary importance. Properties were built very close together, separated by narrow streets and common courtyards. An unchecked fire in one property could quickly spread and engulf a whole street.

The Island was fortunate because most of its buildings were made of stone, although straw thatch was more common than slate as a roof covering. Properties were remote in the country districts; if fire broke out the occupants had either to watch it burn or rely on limited supplies of water from wells or streams and, occasionally, help from neighbours. Townsfolk were in a better position, as there were more people ready to fight a fire — if only to stop it spreading to their own properties.

The earliest records of fire watching appear in the orders and duties of the soldiers at Castle Rushen and Peel Castle, which stated that "the nightbell be runge a little after sunsetting and that by the porter, and the constable with his deputie, with a sufficient guard, be in the castle for the safe keeping and defence of the same". Further, the porter was instructed to go about the walls and see that all was clear and that "every soldier, at the sound of the drum or ringing of the Allarum Bell, shall forthwith make his presence at the gate". Clearly, these men were disciplined, ready to meet any contingency, including fire, as is apparent in some of the early reports of fires.

There were barracks in Douglas in the early part of the 19th century and the same garrison orders applied. On Saturday 20th August 1803, the miller at the Nunnery Mill, just outside Douglas, left work and closed the door behind him. He did not know that barley, left to dry on the second floor, had begun to smoulder. The heat in the store built up overnight; at 8.30am on Sunday fire broke out. The miller sent a lad into town to raise the alarm. A number of active people soon assembled at the mill and managed to extinguish the blaze in two hours.

Contemporary reports do not specifically mention the militia's presence at this fire, but they do record that the fire engines had not yet arrived on the Island, having been detained at Liverpool by the Sun Fire Office for want of mechanics to complete their assembly.

Since 1801 the Sun Fire Office had been offering insurance in the Island, through its Douglas agent, at the rate of four shillings (20 pence) for every hundred pounds insured. It was through the demands of local subscribers that pressure was brought to bear on the Sun Fire Office in London with the result that two fire engines were sent to the Island in 1803.

There was still no organised fire brigade and the local agent relied on volunteers to man the engines whenever they were called out. People living in the out-of-town areas were still no better off, because of the time required to send word to Douglas and then drag the engine to the scene of the fire.

TROUBLE AT MILLS

The need for those outside Douglas to fend for themselves is well illustrated by events surrounding a fire at the mining village of Laxey, six miles north of Douglas, on Saturday 9th May 1804, when Brockbank's spinning mill caught light. Miners in a nearby pub quickly organised a bucket chain and managed to put the flames out before they reached the machines, though most of the stock was damaged. The fire had been started by a young boy employed at the mill, playing with a candle.

Bakehouses and mills presented a high fire risk through the very nature of their business. In February 1805 such a fire occurred in Oates Lane, Douglas, when an oven flue overheated and set fire to the thatch. The Manx Advertiser reported that "...although considerable alarm was at first created in the neighbourhood, we are happy to add that the fire was extinguished without doing more than unroofing the Bakehouse".

Two years later another fire broke out in a bakehouse, again setting fire to the thatch. This time there was considerable panic as a large quantity of gunpowder was kept in the ordnance storehouse nearby. The fire engine was brought to the scene of the fire and operated by the crowd while the militia moved the gunpowder. James Moore directed the helpers and got the fire under control, but not before the building was gutted and adjoining properties damaged. It was fortunate that the fire happened in the daytime; a fire at night would have proved disastrous.

Fire broke out again in the drying kiln at the Nunnery Mill on Friday 1st April 1808. Mr Hastings, the miller, discovered the blaze at about 2am and sent to Douglas for help. The alarm was raised by ringing the chapel bell and sounding the drum at the Barracks. Soldiers and townsfolk took the engines to the mill and prevented the fire from spreading to the rest of the mill although the kiln was gutted and grain stocks damaged. Men were still there in the afternoon removing smouldering grain, and they were rewarded for their efforts by two barrels of ale.

It is difficult to be certain of events that happened so long ago, but it would seem that one of the two engines which arrived at Douglas in 1803 was sent to Ramsey. The minutes of the Management Committee of the Sun Fire Office in London record that five guineas were spent on repairs to the engine at Ramsey in February 1806. Yet by 1808 both engines were back in Douglas.

A minute dated 21st February 1811 states "resolved that James Moore, agent of this office at Douglas in the Isle of Man, be allowed in future to charge in his account annually the sum of eight pounds for working and keeping the engine in good order and other expenses. Also that four Firemen's Badges of the common sort be forwarde to him".. James Moore selected four men, issued them with badges and put a man named Clarke in charge as foreman. It was the first

Chapter 1 THE BEGINNINGS

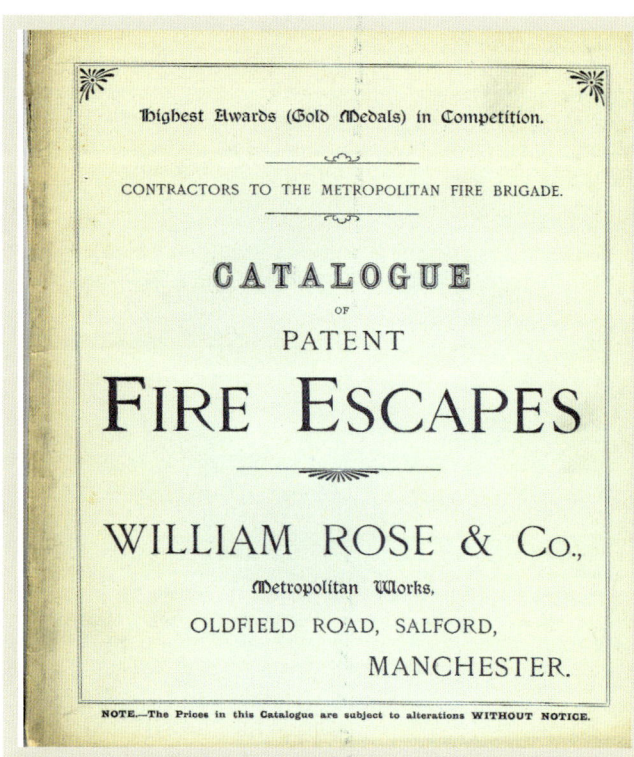

No photographs of the early Wheeled Escapes in use in Douglas have been found: however, the illustrations from the William Rose & Co catalogue of fire escapes does give a clear idea of what they were like. An "Improved Kingston" combination hose cart and fire escape was ordered by Douglas Corporation in 1895 and it was still in use during the Second World War. No records of it exist after the cessation of hostilities.

organised fire brigade on the Island.

These early engines were normally drawn by hand and could take water from a stream or pond. If such a supply were unavailable, the body of the engine — which acted as a cistern — could be filled from leather buckets passed by hand. The larger of the two engines at Douglas could be drawn by horse if required. The pump needed between sixteen and twenty men to operate it.

Not everybody was insured against fire, but this did not limit the use of the engine. Mr Leeson, a draper living above his premises in Lord Street, found this out to his cost when, at 7pm on Wednesday 27th December 1815, a servant's candle set fire to his bedroom curtains. The fire soon took a firm hold. On the first alarm, the chapel bell was rung, the drum beat to arms and a detachment of the Manks Volunteer Infantry was despatched from the Barracks. The fire engine was soon on the spot and "many gentlemen of respectability were actively employed in bringing water to the engine".

There was no mains water supply at this time; water had to be passed by leather bucket from the nearest well or other source. The Douglas Waterworks Act, which was to give the necessary power for the provision of a piped water supply, was not introduced until 1834.

The fire was fierce and threatened adjoining property. Mr Leeson's neighbours helped to remove most of his valuable stock, but his living accommodation was completely gutted by the time the fire was put out some three hours after it had started. Mr. Leeson had insured the building, but the policy had lapsed and his stock had not been insured.

During this period it was a common occurrence for candles to set fire to curtains and bed-drapes. For all but the very wealthy, a candle was the only source of light,

A similar fire occurred in January 1832 at Knockan House, a country farm belonging to a Mr Thompson. Mr Richmond and his family, friends of the Thompsons, were staying at Knockan House and, on New Year's Day, Mrs Richmond gave birth to twins. Three days later, Mrs Thompson was reading a letter to her by candlelight. The flame caught the flutings of the bed-curtains, which were instantly ablaze. Mrs Richmond leapt from the bed; she and the nurse carried the twins downstairs, while Mrs Thompson tried to beat out the flames with pillows. Mr Thompson, some distance away at the stables, rushed to the house and, with Mr Richmond and some farm labourers, organised a bucket chain from the pump in the yard. Fortunately the fire was out very quickly, but Mr Thompson's plight was typical of many in country districts; help was too far away to be of any use. If you were not quick and resourceful, there was little alternative but to stand and watch your property burn. Mr Thompson was also prudent in being insured by the Norwich Fire Office.

A fire of a different kind occurred in Douglas the following year. It was to test the town's fire-fighting resources to the limit; had it not been extinguished quickly, or at least contained, then a large part of the town would surely have been engulfed. The harbour was the heart of Douglas. Many merchants had fine homes fronting onto it, with warehouses close by and the houses of the town huddled tightly behind.

A bakehouse owned by a Mr T Kinrade and a joiner's

shop occupied by Mr N Moore adjoined one another in Queen Street, which led off the quay. These properties backed onto Mr W Stephen's property on the North Quay. At the other end, a narrow yard separated them from Forbes' warehouse, stocked with grain, tallow and spirits, and houses belonging to Mrs Dumbell and Mr Curphey. On Sunday 24th March 1833, at 7pm, someone in Mr Curphey's house saw flames coming from the roof of the joiner's shop. The flames, fanned by a strong north-east breeze, soon embraced the bakehouse. The alarm was raised and messengers sent for the Sun Insurance Company's engines. They were quickly on the spot, but flames were already beating against the adjoining houses and burning embers were being carried over the town by the wind.

His Honour Deemster Heywood was one of the first to arrive. He took charge, issuing instructions to the men working the engines, and Messrs Moore and Clarke of the Sun Office organised water carts between the harbour and the engines. A good water supply was obtained, despite it being nearly low water. Word spread rapidly through the town and into the various places of worship. Such was the panic that people were jammed in the doors of St Barnabas' Chapel, as they rushed to see if their properties were affected.

It was soon apparent that nothing could be done to save the bakehouse and joiner's shop, and so efforts were made to stop the fire spreading. Household furniture and personal belongings were removed from adjacent houses, but some of the several hundred onlookers were less than honest. The Chief Constable had a hard job to control them and stop them hindering the progress of the water carts. At 8.30pm the roof fell in and the firemen were able to gain better control of the blaze, Shortly after 9pm, the fire, which had been leaping across the yard by Forbes' warehouse, set light to a wooden downspout which in turn kindled the roof. Efforts were quickly directed onto it and by 9.30pm it was put out. Shortly afterwards the gutted remains of the bakehouse were damped down and the fire finally extinguished. Small fires on the roofs of nearby properties, started by flying embers, were put out by patrols carrying water buckets. Douglas had had a close call.

The fire was presumed to have been caused by sparks and burning soot falling from the flue of the bakehouse into the flue of the joiner's shop. Both were in the same stack and, in the manner of the period, separated by timber boards or "mid-feathers". The sparks ignited sawdust on the floor of the joiner's shop, which smouldered for some time before setting fire to the roof.

OUT IN THE COUNTRY

The following year, a number of country fires occurred where no help was available. In March, Gelling and Moore's new corn mill at Cregwillysill was completely destroyed by a fire which started in the drying kiln. June saw a serious fire at Ballakissack, in Santon, where the farmhouse was destroyed after bed-hangings caught fire. The next month, neighbours returning home from Arbory Fair found one of the houses at Ronague on fire and, with some difficulty, raised the inmates. Despite the number of people on the scene, the fire spread quickly to the thatched roof and then to the neighbouring house; both properties were gutted.

Thatched roofs were clearly a high fire risk, a risk made greater by the isolation of country properties. A woman by the name of Crellin, who lived in Ballaugh, left her son in the house while she went into the yard to pound gorse, used for dyeing wool. Unsupervised, the boy put more fuel, also gorse, on the fire. It flared up and set fire to more gorse stacked in the alcove of the hearth, and within minutes had spread to the thatched roof. The cottage was reduced to four bare walls.

On Sunday 14th January 1844, another fire occurred which further illustrated the problems faced in isolated country districts. It happened at King William's College, a private school for boys on the outskirts of Castletown. The fire started in the dining hall of the Principal's house. It was discovered at 3.30am, and immediate steps were taken to rescue the boys in the dormitory, but so fierce was the fire that the flames spread rapidly up the staircase, forcing some to retreat and escape by a communicating attic door through the Vice-Principal's house.

The fire was seen from Castle Rushen, about a mile and a half away, by the sentinel on guard duty and the alarm raised. A detachment of the Sixth (the King's) Liverpool Regiment turned out in double-quick time under the command of Captain Griffith and Lieutenant Staunton. They were almost the first on the scene and rendered prompt assistance in saving College property from the flames. A roll-call was taken and everyone was accounted for. Masters and boys then set about preventing the spread of fire by packing wet blankets at the doors and removing the intervening roof.

It was apparent that expert help was needed and so the Captain sent a courier to Douglas on horseback to summon the engines of the Sun Fire Office. The Governor of the Island was soon on the scene and he directed attempts to halt the fire, which was being fanned by a north-westerly gale, but it was to no avail. At 6am flames broke through the west door of the chapel and engulfed it. Half an hour later the whole of the College, except the Vice-Principal's house, was on fire and flames reached 125ft up the central tower.

Once word had reached Douglas, the engines immediately set off. However, because of frost and the slippery state of the roads they did not arrive at the school until 9am — five hours after the courier had left Castletown. The wind died down, enabling workmen to block up communicating doors between the schoolrooms. This, together with the efforts of the firemen, enabled the fire to be contained and eventually extinguished.

Once again the main problem facing the firefighters was an inadequate water supply, a well being the only source. The nearest fire-fighting appliances were at Douglas, a fact that highlighted the need for improved communication between the towns and the provision of more equipment. The College lost an irreplaceable library of books given by its founder, Bishop Wilson, together with most of its buildings. Damage amounted to £4,000, but it was insured for only £2,000 with the Sun Fire Office.

Chapter 1 THE BEGINNINGS

The fire was a sobering experience for all who witnessed it. The incident also reflected badly on Castletown which was, after all, the seat of government and capital of the Island. The matter was discussed between the Governor and the militia and in 1845 the garrison took delivery of a fire engine built by J Stone of Deptford.

Two years later, in Douglas, concern was being expressed at the inadequacy of the insurance engines in the event of fire in the town; this was at a time when communications between the towns were improving. Coaches left the Market Place every day for Castletown and Peel; the public could travel in the *John Bull* or the *Falcon* and return the same day. The coaches *Prince of Wales* and *Regulator* left Douglas on alternate days for Ramsey and returned the following day.

The year 1847 was particularly bad for mill fires. The worst one was at Peel: the windmill at Ballaquane was completely destroyed, there being no fire engine in the area.

In June of the same year a fire broke out in Mr Stowell's druggist's shop in Malew Street, Castletown. A young shop assistant was sent with a young girl to the cellar to get some oil. He took a candle but, being inquisitive, stopped to look in the bottles stored there. He opened a bottle of naphtha and the vapour ignited from the candle flame. The bottle exploded and both were injured. Fire immediately spread and clouds of black smoke filled the shop and the house. Mr Stowell's sister was on the third floor of the house and, on hearing the commotion; she panicked and tried to jump out of the window. A man ran through the smoke and rescued her. The boy and girl were dragged from the cellar and the alarm was raised at the Barracks. The garrison engine was soon on the spot. The floor was broken by the officer directing the soldiers, who played the hose through it and onto the fire. The engine was worked by the soldiers and, with the assistance of the inhabitants of the town, a bucket chain was formed between a public pump and the engine. The fire was eventually put out, but damage was considerable and the adjoining grocery and spirits shops had been endangered.

At 2am on Tuesday 27th September the following year, a fierce fire was discovered in the Fleetwood Hotel on the North Quay, Douglas. The guests were roused and the alarm given. The small engine belonging to the Sun Fire Office arrived but it proved totally inadequate against the fire, which was by now threatening adjoining property. Another machine, built privately by John McGhie, a Douglas brass-founder, was also brought to the fire and proved to be a powerful engine. It was manned by fishermen and marines from HMS *Torch*, moored in the harbour. After a lot of strenuous work the fire was put out.

SETTING SUN

The Sun engine was much criticised following this fire and people deplored the fact that the town did not have an efficient engine of its own. The era of the insurance brigades was clearly coming to an end.

A public meeting was called in Douglas Court House on 11th October 1848, by High Bailiff Quirk. The meeting resolved to purchase the Grampus engine, manufactured by Messrs McGhie, Teare and Lewthwaite, for £80, and to provide a further £50 for hose, buckets and branch-pipes. A committee was elected under the chairmanship of the High Bailiff to administer the engine and raise the necessary money by public subscription. The committee included Mr Dumbell and Messrs Bluett and Harris, both of whom later became High Bailiffs of Douglas. The Sun Fire Office was among the subscribers, donating £15 towards the cost of the new engine. On 2nd November, the insurance company sold their own engine for £5-19s-6d and donated the proceeds to the fund for maintaining the new engine, in the process ending the Sun Insurance Brigade in Douglas.

During the same month, the Grampus was purchased and housed in Lower Church Street below the Court House for the use of the town. The old engine was removed, having been found to be useless.

The last fire attended by the Sun Insurance Brigade was at the premises of Mr Qualtrough on the North Quay on 1st November. Water was again a problem and the turnkey, or waterman, did not arrive until after the fire was put out. It was the waterman who held the key to the fireplugs positioned around the town. The press urged that the alarm should be given to the waterman at the same time as, or even before, the firemen. The importance of this was realised later when duties were laid down for police constables in 1879. They had to know the position of all fireplugs and constables who had the officers of the waterworks living on their beat were instructed to give the alarm to the engineers or persons in charge of the waterworks before doing anything else.

The first fire attended by the new Douglas town engine was at Duke Street in December when a strong wind made conditions difficult. Unfortunately, the engine was slow in getting started because it was the first time a new hose had been used. Once it was in operation, the fire was soon under control.

The small Sun fire engine, sold in 1848, did not leave the Island. It was bought by the Moore family, who had been the Douglas agents of the Sun Fire Office from the outset, and it was used by them at their Tromode sailcloth works.

Fire broke out on 19th April 1856 at premises in Hanover Street, Douglas, used by William Kelly, a soap-boiler and tallow-chandler. It was discovered shortly after 2am and Chief Constable Sayle together with other constables, brought the fire engine from the Court House. There was some delay in getting water from the town mains, but once the engine was working it was put to good effect. The fire, however, continued to burn fiercely, being fed by the tallow in the works. Mr W F Moore, still the agent for the Sun Fire Office, heard of the fire and immediately sent his private engine from Tromode, coming down with his men to work it. Finding that nothing could be done to save the building, their efforts were directed at saving adjacent properties. A large warehouse opposite was in great danger; plaster on the gable of the building cracked with the heat, paint blistered and windows shattered. The fire was eventually extinguished at 6am. The premises were insured for £2,000 and the stock for £1,750 with the Sun Fire Office. It is interesting to note that the old Sun engine was still serviceable, although in private ownership, some eight years after it had been the centre of fierce criticism. Clearly this criticism had been directed at the larger of the two original engines, of which no further record exists.

Now it was the turn of the Grampus to give cause for concern. There was no one appointed to look after it and the only time it was taken out of the engine house was when it was needed for a fire. It was only then that the problems of neglect became apparent. The engine was in the care of the High Bailiff and, in his capacity as the town's administrator, he called a meeting of insurance agents and other interested people to inspect and repair it. The meeting was held in September 1856; by October, the engine had been repaired by John McGhie, one of those who originally built it. A hundred yards of 2½ flax hose in four lengths — complete with branches and couplings — were supplied by the Liverpool & London Insurance Company through their local agent, Mr H Johnson. The engine was thoroughly tested in front of the High Bailiff and found to be in first-class condition.

Though the engine continued to be used, the equipment began to show signs of neglect and the people who turned out with the engine did not always understand how it worked. This state of affairs was deplored in contemporary reports, which advocated a corporate body to manage the affairs of the town. This came about four years later, in 1860.

WHERE DOUGLAS LEADS...

Meanwhile, the other towns were in varying states of preparedness for fighting fire. Ramsey and Peel had no cover, while Castletown had the militia. Outbreaks of fire drew attention to this potentially perilous situation and highlighted the need for fire-fighting organisations which would be enabled by the various Town Acts.

The Sun Fire Office had spent money on repairs to their Ramsey engine in January 1827 and October 1831, but there are no references to the engine being there after 1850. Ramsey no longer had an engine, and the town made no efforts to provide one by public subscription.

In August 1856 there was a fire in Ramsey. It could have had very serious consequences and provoked criticism about the lack of a proper fire brigade. The fire broke out in Lane & Company's brewery; flames were seen coming out of the upper windows shortly after 10.30pm, when the alarm was quickly raised. Mr Bennett, Head Constable of Ramsey, was one of the first on the scene. He organised a bucket chain from a nearby public pump. Another bucket chain was set up from a well inside the brewery yard, but the flames, fanned by a strong breeze, soon gained the upper hand. Wind-borne embers soon threatened adjoining property. A wooden downspout on an adjacent house caught fire and was pulled down to stop the fire spreading. The police organised patrols to protect property and extinguish small roof fires.

The fire had started when a timber floor ignited from contact with an overheated boiler flue. Brewery employees, realising the fire was still under the boiler, fought their way in and drew the boiler fire. The boiler was glowing red and, fearing an explosion, workmen climbed to the top of the

The 60ft Shand Mason Curricle Wheeled Escape purchased by Ramsey Commissioners in 1895 survived in IOM Forestry Board ownership until the late 1980s. It is presently preserved by the IOMF&RS and is representative of the early Wheeled Escapes first used by the towns. *(Author)*

boiler and managed to lift the safety valve despite burning timbers from the roof falling about them. Their courage prevented a very serious explosion. The roof fell in at 2am, the fire eventually burning itself out two hours later.

Castletown still relied on military personnel for its cover, and they were in action at a fire in May 1857, attended by the Barracks' engine. Fires in Douglas in the same year showed up problems with the water supply. One fire occurred in Hill Street at Radcliffe's cabinet-maker's workshop. The alarm was raised shortly before 10pm. Chief Constable Sayle was quickly on the spot and the fire engine was brought up from Lower Church Street. The fire proved too fierce for the engine to have any effect, due to low pressure in the water mains. The building was gutted and the large number of helpers who had brought the engine were unable to assist.

The press carried criticism that the engine was not working properly for the want of one person to look after it and urged the need for a corporate body to look after the affairs of the town. Clearly it was time for the towns to become organised.

Chapter 2 THE TOWN ACTS

THE TOWN ACTS
Local authorities are given fire-fighting powers

THE FIRST LEGISLATION giving power to a local authority to spend money on fire-fighting apparatus was contained in the Douglas Town Act of 1860. In it the Commissioners were given the necessary means "to hire or purchase suitable premises wherein to keep fire engines, to purchase and support fire engines and all necessary appliances thereto, to appoint a fire brigade and determine their pay and charges".

The Douglas Town (Amendment) Act of 1864 extended these powers to enable the insurance companies to be charged for the services of the town's brigade and appliances attending fires at insured premises. There were provisions for apportioning costs where more than one company was involved, and means of recovering costs in the event of disputes. The Commissioners were also empowered to permit the fire engines to attend fires outside the town boundaries, and to charge for this service. For the first time, powers were given to constables and firemen to break in to properties thought to be on fire, without the consent of the owner, for the purpose of extinguishing fire and protection of chattels.

Hitherto Castletown had been the centre of government and ancient capital of the Island, but in 1862 Douglas became the administrative capital. These towns, together with Ramsey and Peel, were still the four principal centres of population.

Town Acts followed, for Ramsey in 1865 and for Castletown and Peel in 1884. They all incorporated powers similar to those in the Douglas Act. Legislation was also introduced in the same period to authorise the formation of water supply companies. It required these companies to provide fireplugs and to permit water to be taken free of charge at all times for fire-fighting. These water companies were later to provide hydrants of the "ball" variety.

Douglas Town Commissioners were the first to implement the provisions of their legislation. The first meeting of the newly-elected Commissioners was held in August 1860 at the Court House in Athol Street, where it was agreed that a brigade should be set up. The fire engine, it was decided, could be stored under the Commissioners' new offices in St Barnabas Square, which were to be rented from Samuel

The Douglas Brigade pose with their fourteen Manual Engine supplied to the Douglas Town Commissioners in 1884 by William Rose & Co. The location is unspecified but is likely to be at Hill's Brewery where the fire station was located at that time and before the new station was built at John Street. *(Author's collection)*

MANN ABLAZE

Harris. High Bailiff Bluett attended the meeting and informed the Commissioners that the fire engine, which had been purchased by public subscription in 1848, was still in his charge; he felt it proper that he should hand it over to their care.

The High Bailiff also attended the next meeting and told the Commissioners that he wanted the engine moved from the Court House, where it had been kept since its purchase. The Commissioners were anxious to take it into their charge, but had nowhere to keep it. The engine was temporarily housed in Callister's Yard at the west end of Athol Street and initially placed under the care of the Town Clerk. The Commissioners decided to form a brigade of some twenty to thirty men and to purchase a length of hose and a standpipe.

The Water Engineer was instructed to prepare a list of fireplugs on the fourteen mains serving the town. He produced a list of seventy-four plugs of which six were on the large mains. It was pointed out, however, that some plugs had been paved over and that their exact location was not known. These plugs had been provided under the provisions of the Douglas Waterworks Act 1834 and the Joint Stock Companies Act 1856. Chief Constable Sayle and the Town Clerk kept keys for these plugs.

The first properly-constituted fire brigade for Douglas was formed in 1871. Before this date the brigade consisted of men employed by the Commissioners and any volunteers that could be mustered. The engine and equipment were maintained by the overseer under the direction of the Town Clerk.

On the evening of Tuesday 5th January 1864, the Chairman of the Council, John Mylrea, interrupted a meeting with a report of a fire in a stable at Derby Castle. Charles Craine, the Town Clerk, and John Robertson, the overseer, immediately rushed out into St Barnabas Square to accompany the engine to the fire. The stable roof had fallen in by the time the fire brigade and the engine arrived, but contemporary reports tell us that the engine was used to throw water on the smouldering ruins. Captain Goldie and Inspector Sayle, together with other constables, controlled the crowd and helped to fight the fire.

Later in the month the Town Clerk was walking along the quay, as was the fashion, when he saw smoke pouring from the forepeak of the schooner *Jane and Agnes*, moored alongside. He quickly ran to the stores and brought the hose from the fire engine. With the help of passers-by, he connected it to the hydrant normally used for replenishing Steam Packet vessels. Members of the brigade were soon on the spot and broke through a bulkhead into the crew's quarters. After an hour they had extinguished the fire, which had been caused by a stove overheating.

So Douglas now had an efficient fire brigade under the charge of the Town Clerk. Tradesmen employed by the Council made up most of the retained brigade, their knowledge of the construction of buildings proving invaluable when dealing with fires,

The lower part of Douglas, huddled round the harbour, was densely populated; many houses were built back-to-back, with a common yard serving two or three properties. Others were built around a courtyard. In such circumstances, fire could be very hazardous, and the priority of these early firemen was to stop fires spreading. An incident later that year illustrates the point. Two brothers by the name of Kaye ran a dye and silk-processing works at the rear of a shop (owned by a Mr Johnson) in Duke Street. Fire was discovered at 10.30am on Monday 12th June. The alarm was raised and the fire brigade were soon at the scene with a hose. The men attached the hose to a plug in King Street, to the rear of the burning building. Helped by a good supply of water, the fire was prevented from spreading to nearby premises and the flames were extinguished in half an hour, but the three-storey building was gutted and the mangles, presses, washing machines and rollers, used for pressing shawls, were all destroyed. A horse stabled in the lower part of the building was rescued and two other horses owned by Mr Clague, the coal merchant, were moved from a stable in the lane opposite. The contents of the building were insured with the Provincial Fire Insurance Company but the building was not insured.

FEAR ON FOUR LEGS

The presence of animals, with a natural fear of fire, was another hazard for the firefighters. Nine horses were less fortunate when fire struck at Ballamoar, Patrick. Sparks from a portable steam engine used in threshing were thought to have set light to straw. The resulting fire spread through the stackyard and engulfed the adjacent buildings. The horses suffocated before they could be rescued, but twenty cattle were saved. The fire was fought by the owner and his farm-hands helped by the neighbours who were present for the threshing and the fire was contained. The prudent owner had insured his buildings and stock with the Royal Insurance Company.

Thomas Kinrade, of Ballafageen Michael, had an even more unfortunate experience. He went to Ramsey for the day on business; soon after he left a fire started in a haystack and quickly spread through the stackyard. The smoke alerted neighbours who ran to the farm and tackled the fire. Despite their strenuous efforts, the corn in the stackyard, valued at £300, was destroyed. Mr Kinrade discovered his loss on his return in the evening, it was made worse by the fact that he was not insured.

Ramsey received its Town Act in 1865 but it was no help to Daniel Kelly and William Corlett who were in partnership as joiners, millers, agricultural engineers and general dealers in Kirk Michael. Late in May 1866 their premises were destroyed by a fire which started in the sawmill and quickly spread to the tower of the windmill and the threshing mill. The machine shop, housing several partly-completed threshing machines and other agricultural implements, was soon engulfed. Fanned by a strong breeze the flames spread to timber stored in the yard to the rear of the cottages in Windmill Terrace. The villagers could do nothing to save the mill and so they set about trying to save their houses.

While they were busy at the cottages the fire leapt across the lane at the rear and set fire to outbuildings at the rear of the Post Office belonging to John Cameron. Efforts were

Chapter 2 THE TOWN ACTS

then directed at saving cattle housed in these outbuildings and in the confusion one cow perished before she could be reached. The spread of fire was eventually stopped by the continued efforts of the villagers. The mill was, however, completely burnt out. Damage was estimated at £1,000 but the owners were totally insured. The effect on the village was devastating as the yard was the principal employer.

An inquiry was held at Kirk Michael Court House on 14th June under the direction of R J Moore, High Bailiff of Peel. After hearing all the evidence, he found that the fire had been the result of arson, and that the motive was revenge. A public meeting at the Mitre Hotel in July opened a fund for Kelly and Corlett. The sum of £40 was immediately subscribed, a clear indication of the value of the firm as employers in the area.

In December 1865, Mr Blackwell, printer and bookseller, of Malew Street, Castletown, was preparing for a family Christmas with his family. He was getting out of bed when one of the servants roused the whole household, having discovered a fire in a child's bedroom. The alarm was raised and the fire engine and military personnel, commanded by Major E J Dickenson, were soon on the spot. By their efforts, and with the help of neighbours, the fire was confined to the upper storeys and extinguished but not without considerable damage to the shop and contents below.

Meanwhile the militia were having more to do with the affairs of the Island than with fighting fires. Major Dickenson wrote to the High Bailiff of Castletown and informed him that he had issued a district order preventing his troops from helping to fight fires outside the Barracks, and advising that their fire engine would not be used for fighting fire in the town or its neighbourhood. The High Bailiff immediately wrote to Governor Loch, informing him of the order, pleading that the only fire engine in the town was the one at the Barracks and asking him to bring pressure on the military to continue to provide a fire-fighting service.

Meanwhile in Douglas the Fire Brigade was now administered by the Lighting and Cleansing Committee of the Town Commissioners. They appointed a sub-committee made up of Messrs Brearey, McGhie and Craine to look into means of making the brigade more efficient. Among their recommendations were the purchase of a reel-cart and additional hose, the replacement of all fireplugs with proper hydrants and to an approach all insurance companies doing business in the town for an annual subscription towards the cost of maintaining the brigade. The Commissioners acted upon all the recommendations.

Early on the morning of Friday 27th July 1866, a fire was discovered in a shop occupied by Mr Moore, a baker. It was situated in Market Place and formed part of the Douglas Hotel. The alarm was immediately raised and messengers sent for the fire brigade; they soon arrived with the engine. When the shop door was forced open, the interior was found to be fiercely ablaze. The flames broke through the ceiling and into the hotel and so the brigade tried to contain the fire by tackling it from inside the hotel. Some of the firemen went into Mr. W Graham's earthenware shop next door and broke through the shop wall to get to the fire. After much strenuous effort, the fire was extinguished. However, the shop interior was gutted and an oyster stall, kept in the basement by John Cowley, was severely damaged. The property was, however, insured at the Western Fire Office.

Although the Douglas Brigade continued to function efficiently, the Governor Henry B Loch wrote in 1869 to Captain Goldie, the Head Constable, asking him to prepare a scheme for the formation of a full-time fire brigade for Douglas. Captain Goldie's reply on 16th March listed the number of fires over the previous three years and the monies paid by the insurance companies for the payment to firemen and the use of equipment:

1866	4 fires	total payments	£33-5s-6d
1867	3 fires	total payments	£22-6s-0d
1868	1 fire	total payments	£10-17s-0d

He also laid down his suggestions for the formation of a fire brigade: "In the event of the Fire Engine, hose etc being placed under the care of and being worked by the police constables I beg to make the following suggestions. That four active constables together with two-first class constables be employed as firemen. These men to have charge of the engine keeping same clean and in working order. One of them always to be on duty to provide for a fire at a moment's notice".

He went on to suggest an increase in pay and an insurance share-out for these men. The Governor replied promptly asking Captain Goldie to progress the matter with the Town Commissioners, but turned down the suggestion for an increase in pay on the grounds that the police already assisted at fires. By December 1869 the Governor authorised Captain Goldie to take charge of the fire engine and form a fire brigade for the town provided that the Commissioners pay an annual sum of £10 to the police together with any payments from the insurance companies.

Nothing came of this as far as the police were concerned and the Island never had a police brigade, although many towns in the British Isles did, even though the Commissioners had agreed in July to all the conditions and to contribute an annual sum of £20.

The Commissioners moved the engine and apparatus to their yard in Fort Street in November 1869, and put everything in a good state of repair. They fixed a revised charge of £5 for the use of the engine and hose, whether used separately or together. The positions of all plugs and hydrants were marked on walls. However, the state of the brigade was not good and this problem was to occupy much of the Committee's time during the next year. The outcome was the drawing-up of the first set of rules and regulations for the fire brigade.

On 12th May 1871, William Kewley, a mason by trade, was appointed the first Captain of the Douglas Fire Brigade.

Over the next few years the brigade functioned well, attending a number of serious fires; two of the most severe occurred in 1875. One gutted the entire coach-building establishment of Cringle & Fell, of Wellington Square. The brigade fought strenuously to contain the fire and stop it spreading to Curphey's grocery warehouse, next door. The

This photograph shows the horse-drawn fourteen Manual Pump outside the John Street Fire Station in 1901. The occasion is a parade to celebrate the Coronation of King Edward VII. The pump is decorated and there is a full complement of men with the Superintendent Richard O'Hara in the white helmet standing on the right. There is also a full complement of four black horses which indicates a special occasion as the usual problem facing the brigade when responding to a call was the difficulty of finding horses! *(Author's collection)*

other fire broke out in a paint workshop on Well Road Hill, belonging to Mr W Nicholson. The brigade arrived within twenty minutes but the flammable nature of the contents meant that little could be done to save the property.

Despite their ability, William Kewley was having difficulty keeping his men together. The reason was simple: they weren't getting paid! In fact, the men were owed a total of £56-9s-3d from various insurance companies for the services of the brigade. Matters came to a head in July when the Commissioners paid the men themselves and instituted proceedings for the recovery of the outstanding amounts. The same year the engine was moved from Fort Street to premises in Hill's old brewery for which a yearly rent of £6 was paid.

Fires in some of the taller houses of Douglas were giving concern to the Commissioners. In January 1877 the Lighting and Cleansing Committee recommended to the full Board that a 50ft wheeled fire escape be purchased. David Munroe, now the Head Constable, sent the Commissioners a copy of Merryweather's illustrated catalogue for their consideration. In June they bought a 50ft Clayton fire escape and fly-ladder, a double standpipe and a felt helmet for the Superintendent of the brigade.

A fire at Pulrose Mill demonstrated that the Grampus manual engine was getting old. It was both heavy and unreliable, and so a recommendation was made in September 1883 to buy a manual fire engine from William Rose & Company. The order, not placed until the following April, was for a 14-man, 18cwt engine, complete with suction mechanism and modern patent coupling delivery hose. The cost was £95.

On 14th July, William Kewley was told at about 11pm that there was a fire at Derby Castle. The brigade borrowed a horse from a Mr. Glashen and took the reel-cart to the fire. On arrival they found no water supply. The cart had to be taken up Burnt Mill Hill to Strathallan Park Road where there was a hydrant. The brigade laid out 400 yards of hose over the cliff to the fire, which was confined to gorse on the cliff face. It was 2am before the fire was out.

It is interesting to compare the names of the firemen who attended this blaze with the subsequent development of the brigade.

Superintendent: William Kewley. Firemen: Richard O'Hara, Mark Kelly, James Caugherty, William Moughtin, George Moughtin, Joseph Moughtin, Joseph Clarke, James Woods, Henry Sayle, Isaac Corlett and Daniel Clague.

The new engine arrived late in August 1884. It was successfully tested in Circular Road, throwing a jet of water over the Templar Hall, and was formally named "The Douglas". Its first active service should have been on 26th August, when there was another fire at Derby Castle. The blaze was discovered at 10pm by the manager who sent a messenger on horseback. Kewley got his men together at the engine house and made the new engine ready. He sent one of the men for a pair of horses and, after trying several places, he reported back that none could be found. Eventually, the brigade used Joseph Moughtin's van with one horse and took its hose and standpipes to the fire. This time the fire was more difficult to tackle and property was at risk. The fire on the cliff was not extinguished until 7am. It was the fifth call of the summer and arson was suspected.

Early in 1885 came the first instance of the Douglas Brigade operating outside the town, as permitted under the Town Act, when there was a fire at Peel. Peel had its Town Act, but it still had no fire brigade; it was to be five months before it was formed, hastened by this incident. At 6.30pm on Tuesday 13th January, a paraffin oil lamp was upset in an upper room of the Marine Hotel, one of the oldest hotels in Peel. Mrs Froy, the licensee's wife, was rescued by some of the men who were drinking in the bar. They raised the alarm and offered what help they could.

The Chief Constable of Peel, Mr Cringle, together with Constables Quirk, Clucas and Callan, was quickly on the spot. Seeing the threat to surrounding property and knowing there was no fire brigade or fire-fighting apparatus in Peel, Cringle immediately telegraphed for assistance from Douglas Fire Brigade. Meanwhile, several of the Peel Town Commissioners, Messrs Joughin, Mylchreest and Keig, organised men to contain the fire. Captain Quigley, of the Royal Naval Reserve, arrived with men from the Battery and gave assistance. The Douglas Brigade, under William Kewley, set off with the new engine and a full complement of men. When they arrived at Peel they found the hotel gutted, but still burning fiercely and threatening adjoining property. By 11.30pm, the fire was under control and it was out shortly afterwards.

This was the first example of Douglas providing cover under the requirements of the Town Act of 1864.

At the end of 1887 the Douglas Town Commissioners bought a new reel-cart, against a background of concern as to the brigade's efficiency. The Commissioners' Lighting and Cleansing Committee reported to the Board that the brigade's manual engine was in perfect order, the fire escape ladders and buckets were being painted, and the old hand-cart and reel-cart were to be repaired at once. They also requested an increase of three in the brigade strength. The report was referred back with the recommendation that further approaches should be made to the police to take over the fire brigade, but Colonel Paul rejected them, having sought advice from various counterparts in England. He also referred to the correspondence of 1881 and pointed out that, at that time, it was the Commissioners who could not agree to a take over of the fire brigade. The Commissioners had another try with the newly-appointed Head Constable, Colonel Freeth, in November 1888, but to no avail. The era of the police fire brigades was clearly over.

THE OUT OF TOWN BRIGADES

The newly-constituted Peel Commissioners held their first meeting on 15th May 1884, and immediately set about implementing the provisions of the Town Act, but it was the following January before any progress was made towards forming a fire brigade, with a quotation for a fully-equipped engine being obtained from Wm Rose & Sons of Manchester.

The engine, comprising just a hand-cart with two standpipes, two reels and 150 yards of hose, was purchased in June. Mr Joughin was the Chairman of the Fire Service Committee and he sought the advice of Captain Quigley, the man in charge of the Rocket Brigade, about forming a fire brigade. The new equipment was stored in the Rocket Brigade House and most of Captain Quigley's men duly formed the new brigade. William Kermode was appointed Captain, at an annual salary of £5, on 1st December 1885.

Castletown Commissioners met for the first time on 13th May 1884, and concerned themselves with improving the town's sanitation. As far as fire-fighting went, the town was somewhat spoilt, having enjoyed the protection provided by the military barracks. However, a fire in the town the following year led to Major Fitz-Herbert at the Barracks expressing concern that his men could not function properly as a fire brigade while they had to rely on their manual engine. He wrote to the Commissioners asking for a standpipe to be provided for use on the plugs in the town. When this was discussed with the Castletown Water Works Company, it emerged that the plugs were not adapted to take a standpipe.

The incident which had given rise to the Major's concern was a fire in Malew Street, at which the military had considerable difficulty maintaining a supply of water to their engine. Mr Wood who lived above his drapery shop discovered the fire about 10.30pm. The fire spread so rapidly that he and his family only just managed to escape. The alarm was raised, the engine was brought from the Barracks and the soldiers quickly brought water onto the fire. Adjoining property was threatened and the shutters and windows of houses on the opposite side of Malew Street were set alight. The soldiers, with the help of townspeople, continued to work the engine until 5am. Water was obtained from a fireplug in the street and supplemented by a bucket chain from a nearby well.

The premises were gutted and several houses damaged. It was the worst fire in Castletown since King William's College burnt down in 1844. Mr Wood's loss was assessed at £6,000 and the insurance was shared between Phoenix and Commercial Union. Houses belonging to Mr. Thompson and Mr. Crebbin were insured with the Isle of Man Insurance Company and the Alliance & Globe.

A dinner was given the following Monday to thank the soldiers and those who had helped fight the fire. In October, John Gilbert, Chairman of the Commissioners, called for the provision of an efficient fire engine for the town. The insurance companies were invited to subscribe towards the cost, but the matter was dropped when no financial help was forthcoming.

Although Ramsey had received its Town Act in 1865, it was nineteen years before the Town Commissioners provided a fire brigade. In February 1884 they opened negotiations with the insurance agents in the town, asking them if they would contribute towards the cost of equipment. The response was poor, with only the Isle of Man Insurance Company offering to put £20 towards the cost of the appliances, which was estimated at £50. A minute dated 3rd February 1885 states that it was resolved that the company would enjoy free use of the equipment. No further details of the equipment in use were recorded.

THE LOCAL GOVERNMENT ACT 1886
Double tragedy prompts new rules

THE PUBLIC HEALTH ACT of 1884 had incorporated many requirements for sanitation and health, and it was the responsibility of the Commissioners of the various districts of the Island to enforce them. It also repeated and amended some of the requirements of the various Town Acts. The authorities were kept busy removing pigs from houses, keeping infectious disease at bay and generally improving the living standards of the Islanders.

The amount of legislation was becoming unwieldy, however, and an Act was introduced to consolidate the various statutory provisions. Whereas previous legislation had given Commissioners the power, should they wish, to borrow money to buy fire-fighting equipment, the Local Government Act of 1886 made it compulsory for them to do so. Section 182 stated that "Commissioners shall within six months after the promulgation of this Act, purchase or provide such engines for extinguishing fire and such water buckets, pipes, hose and other appurtenances for such engines and such fire escapes and other implements for safety or use in case of fire". etc. The Act gave the firemaster the power of entry and to close streets. It was his duty to report back to the Commissioners who, in their turn, were given powers to recover costs.

This was the first mention of the provision of fire escapes and as far as the Island was concerned Douglas was the only authority complying with this requirement.

After their various attempts to interest the police in providing an efficient fire brigade for the town, the Douglas Town Commissioners were now faced with a statutory obligation. In January 1889 a sub-committee presented a report on the reorganisation of the Douglas Brigade, advising

The Douglas Brigade with their Merryweather "Greenwich Gem" horse-drawn fire engine bought new in 1909 for £320 by the Douglas Corporation. The likely location for the photograph is the Corporation yard in Lake Road. The pump was driven by a double-cylinder vertical engine operating at 120 pounds per square inch and although the appliance was intended to be drawn by three horses the Brigade preferred the use of two. *(Author's collection)*

Chapter 3 THE LOCAL GOVERNMENT ACT 1886

that a fire station should be established with a Superintendent permanently on call.

By 1890 Richard O'Hara had become Captain of the fire brigade. He lived in Queen Street, and it was there in October that year that he was to face the most difficult fire since his appointment. The fire broke out in a jam-preserving works in Thomas Cubbon's general grocery stores, which fronted onto the North Quay and backed onto Queen Street. The fire had a firm hold when the brigade arrived shortly after 2am and it was another four hours before it was under control. It penetrated an adjoining grain warehouse and the firemen had to fight the blaze from within the building as well as from the front and rear. The top three storeys of Mr Cubbon's building were completely gutted. Twenty-five tons of jams were destroyed and hams, meat and other groceries damaged by water. The adjoining premises suffered fire and smoke damage. The total loss was assessed at £2,400 - fortunately Mr. Cubbon was insured.

In September 1894, Mr Fielding, the Headmaster of Hanover Street School, was walking down Victoria Street in the early hours of a Sunday morning to meet his daughter from the boat. As he passed the drapery shop belonging to Kneen Bros he noticed that the whole of the shop was on fire. He ran to the police station and raised the alarm and Sergeant James Bell immediately called the fire brigade and ran to the premises. Inside sleeping above the shop were James and Joseph Kneen, their assistants Godfrey Green and Fred Cannell and their housekeeper Miss Corlett. Sgt. Bell blew his whistle to wake them but they could not get down as the staircase was on fire. James Kneen found a rope and assisted from below by Sgt. Bell they managed to escape although Miss Corlett was so frightened that she had to be forced out of the window. They lost all their belongings and the fire was so severe that Mr. Kneen's nightdress was burnt during his escape.

By the time Richard O'Hara arrived, flames were bursting out of the windows. A plate glass window in a shop across the street cracked with the heat, and the occupants of Cowin's bakery could not escape from above their shop as the flames reached across the side street to their only door. Mr O'Hara rescued them from the second-floor window using the fire escape.

Meanwhile the brigade were fighting the fire with a good supply of mains water. Mr O'Hara and Edward Corlett were directing water onto the fire from the wheeled escape when part of the side string of the ladder collapsed. They had to hold on to the remaining side until they could be rescued from this precarious position. The fire was under control by 5am; two hours later it was completely out. The damage to the premises which were insured with the Royal Insurance Co. amounted to £3,000.

The damaged fire escape was repaired and the newly-appointed Town Surveyor, Mr Taylor, indicated that protection from the weather was required for the fire appliances. He was instructed to make the necessary arrangements.

Following this fire, the Commissioners considered the recommendations of a sub-committee for provision of additional fire escapes for the town. In October 1894 they decided to buy a patent Improved Kingston 46ft fire escape and hose-cart for £55 and one patent Curricle 39ft fire escape for £36, from William Rose & Sons of Manchester, The equipment arrived in January on the Steam Packet steamer *Fenella* and was stored in the Villiers Yard until their street locations were decided.

The other escape, now repaired, had a reach of 45ft and an additional 10ft by using its fly ladder. It was stored with the other equipment in the new engine house in Thomas Moore's Livery Stables on the corner of Westmoreland Road and Circular Road. The committee also recommended the installation of street alarms for improving the arrangements for calling the brigade.

During 1895 there were a number of fires that vindicated the choice of Circular Road for the engine house. Mr O'Hara now lived in Circular Road and eight of his men lived within 100 yards of him. With a downhill run into town, the attendance times improved tremendously. There were still occasions, however, when the police had put the fire out before the brigade arrived. One such incident happened when fire was discovered at No.57 Derby Road. Superintendent Boyd and four Constables were quickly on the scene and soon had the fire extinguished. O'Hara was telephoned but the fire was out before the brigade arrived.

In August a fire was discovered at 2.30am in a tobacco factory in Seneschal Lane. The fire brigade were quickly on the scene and assisted by Sgt. Fayle and Constables Faragher, J. Kelly and R. Kelly. The fire was confined to the rear of the building, which was gutted and had to be demolished for the sake of safety.

Later that month, Sgt Corkish was on his walk (later known as a beat) when he saw smoke coming from the top storey of Mrs Butterfield's lodging-house in New Bond Street. His attempts to warn the landlady were met with abuse, and she slammed the door shut saying that the house was not on fire. By this time flames were coming from the upstairs windows; people living on the upper floors could not get down the staircase and were calling for help. The fire brigade came to their rescue with the reel-cart and the fire escape. People were rescued and the fire quickly put out. Burning bedding and clothing was thrown into the street and extinguished with buckets of water. The fire had been started when an old woman knocked over a candle and set fire to her bed. Though overcome by fumes, she was eventually revived with some difficulty.

DEATH FIRE BRINGS CHANGES

A fire on 13th September 1895 had tragic and far-reaching consequences. Sgt Fayle and Constable Faragher were walking down Victoria Road early in the morning when they smelled burning. Hearing screaming they ran to the corner of Broadway and saw that one of the boarding-houses in Sherwood Terrace was on fire with flames coming out of the roof. The policemen roused the house and were told that two servant girls slept in the attic. The officers ran upstairs but on the top landing were beaten back by flames. Constable Faragher was sent to raise the alarm and fetch the fire brigade. Half an hour later Supt O'Hara arrived with the reel-cart. The fire escape arrived shortly afterwards and was pitched against the building. Water was played on the fire, which had now spread to the adjoining building. With the fire subdued, the men could force their way into the attic bedrooms and put the fire out.

The two servant girls died in the fire. The inquest heard that their only means of escape was a trap door. It also found that the party-wall between the adjoining buildings had been reduced to a timber lath-and-plaster partition in the roof space; this had allowed the fire to spread to the neighbouring property. These two facts had important legal repercussions. Regulations were introduced to govern habitable rooms and byelaws were prepared to cover the design of new buildings.

The efficiency of the fire brigade was also questioned and George Taylor, Civil Engineer to the Town Commissioners, indicated at the inquest that a fire station was to be incorporated into the new municipal buildings, and so bring the brigade nearer the centre of the town. The wheeled escapes were also relocated, after the fire, to different parts of the town. The tallest escape was placed at the Villiers Yard, convenient for the highest buildings on the promenade. The 45ft escape was placed at the foot of Broadway and the smallest one was positioned in Kensington Road, to serve upper Douglas and the Bucks Road area.

Meanwhile, things began to happen in the village of Port Erin, a quiet place until the railway arrived in 1874. A breakwater was constructed, large hotels and boarding-houses were built and suddenly services were needed. To organise this, the Port Erin Sanitary Authority was formed in 1884, later becoming the Village Commissioners. In June 1896 they petitioned Tynwald for borrowing powers to purchase a fire escape and appliances. They were doubtless inspired by memories of an incident thirty years earlier, when there had been a very serious fire in outbuildings at the Falcon's Nest Hotel. Mr.Geary, the proprietor, sent a messenger to Castletown to summon help and soldiers under the command of Major Dickenson were dispatched with the Barracks engine. They arrived about 10pm, but it was 4am the following day before the fire was put out, due to the difficulty of getting water.

In March 1897 tenders were invited from Wm Rose & Company for the supply of suitable fire escapes. A 60ft Metropolitan Pattern escape was delivered in September at a cost of £91-4s and inscribed 'Port Erin Commissioners No.1'. William Harrison, who was employed by the Commissioners, was put in charge of it and, by 1903, a brigade of twelve men had been formed.

Port Erin continued to expand and the Commissioners kept improving the public services, providing new sewers and water mains. By 1914 the reservoirs serving the district proved inadequate and the Commissioners petitioned Tynwald for borrowing powers to take over and expand the water undertaking. This expansion had its effect on the fire brigade which had continued to function under Mr Harrison, relying mostly on his friends and fellow employees to assist as required. The escape had been kept in the Commissioners' yard and its condition was giving cause for concern. It was time for the brigade to be put on a proper footing.

In May a special meeting was held to discuss reorganisation and the purchase of additional equipment. After considering tenders from Shand Mason, H Simmis & Co and J H Newsham, the Commissioners agreed to buy a 45ft extending ladder and cart from Simmis at a cost of £72-9s. A letter was received five months later, in September, apologising for the non-delivery of the appliance due to pressure of work for the War Office. It eventually arrived on 8th December 1914.

In February a sub-committee under the chairmanship of J.J.McArd drew up a set of rules and charges after consultation with Peel, Ramsey and Castletown and these were adopted by the full Board. The new brigade which was appointed in March was made up of nine members, including the Captain who was to be retained at an annual fee of £2-10s. William Harrison was appointed Captain and the brigade members were G Costain, H Costain, J Costain, J Kelly, W Quilliam, A Cregeen and S Duke.

Port Erin now had an efficient brigade with a reasonable amount of equipment, including a wheeled escape and combined ladder-cart and implement van. They were concerned about the insurance of their brigade members against personal injury. They consulted with the other local authorities and terms were eventually agreed with the Commercial Union Assurance Co. at a premium cost per member of 5s. They are worth noting, as they were similar to those applying to Peel and Ramsey:

> £200 on the death of the insured
> £200 for the loss of both limbs or eyes
> £100 for the loss of one limb or eye
> 20s per week for total disablement
> 5s per week for partial disablement
> (weekly payments to be limited to 26 weeks
> for any one accident)

All was not well in Peel, however, as the entire brigade had resigned in January 1887. The problem centred on pay and equipment and the Captain was summoned to the next Commissioners' meeting for an explanation. His reasoning was accepted and he and the rest of the brigade were reinstated. The Commissioners ordered a new 30ft ladder together with spades, picks and four-and-a-half dozen buckets.

By 1890 the brigade was holding quarterly practices and functioning efficiently. The brigade members were William Kermode(Captain), R Callister, A Radcliffe, H Caine, T Kermode, J Kelly and T Quilliam.

The first record of attendance at a fire in Peel involved the premises of G B Kermode, cabinet-maker, in Market Street. The account for £7-17s was paid by the General and the Manchester Insurance Companies. Over the next two years the brigade negotiated increased rates for attendance and in July 1894 the Commissioners published the revised rates, charges and conditions of service. In the same month the Commissioners purchased a 40ft telescopic ladder and additional hose.

William Kermode resigned as Captain of the brigade in August 1895. Henry Quayle succeeded him, with Messrs

Chapter 3 THE LOCAL GOVERNMENT ACT 1886

Cowell, Wilson, Quirk, Jones and Thomas Watterson the members of the brigade. At the same time the Commissioners broke their ties with the Rocket Brigade and moved the fire-extinguishing equipment to Philip Clucas' store in Station Road.

At a little after 2am on 7th November 1896 the brigade were called to a fire at the Fenella Hotel at the foot of Peel Hill. It illustrated the widespread problem of low water pressure as the towns began to develop faster than the water companies could improve their services.

In the case of the Fenella Hotel fire, the brigade had to run their cart three-quarters of a mile to the blaze, but there followed another, more graphic, demonstration of the problem.

Peel was a small town and was the centre of the Island's herring industry, and houses rubbed shoulders with warehouses around the quay. Ships' chandlers and those engaged on net -and sail-making occupied the larger warehouses. Early in the morning of 6th July 1901, a warehouse belonging to William Teare, in Keown Lane, caught fire. It adjoined another warehouse belonging to John Keown and backed onto yet another owned by a Mr Higgins. PC Cornish discovered the fire and called the brigade who were quickly on the scene and connected up to a hydrant. Access was difficult through back yards and lanes, and the water pressure was so poor that the firemen could not get near enough for the jets to reach the flames through the fierce heat. The warehouse was ablaze from top to bottom and the brigade could do nothing except concentrate all their efforts on stopping the fire spreading. Henry Quayle was quick to enlist the help of bystanders to move flammable material from the adjoining warehouses; they took buckets and extinguished the many small fires started by flying embers.

In his report, the Captain of the brigade expressed his frustration at being unable to fight a fierce fire effectively because of the low water pressure.

Thomas Watterson succeeded Mr Quayle as Captain in December the same year. He continued the fight to improve pressure in the mains; the brigade had no pumps and relied on mains pressure to throw water any distance.

In March 1902 Mr Watterson received a call to a fire at the station refreshment rooms. Within minutes the brigade were at the fire. There was some delay in finding a hydrant and there was poor pressure, but the men were able to get straight to the seat of the fire, which was out within half an hour. Once again the building, which was gutted, was not insured but the fittings were with the Commercial Union. However, in his report to the Commissioners, Thomas Watterson complained again about the lack of pressure in the mains and the fact that hydrants had been covered by road metal. The Commissioners' Committee of Improvements, Finance and Fire Brigade acted and by 1904 the water company had made some improvement. With the co-operation of the company's turnkey, the brigade now had the ability to throw water over the houses on Marine Parade.

Subsequent reports reflect how efficiency increased with the improvement in mains pressure. For example, a straw fire in cowsheds at the rear of the Vicarage in April 1906 was quickly extinguished. Contrast this with problems outside the town when the brigade had been called two years earlier to a fire at Knockaloe Mooar, Patrick. The brigade ran some two miles to the farm with their hand-cart. When the men got there they could not use their hose as there was no piped water supply and they had no pump. Thomas Watterson reported: "We did all that was possible for us to do with our ladders and buckets until four in the morning". That was seven hours after the alarm had been raised. The building was gutted but the brigade had at least stopped the fire spreading to the farmhouse.

The brigade continued to operate out of their increasingly inadequate premises in Station Road — there was no facility for drying hose and it was difficult to get in and out with the ladder.

In 1912 the brigade were called to a fire in the Railway Hotel and, although it was quickly extinguished, some of the men were overcome by smoke. Thomas Watterson pressed the Commissioners to provide smoke helmets and two were subsequently bought from Eeds & Company, of Manchester.

RAMSEY FOLLOWS

Ramsey Commissioners were now under pressure to comply properly with the provisions of the Local Government Act. They elected a sub-committee of three under the chairmanship of Mr Cruickshank in 1887 to look into the whole matter and report back. This they did and, in June, the Commissioners bought from Wm Rose & Co a fire hand-cart, 25 yards of hose and two ladders to add to the equipment they already had. In October the Commissioners appointed Alfred Wall as Brigade Captain at £4 a year.

A portable fire brigade engine with 30ft of suction hose and 12ft of delivery hose was ordered from William Clague's ironmongery warehouse on East Quay. Uniforms, ladders, 150ft of canvas hose and a jumping sheet were also obtained. The brigade operated out of the old brewery until the completion of the proper station that was to be incorporated in a new Town Hall planned for Parliament Square.

Like their counterparts in Peel, Alfred Wall and his Chief Officer, William Boyd, were soon complaining bitterly about the lack of water pressure in many parts of Ramsey and the fact that some hydrants were set too deep for their standpipes, as well as requesting more hoses, helmets and boots.

Subsequently, the Commissioners bought a second-hand manual fire engine for £30 from Stourbridge Fire Brigade, Worcestershire. It was repainted and lettered at an additional cost of £10 and delivered in April 1888.

The brigade continued to function with the hand-cart and manual engine, dealing with the small number of fires that Ramsey had come to regard as normal. However, neither Ramsey nor Peel could help when a fire at Bishopscourt caused considerable damage to the main part of the building, illustrating that country districts were still very much on their own.

In 1895 a spate of fires in Ramsey, most of them in the built-up area of Maughold Street, led to disputes with the insurance companies as to apportionment of costs. One

Whenever a fire occurred in the country the inevitable result was total loss due to the difficulty the nearest brigade had in getting to the blaze. *(Author's collection)*

such argument with the Liverpool, London & Globe Insurance Company dragged on for months in respect of charges amounting to £5-16s for a service to No.6 Maughold Street.

The Commissioners' Lighting and Cleansing Committee, which now administered the brigade, recommended that a fire escape should be bought in the interests of public safety. A Shand Mason Curricle Escape was ordered in November 1895 at a cost of £69-7s, but it was to be almost six months before it arrived at Ramsey on the ss *Ellan Vannin*. The ladder, which could extend more than 60ft, comprised four sections, each of about 18ft. The lower two were braced externally and one slid within the other, whereas the top two were conventional. The whole assembly was carried on two large wheels and a hose-cart with room for branches and standpipe. The new escape was demonstrated to civic dignitaries and a large crowd of townsfolk at an unfinished property next to the Premier House on the North Promenade. Not only did it give access to a sixth-floor window, but also three firemen demonstrated the ladder's strength by climbing it in close order. Another man climbed the ladder as it stood clear of the building with two firemen holding the heel of the ladder.

Later the same year the Ramsey Brigade was called to a fire outside the town that underlined the sort of problems of communication and access that faced both the public and the fire service. George Morris was the tenant of the Slieau Lewaigue Hotel; on Sunday night 13th September 1896 he was sitting in the living room behind the bar and, taking a fit of sneezing, found he had no handkerchief. Taking an oil lamp he went upstairs to his bedroom which was above the bar, the lamp spluttered and flames shot up from it. He put it down and tried in vain to extinguish the flames. Suddenly it exploded and burning oil was spilt over the carpet and bedroom furnishings. The alarm was raised at once and Mr. Morris' family ran outside. It was about 10.30pm.

Mr. Kaneen, a neighbour, sent his son to summon the Ramsey Brigade. Meanwhile he and the Moores from Ballaberna gave what help they could, passing buckets of water upstairs to Mr Morris who was trying vainly to extinguish the fire. The burning oil was seeping through the floor into the public bar causing spirit bottles to explode, feeding the fire which now had a good hold on two floors at the west end of the building.

Kaneen's lad had run all the way to Ramsey and set off the alarm at Queen's Pier. The brigade turned out with the escape but on learning of the location of the fire two horses were obtained from Mr. Lindsey of Parliament Street and the brigade set off for the fire with the engine.

The hotel was at the top of a very steep hill two miles from Ramsey and the road was rutted. Hence the brigade arrived with some difficulty shortly after midnight — one and a half hours after the fire had broken out. The whole front of the building was found to be alight and part of the roof had fallen in. Captain Wall took the engine round the back of the building and positioned it alongside a small dub, or pond, fed by a stream. Two hoses were employed at once, but the water supply dried up just as the firemen were making some progress. The engine emptied the dub faster than the stream could fill it. By 2am the building was completely gutted and the brigade could do little more than damp down with the limited water available.

It is hard for us in the 21st century to comprehend the difficulty facing most people, particularly in country areas, in summoning help in the event of fire. The mobile phone could not even be imagined! They had to be self-sufficient and rely on help from neighbours. For many insurance was not even affordable. In this case, however, both the building and the contents were insured. The charges for the brigade's services amounted to £23-3s-6d.

The Lighting and Cleansing Committee took great pride in their brigade, but late in 1897 it was transferred to the newly-constituted Stables and Stores Committee under the chairmanship of Mr W T Crennell. He quickly asserted his authority and initiated the first of many surprise practices by

Even in the town and village districts the local fire brigade were often unable to save property due to insufficient water or equipment as this blaze in Peel illustrates. *(Author's collection)*

Chapter 3 THE LOCAL GOVERNMENT ACT 1886

pulling the alarm outside the station. The clerk timed the arrival of each fireman and a practice call was staged at Liverpool House on North Promenade. The police were the first to arrive six minutes after the call was initiated and several firemen shortly after. The average turnout time was ten minutes. The escape was pitched against the building twenty-seven minutes after the call and two minutes later hoses were playing on the building.

The continuing problem of water pressure became so severe that Captain Wall and Superintendent Boyd decided to test a number of hydrants in the town during February 1900. Pressure at Lezayre Mount, Windsor Road and St Olave's was found to be good and a ¾" jet was sent over the steeple of the church. Pressure in the lower part of the town was not so good and, on the South Promenade, it was only sufficient to throw a ¾" jet a distance of 10ft. With a ½" branch, water could barely reach the eaves of a two-storey house. The manual engine was connected up, but after half a minute it was starved of water. The matter was taken up with the Waterworks Company.

The Committee were also conscious of the fact that the Queen's Pier was a high fire risk, having timber decking and frequent ship calls. Accordingly, arrangements were made with the Isle of Man Harbour Commissioners to hold three practices a year on the pier.

Captain Wall retired in 1900 and the brigade carried on under the leadership of its Superintendent, William Boyd.

In June 1887, the question of providing suitable fire-extinguishing appliances for Castletown was again considered and quotations obtained by the Commissioners, who nonetheless voted against purchase. Instead, they instructed their Chairman, Mr J Mylchreest, to discuss with officers at the Barracks to what extent the engine there could be relied upon for the town's use.

By August 1890 the Commissioners had still not complied with the statutory requirement to provide a fire engine for the town and the matter had been drawn to their attention by a letter from the Chief Constable of Castletown. A meeting with the water company was hastily convened and agreement reached for the conversion of the seventeen existing fireplugs to ball hydrants and for an additional twenty such hydrants to be placed around the town.

At a special meeting of the Commissioners in August it was agreed to spend £50 on a hose and implement box, complete with tools and 450ft of hose, from Morris & Company; of Salford, also included were one Regent hand-pump (Government pattern) and one set of Morris telescopic ladders to reach 30ft. Premises were rented in the Union Hotel yard and Robert Clarke, the Town Clerk, was appointed Firemaster.

The Commissioners meanwhile sent a deputation to Captain Gore at the Barracks to ask if the military authorities would reconsider giving their services and allowing the use of their engine at any fire which might occur in the town, pending formation of the brigade and completion of the hydrant conversion. The Captain agreed, subject to their being allowed to connect the engine to the new hydrants and that the Commissioners paid for any damage to the soldiers' uniforms.

By April 1891 the town had been unable to raise a fire brigade despite having advertised for men. The Commissioners were obliged yet again to ask the military for assistance. Agreement was reached with Captain Ayde, the new Commanding Officer, that the military would provide a fire brigade for the town using the Commissioners' equipment or their own as required.

The same terms had to be agreed with each succeeding Commanding Officer. In 1893 Lieutenant Hawks, then in charge at the Barracks, asked for a key to the apparatus to avoid unnecessary delay in turnout. This was agreed to with the condition that the equipment should not be used for practice without the prior permission of the Town Clerk!

The following year the new officer-in-charge, Major Conran, sent an account for services to a fire in Laughton's stockyard in the town. Up to this time the Commissioners had enjoyed the services of the military free of charge. Now faced with a charge for their services they asked the Ramsey and Peel Commissioners for advice on how they dealt with charges and insurance claims, but in February 1896, the military authorities announced that personnel were being permanently removed from the town and that the Barracks were to close. Suddenly the Commissioners were faced with the problem of having to form their own fire brigade. A committee comprising Messrs Collister, Fell and Cannell was given the task. Necessity proved the mother of invention and a brigade, under the captaincy of John Cubbon, was ready to take over from the military on 14th February, the day after the troops' departure.

The manual engine in the Barracks dated from 1845; it had been left behind when the detachment of the North Lancashire Regiment left aboard the ss *Snaefell*. The Commissioners wrote to Colonel Hope, General Commanding Officer of the Western District at Chester, offering £10 for the engine, which had been made by J Stone & Company of Deptford. The offer was accepted in June and the brigade had their first practice with the engine in July.

In December the following year, a farm worker discovered a fire in the threshing mill and the adjoining barn at Ballaglonney Farm, Malew. A lad was sent three-quarters of a mile along the railway track to the station at Santon, where the Stationmaster telegraphed Castletown. It took the brigade an hour and a quarter to cover the five miles to Ballaglonney, with the engine often sinking in the mud and deep ruts on the climb out of Ballasalla. By the time it arrived, the mill and barn were gutted, but the brigade were at least able to stop burning embers, blown by the wind, from igniting other buildings. The damage amounted to £500, the building being insured with the Palatine Insurance Company. Following this fire the Streets Committee fitted shafts to the engine to allow for it to be more easily drawn by horse.

Towards the end of 1898 the fire station was moved to premises in Hope Street and responsibility for the brigade was transferred to the newly-formed Stores Committee. Various pieces of equipment were purchased between then and 1911 when the brigade was reorganised. The most important were a standpipe and new hose fitted with patent instantaneous couplings purchased in 1910 from John Morris & Sons. About the same time, the Commissioners opened negotiations to buy the old Barracks and drill ground, and took possession on 22nd January 1912.

TOURIST PRESSURES

Douglas was expanding rapidly as a Victorian watering place, and as the end of the 19th century approached the number of seasonal visitors was nearing half a million. Most of the town's large houses were used as lodgings and many streets were given over entirely to boarding-houses. The Loch Promenade was complete and the largest hotel on it was the Villiers. All these buildings, and the many large places of public entertainment, presented a formidable task for the Superintendent of the fire brigade, Richard O'Hara, and his men, with their manual engine, ladder-cart and street escapes.

The brigade were severely tested by a large fire in May 1898. Three young men walking along Duke Street in the early hours spotted flames on the ground floor of No. 55 and sounded the alarm at Villiers Corner. The brigade arrived at 2.30am with the reel-cart to find that the fire had taken a fierce hold. The young men who had raised the alarm had, with great presence of mind, run the wheeled escape up from Villiers Corner and had it ready for the brigade.

John Harvey and his niece were sleeping on the fourth floor of their house. Once awakened by Constable Ellison blowing his whistle they tried to make their way down the staircase, only to be beaten back by flames and smoke. Next door, Walter Halsall had been wakened by the commotion and was quick to see his neighbours' plight. He opened a third-floor window, shouted to Mr Harvey and helped the pair out of the landing window onto the outlet roof and into his house. He acted none too soon, for the flames quickly engulfed the building and the rescue, despite the best efforts of the young men, would have been too late. The brigade soon had two hoses in use at the front of the building. There was no access to the rear of the property from Duke Street Lane, so a third hose had to be brought through Mr Halsall's property and the fire fought from a small yard at the rear.

The heat of the fire was intense and soon the roof collapsed. Four large panes of glass were broken in Messrs. R C Cain's premises; other adjoining property was severely damaged and the brigade were hard pressed to contain the fire. By 4am, however, it was under control and extinguished shortly afterwards. All the premises were insured but with several companies which, together with the charges for the brigade, was to provide a headache for the insurance assessors.

The fire had been tackled by hose with a good pressure of water direct from the mains, the head for which was provided by the town reservoir located in Summerhill Glen.

THE TAR WORKS TRAGEDY

Shortly after 5pm on 28th December 1899, two apprentices were installing a new engine in the tar yard at Douglas Gas Works. One of the men borrowed a small moulder's lamp to soften some lead piping. As he walked past the ammonia tank, the naked flame ignited the vapour escaping from the vents. The tank exploded, lifting the 4ft-thick concrete top high into the air. This was followed quickly by a second explosion in the washers and a third in the pipes between the purifiers and the retort. The gas flared up in a tremendous fireball and the adjoining tall building housing the scrubber, a cast-iron cylinder surrounded with brick, exploded. Portions of this building flew across the harbour and landed in Quiggin's yard almost three-quarters of a mile away. A jet of gas from the damaged scrubber was burning freely, the flame rising to more than 100ft. A deafening roar could be heard all over the town. Gas works employees, working in great danger, had to close valves leading from the gasholders. The retorts were drawn and the escaping gas from the mains extinguished as, one by one, the valves were closed. As soon as the works were rendered safe, the fire brigade entered. The men extinguished the burning buildings and assisted with recovering the bodies of three men who had been killed.

A fire on Douglas Head in September 1900 highlighted some shortcomings of the brigade's equipment. The ability of the men, however, was not in doubt. The Warwick Tower Pavilion was an iron bird-cage-like structure 200ft high, with rotating observation lifts in which people rode. At its base was a boiler house and pay desk. There was a dance pavilion, amusement arcade and sideshows, all built in timber. The engine house for the revolving lifts was also housed in a timber match-boarded building.

Piermaster Target first observed the fire about 10pm, almost the same time as Mr Wallis of the Douglas Head Hotel who telephoned Captain O'Hara. The brigade arrived with the manual engine less than half an hour after the alarm. The building was a mass of flames, with oil and grease in the boiler house fuelling the fire. Water was, as ever, the real problem as the town main finished some distance lower down the road opposite the Fort Anne Hotel. Captain O'Hara first used the roof storage tanks of the Douglas Head Hotel as his water supply, while the manual engine was connected to the end plug of the main. The brigade commandeered extra help but, with the manual pump working under full pressure, it could not lift the water sufficiently to throw a jet on the fire. Captain O'Hara found a well serving the Fort Anne Hotel and got permission to draw from it. He was able to lift water half a mile to the fire using the manual engine. By this time the buildings were engulfed in flames reaching half-way up the tower. The lift counterweights, each weighing five tons, came crashing down from the top of the tower. The impact sent sparks and burning embers flying over the Douglas Head Hotel. The brigade concentrated their efforts on protecting the hotel, but the pavilion was gutted and the tower and lifts severely damaged.

Meanwhile, the new Town Hall had been built and opened at the beginning of May. The buildings included a fire station, which housed the manual engine and a ladder-cart. There was a parade room at the rear of the station where the uniforms were kept. The Clayton escape was kept at the Villiers Yard and the other two escapes remained at Broadway and Kensington Road. Covers were arranged for these escapes to protect them from the weather.

Chapter 3 THE LOCAL GOVERNMENT ACT 1886

The Secretary of the Fire Brigade was Stephen Caugherty, the son of the Turncock in the first brigade. He took issue with the Highway Committee, who now had responsibility for the brigade, on the question of insurance against injury or death to firemen on duty. This followed a serious accident to fireman Edward Skillicorn at a fire in Upper Church Street. The outcome was that Skillicorn was paid 7s-6d a week by the Corporation until his return to work, subsequently firemen were insured whilst attending fires.

FIRE UNDERGROUND

1900 was to end with a fire of a very different nature though with no loss of life.

Foxdale was a remote mining village in the parish of Patrick, six miles from Peel and eleven from Douglas. It was the centre of the Island's mining industry; twelve mines worked the productive lead veins which also yielded a high silver content. Christmas Day was the miners' only holiday. The mine buildings were quiet and only the watchmen were about. Shortly after daybreak, smoke was seen pouring from the top of Beckwith's shaft at the Old Flappy mine. The watchman raised the alarm and woke the Mine Captain; word soon spread around the village. Men rushed to the mine and assembled at the head of the shaft, concerned as much for their livelihood as for the investment of the owners. Remote from the towns and accustomed to fending for themselves, the miners formed teams and set about finding the seat of the fire. The first men to enter the mine were driven back at the 35-fathom level by the dense smoke.

The three principal shafts at Foxdale all connected at various levels. Captains Kitto, Lean and Collister took men down Bawdens and Potts shafts, securing each level as they went, until they reached the 170-fathom level. Here the fire was discovered, in a sump head in a cross-cut. Water was a problem as well as the heat, and only one man at a time could get in to fight the fire. Water was let down from a higher level and, by scooping it up in buckets and throwing it on the fire, the miners managed to contain the blaze in the one level, although it continued to burn for three days. Miners fought the fire in relays and many were overcome by smoke. They had to be carried 1,000ft up ladders by their colleagues to reach the surface.

Luck was on their side because on the third day the fire burnt through timber roof supports; the resulting rock fall smothered the flames. The fire had been caused by two men leaving their candles burning in their rush to get away on Christmas Eve.

In September 1902, a large fire at the Palace Pavilion in Douglas highlighted another problem for the Douglas Brigade to add to its difficulties with water pressure. The alarm was raised at about 2am and very soon the whole of the north gable of the huge ballroom was on fire. The seat of the fire was in the refreshment bar and it was thought to have started in a mineral water works at the rear of the Pavilion. Soon the roof was alight and fire broke out at both ends of the building. Water was eventually obtained from a hydrant near Empire Terrace, but the brigade were handicapped because their ladders could not reach the roof, 85ft above floor level. Eventually, a long ladder normally used for servicing the arc lamps was obtained and the men were able to make some impression on the blaze.

By 8am the fire was out - Supt O'Hara and his men had extinguished the fire. The damage was estimated at £3,000 to £5,000 but the building was insured with the Sun Fire Office.

In 1903 the brigade was again reorganised with a new set of rules being drawn up by the Town Clerk, Alexander Robertson, and the Borough Surveyor, A E Prescott. The brigade was styled "The Douglas Corporation Fire Brigade" and was placed under the control of the Highways, Sewering and Works Committee and the Borough Surveyor. Richard O'Hara was appointed Superintendent and Station Keeper and paid 30/- per week; William Pickett was made Captain on a retaining fee of £5 per annum. The National Telephone Co. installed a system of call-bells in the men's houses with a switchboard at the Fire Station.

BLAZE AT LAXEY

Just before midnight on Sunday 5th February 1905 William Kinrade woke up choking and found his bedroom full of smoke. His mother was the licensee of the Queen's Hotel and he lived there with his mother, his wife and the servants. He quickly raised the household and got them outside. His mother who had not been well was taken down the staircase with difficulty. By this time the flames were breaking through the floorboards of the bedrooms.

William Kinrade raised the alarm in the village and the Douglas Fire Brigade was called by telephone. Mr Kinrade and friends tried to salvage what they could, but the fire spread quickly and soon they could not get near the bar or any of the upstairs rooms. The brigade received the call shortly before 1 am. Supt O'Hara obtained horses and left with the Douglas for the fire. They arrived at Laxey at 2.30am and once again their first problem was lack of water. The engine had to be moved further down Rencell Hill to the river, where twelve Laxey men took the handles to help raise water to the fire. Their efforts were in vain; the fire had been too well established before the brigade arrived and they could do nothing to save the building. The local press carried leaders criticising the fact that Laxey had neither fire-fighting equipment nor mains water and this provoked calls for the establishment of fire cover at this important village, mid-way between Douglas and Ramsey.

Things were a little better in Port St Mary, a village in the south of the Island which had grown around a busy harbour with a healthy fishing and boat-building industry. Commissioners had been elected for the village district; they held their first meeting in April 1890. By 1900 the Rushen Water Works had some mains in the village and there were a number of hydrants. Two Commissioners were deputed to look into the question of fire-fighting and, in December, a hose and standpipe were bought. Agreement was eventually reached with the Chief Constable for the hose to be kept at the police station and they provided a box for it. Sgt. E H Corkill was quick to point out that there was no hydrant key and one was provided without delay.

A fire in Port Erin was attended by men from Port St Mary using the Commissioners' hose and they sent an account

MANN ABLAZE

for £3 to the Hand in Hand Insurance Society, The Royal and the London & Lancashire. The ensuing wrangle over payment was to go on for more than a year. The Commissioners considered forming a fire brigade in 1910 and asked the local police to supervise it, but nothing more came of the idea.

In Douglas, however, the fire brigade was being developed. Following strong representation from the fire brigade Superintendent, the street alarms were removed in 1908. Complaints were being heard yet again about the poor water pressure in certain parts of the town, making it impossible for the brigade to function effectively.

The Borough Surveyor understood Richard O'Hara's predicament and asked the Highways Committee to provide a new fire engine, additional hose and two Pompier ladders. The result was the purchase, in 1909, of a double-cylinder vertical Greenwich Gem fire engine from Merryweather & Company at a cost of £320. The Governor, Lord Raglan, gave his consent for the new engine to carry his name. The new steam engine was ready to be inspected by the full Douglas Council on Thursday, 4th March and was to take the form of a full-scale drill at the Villiers Hotel. Already the brigade had come up against snags: the engine was large and heavy and some of the town's streets were very narrow. It was designed to be hauled by three horses hitched abreast, but this presented difficulties when taking tight corners.

At at 3pm the new Merryweather steam engine was rolled out of John Street Station. Supt O'Hara was in charge of the brigade, but the machinery was under the direction of a representative from the manufacturers. Two horses from Gribbin's stables, normally employed on the Peel Road omnibus service, were yoked to the swingle trees and a lead horse to the pole in front of the other two, the fire was lit and the engine raced to the scene. A fine sweep was made into Prospect Hill and the Superintendent blew his whistle to clear the way. The hill was climbed at a hard gallop and the engine turned into Finch Road. It gathered speed going down the hill and, on turning into Church Road, had to swerve to avoid a slow-moving coal cart. The back end of the engine skidded sideways into the pavement, lurching over and throwing two firemen and the Merryweather engineer off against the steps and into the railings of the houses in Church Road.

The engine was brought to a halt and Richard O'Hara ran back to check on his men. One had a sprained wrist; the other had injured his hip and could scarcely walk. Merryweather's man had a nasty gash in his right arm, but the jolt had also thrown the fire out of the boiler. They got back on the engine and were quickly under way again, running at full gallop down the centre of the Promenade. As they pulled across to the Villiers, a timber cart failed to give way and the driver had to swerve again, bringing the engine to a stop with the lead horse on its haunches and in danger of being run over by the pole horses.

Despite the eventful journey, the rest of the exercise went perfectly. The horses were unhitched, the fire was re-lit and two hoses connected to a hydrant and led into a canvas reservoir into which the engine suction was put. In four minutes the boiler pressure had reached 20 lbs per square inch and after seven minutes a full pressure of 120 lbs was reached.

The demonstration proved that the new engine could deliver more water than the mains could supply. The brigade were able to become proficient in the use of their new engine before it saw use at a serious fire. This occurred at the site of its near disastrous skid on the first demonstration run.

The curate of St Thomas' Church was conducting the evening service on 11th February 1912, when he and members of the congregation smelled smoke. They thought no more about it, as fumes often came from the central heating boiler under the main part of the church. The organist, Mr Poulter, played the recessional hymn at 7.40pm and he too noticed a strong smell of burning wood. He assumed it was coming from outside. The Rev Robinson bade goodnight to his congregation and closed the main doors. Mrs Poulter joined her husband and was chatting to the sidesmen when they noticed that the burning smell was getting stronger. One of the men opened the door leading to the belfry; to his surprise and horror the whole of the belfry appeared to be on fire.

Mr Poulter and Mr Myerscough ran to the police station to raise the alarm. Some of the congregation talking outside the church looked up to see flames flickering through the louvres in the belfry, high in the tower above Church Street. Suddenly there was a tremendous crash as one of the bells plunged through the floor of the belfry. Burning debris blocked the staircase which people had made their way down just minutes earlier. The fire must have been smouldering on the floor above them during the service; it was the inrush of air when the main doors were opened that caused the belfry to burst into flames. They had all had a lucky escape. It was fifteen minutes before the fire brigade arrived. The first appliance to appear was the hand-cart, accompanied by six firemen. They connected a hose to a hydrant in Castle Street some distance from the church. The crowd which had gathered heckled the firemen, shouting at them to use a hydrant in Church Street that was right outside the church — but the firemen were right. They had seen the flames leaping out of the tower as they ran along Strand Street and knew that they would need a lot of water. They also knew that there was an eight-inch main in Castle Street and that the one in Church Street was only a three-inch main.

Within a few minutes a jet of water was being played up the tower, but the strong easterly wind fanned the water into spray before it could reach the belfry. Another hose was run into the church and a ladder taken from the ladder-cart, which was the next appliance to arrive, so that access could be gained to the gallery. From the gallery the firemen were able to direct water into the heart of the fire, in the ringing chamber below the belfry, but with little effect. They also played water on the back of the organ to stop the fire spreading into the church. Within half an hour another of the great bells came crashing down and wedged itself in the head of the stairway. It was glowing red-hot.

The men who had brought the ladder-cart ran to

Chapter 3 THE LOCAL GOVERNMENT ACT 1886

Broadway and brought the wheeled escape; it was pitched on the north side of the tower from Church Road. The escape was not long enough to reach the belfry and Fireman Crosby was standing on it when a roof-slate fell onto the escape below him. Supt O'Hara decided it was unsafe to use the escape and it was withdrawn. He put two men on the roof of the old vicarage; from here they could aim a jet into the louvres of the belfry.

Meanwhile concern was growing at the hospital, a quarter of a mile away at the top of Crellin's Hill. When the first bell crashed down it sent showers of sparks high in the air which were blown over the hospital. A hose was made ready and hospital staff, under the direction of Dr Lionel Wood, extinguished embers as they landed.

Shortly after 8.30pm the steam fire engine arrived, drawn by two horses. The boiler was lit to provide a head of steam. Hoses were connected but the wind was still turning the jets to a fine spray. The escape was brought back and pitched against the east side of the tower; from this position water from the steamer was poured on the fire, which was under control by 9.30pm.

One of the bells had fallen on the organ loft and efforts were made to stop the fire spreading into the main body of the church. The red-hot bell was igniting the tinder-dry timber of the organ faster than the firemen could cool it. The heat from the bell melted the lead gutter between the tower and the chancel roof, which led to another minor outbreak of fire about 10pm. The firemen, who were now able to get closer to the fire, stopped it spreading to the main roof but in the process caused further damage to the organ. The fire was the most difficult that the brigade had tackled; it was also the most spectacular. The sound of the bells crashing from the belfry, and the sparks shooting high in the air, soon attracted a large crowd.

The Douglas Brigade had a full turnout at this fire and all their equipment was in use. Three of the appliances belonging to the town were at the fire: a hand-cart (also known as the reel-cart, which carried hose, some tools, standpipes and a small 18ft folding ladder); a ladder-cart with two Pompier ladders and three scaling ladders; and the Merryweather steam fire engine. One of the three-wheeled escape ladders which were positioned around the town was also present.

The old manual engine was now redundant and M. F. Cottle, the Borough Surveyor, had written to Port St Mary Commissioners offering it to them. They wrote back declining the offer stating "..they did not require a fire engine at present". This was despite the problems they had in trying to form a brigade and the small amount of equipment they possessed.

In August the following year the Douglas men again found themselves at Laxey, to fight a fire at the Glen Gardens Pavilion. Within minutes of the brigade's assembly, the Captain, W J Pickett, procured a motor car. He took five men, some lengths of hose, a standpipe and some hand tools and left for Laxey. They arrived shortly after 1am, half an hour after receiving the alarm. The speed of turnout was commendable, but they were unable to do any useful work due to low pressure from the hydrants. The whole building, more than 100ft long and built of pitch pine, was one mass of flames. Captain Pickett realised there was little that could be done until the steam fire engine arrived, so he left his men to contain any spread of fire while he surveyed the area to find the best location for the engine. On arrival an hour later, the engine was taken through Corlett's Flour Mills into the gardens and placed beside an ornamental lake. With a good supply of water the fire was quickly brought under control. The pavilion, however, was totally destroyed, the damage amounting to £4,000. It was insured by the Commercial Union.

Another fire, in April 1914 at Government House, is of interest. It was discovered about 11pm by Lady Raglan, who noticed a smell of burning coming from the servants' quarters. She and Lord Raglan immediately roused the household. The fire was beneath the servants' quarters and the smoke caused some panic. A footman was overcome by smoke and had to be carried out by a manservant; a housemaid escaped through a window and down a ladder. The Government Property Trustees had installed hydrants and hose eight months previously. Lord Raglan soon had his staff organised and the alarm was raised.

The Douglas Fire Brigade received the call at 11.15pm and Captain Pickett left by car with ten men. On arrival they found the Governor's staff were holding the fire in check. However, it broke through into the roof and proved difficult to control; a gas explosion injured Firemen Quirk and Faragher. The fire was extinguished by 8am next day, but damage was considerable.

With the advent of the motor bus, the days of the horse bus were numbered. As a consequence Douglas Brigade now found it difficult to find horses for their steam fire engine. The Council deliberated at length on the matter and, having lost a number of tram horses for war purposes, eventually resolved to supply horses from their depot in Lake Yard whenever required.

The annual report for that year tells us that there were 24 calls, two of them outside the town. In an effort to improve the brigade's efficiency, the Council had authorised a night attendance at the fire station during the holiday season which increased the cost of the brigade to £350 for the year. This is interesting when viewed in the context of a meeting which had been held at Government Office on 20th April 1912, attended by the Government Secretary, Mr B E Sargeant, and representatives of all the local authorities. The purpose of the meeting had been to discuss a proposal to establish a professional fire brigade with two modern high-speed motor engines, stationed centrally to serve the whole Island. The villages and towns would retain only first-aid appliances. The fire brigade would be under the control of the Chief Constable and the whole scheme would be funded by an Island-wide penny rate. This would have produced an income of £1,650, which was considered sufficient to meet the expenses of a full-time brigade made up of a chief officer, second officer, two mechanics and eight firemen. The idea was clearly judged ahead of its time and rejected by the proud towns.

DEFENCE OF THE REALM
The Local Government Consolidation Act 1916

THE FIRE at Government House in the spring of 1914 had obliged the Governor and his family to move out until the damaged wing was rebuilt. They were accommodated by the Government Secretary, in whose residence they were living when war was declared in August.

The Defence of the Realm Regulations of the Imperial Government were adopted in the Isle of Man and the War Office immediately requested the Island to house alien prisoners. Emergency plans were drawn up involving the police, local authorities and fire brigades and, during October 1914, a Bill to consolidate all previous town and local government legislation was introduced in the House of Keys.

Cunningham's Holiday Camp in Douglas was requisitioned and converted into an internment camp for "enemy agents". By October 1914 a total of 3,300 men, mostly merchant seamen, were kept there, four to a tent.

The Island was at war and the presence of so many aliens made for an uneasy awareness of the world situation. The coast of the Island was being patrolled by an Admiralty yacht HMS *Dolores* manned by RNVR personnel. In August 1915 the yacht caught fire in Douglas harbour and despite the best efforts of the Douglas Brigade the vessel was burnt out. The Council had some difficulty in getting paid for their service but eventually settled for £7-16s.

Douglas lost a leading public figure on Sunday 23rd January 1916 when Richard O'Hara, the Superintendent of the fire brigade, died. Soon after his death, the alarm bell system for calling the brigade was transferred to the fire station and by June the system was centralised, with extensions in the Town Hall and the caretaker's flat.

Mr. T E Watterson, Captain of the Peel Brigade, with the horse-drawn manual fire engine which was built by Shand Mason & Co. and purchased second-hand by the Town Commissioners in 1921. It required twenty-two men to operate the pump handles which folded out on each side. Although intended to be horse-drawn the Brigade preferred to manhandle the pump through the narrow streets of Peel. *(Author's collection)*

Chapter 4 DEFENCE OF THE REALM

As the war progressed the Douglas Brigade found itself short of firemen attending drills and fires. It was found that the men were being called for military service with the Isle of Man Volunteers, principally on guard duty at the internment camps.

On 26th September 1916 the Island received its first air raid warning against an impending Zeppelin attack. The fire brigades went to their allotted posts, but the alert passed without incident.

The Local Government Consolidation Bill eventually became law on 5th July 1917, after two years of the disruption inevitable for those living on a small island on the periphery of a World War.

THE RISE OF KNOCKALOE

The Douglas camp was not the only, or indeed the largest, centre for internees. In 1914 the estate of Knockaloe, in the parish of Patrick, was requisitioned as an internment camp. Eventually it comprised 23 compounds, housing 1,000 men in each. By the end of 1915 its population was 26,000, including guards, engineers and civilian staff. A branch railway line was built to service the camp and to convey the internees who were brought to Peel by ship. The nearest fire brigade was at Peel and its equipment was one small hand-cart, a few buckets and ladder.

Notwithstanding the huge new population on their doorstep, the Peel Brigade continued in much the same way as before. In March 1916 they were called to a fire not far from the camp at Knockaloe Farm. The men ran with the hand-cart almost two miles to the farm, and managed to contain a fire in two haystacks and prevent it spreading to the farm buildings.

Knockaloe was outside the town district and the Commissioners had no scale of charges for this type of service. They met, fixed a special scale, and sent an account for £6-11s-6d to the Commercial Union Assurance Company through its agent, Mr E T Christian. The company refused to pay and a legal argument began.

Meanwhile, the brigade had bought additional lengths of hose, fitted with 2½"Morris couplings, from Keddaway & Company. Members were also issued with armbands. Further argument ensued with regard to charges at other fires and in March 1917 Messrs. T. Theodor Bowler & Co., fire assessors, made representation to the Commissioners urging them to reconsider their scale of charges. This they did the following month – upwards!

At the end of the war the internees left the Island. The camp at Knockaloe was dismantled and the materials put to new uses. Some of the hut sections were still in storage at Walter Quayle's sawmill in Mill Road, Peel, in September 1920 when the brigade were summoned to a fire in the yard early one morning. The huts, bought from the Government by Roberts & Armstrong of Belfast, were well ablaze. The intense heat made it the worst fire the Peel men had tackled. Their limited resources were severely tested as the fire spread to adjoining property; concern was even expressed for the safety of the gas works. Members of the brigade were sent to extinguish burning embers falling near the gasholders. The fire was eventually brought under control but, as dawn broke, the extent of the damage was seen to be considerable.

Later the same year the brigade found themselves called to another farm fire outside the town boundary, this time at Shenvalley farm, Patrick. Knowing the difficulty in obtaining water in this area they only took buckets and hand appliances. On arrival they enlisted as much local help as they could and organised a bucket chain from a well. Altogether a total of twety-two men fought the fire in a two-storey cow shed, putting it out after two and a half hours despite the lack of a good water supply.

In his report, Thomas Watterson requested the Commissioners to provide a manual pump if they wanted the men to keep attending fires outside the town boundary, where water could only be drawn from wells or streams. The Commissioners did not act on the report and seemed unaware that their brigade had been tested to the limit on a number of occasions. The Local Government Board, however, were more aware of the situation. On 21st January 1921 they held a public inquiry that resulted in a reprimand for the Peel Commissioners for not enforcing their theatre regulations properly. They were also told to provide a fire engine, as required under Clause 271 of the Consolidation Act, and given three months to comply. The Commissioners lost no time in obtaining quotations for an engine. They eventually accepted a quotation from Shand Mason & Co. for a second-hand London Brigade-pattern manual fire engine, fully reconditioned, for the sum of £135.

The engine was a manual pump with two 6" gun-metal barrels fixed in a hardwood cistern with side lockers, hose and suction, designed to be operated by 22 men, It was intended to be hauled by a sway bar and pole with two horses. However, shortly after its delivery in June 1921, the brigade acquired drag ropes to allow it to be pulled by twenty men, it being found quicker to manhandle the engine within the narrow streets of the town. On the first practice the engine threw a jet of water to a height of 120ft and was found to be entirely satisfactory. It was kept in the Commissioners' new yard at Boilley Spittal. The hose and ladder-cart were also retained. The Brigade Captain's retainer was increased to £10 per annum and the brigade strength went up to twelve.

In 1932 W. Oates was appointed Sub-Captain of the Brigade. Little change took place until 1939 when the Commissioners were informed that it was the intention of the Local Government Board to submit a proposal to Tynwald, when discussing the Local Government Fires Bill, for sufficient money to be allocated for the purchase of a Fordson fire brigade tender and trailer pump.

SOUTHERN CHANGE

The Commissioners at Castletown had drawn up a set of theatre regulations in 1912, They set about enforcing their provisions, having acquired the redundant barracks and moved in their two appliances. On the introduction of the new legislation, the Commissioners reviewed their equipment and satisfied themselves that they had adequate fire-fighting appliances. They considered the addition of a ladder but deferred its purchase.

A further review of the brigade was made in 1920 following a conference in Douglas which looked at the whole question of fire-fighting throughout the Island. The conference prompted the Commissioners to decide that their brigade should comprise younger men; they were concerned that interest in the brigade among its men was waning. On 23rd March 1921 the old brigade was therefore disbanded and a new one appointed, with James Kneale as Captain. Following his death, in May 1928, Thomas Corkill was appointed Captain. His several requests to the Commissioners resulted in the purchase of an additional 100 yards of hose, chemical extinguishers for oil fires and a 40ft Ajax extension ladder. In the closed position the ladder was 24ft long and the fire station had to be altered to accommodate it. In 1932 the position of Sub-Captain to the brigade was created and W Oates appointed.

There were few further changes in Castletown until 1939 when the Local Government Board advised the Commissioners that they intended to allocate funds to the town, under the Local Government Fires Bill, which was before Tynwald, for a Fordson fire brigade tender and trailer pump similar to that proposed for Peel.

Meanwhile, the Local Government Board had also become aware of declining standards at Port Erin and reminded the Commissioners in 1927 of their statutory duty. The Commissioners quickly recommended the appointment of a new eight-strong brigade with a Captain on an annual retaining fee of £8. They appointed Police Constable A Corris as Captain, subject to his Chief Constable's and the Government Secretary's approval. PC Corris took charge of the brigade in July but was deprived of his retainer on account of his police position.

After two practices, the Captain requested the purchase of four extra lengths of hose and miscellaneous hand equipment including two Pompier ladder-belts. He also reported that a number of hydrants had been covered over and should be exposed and marked by hydrant plates. The Commissioners agreed to both requests. Their wheeled escape, which had been kept in the open in the Commissioners' yard at the Lower Rowan, was found to be in need of repair. It was stripped down, repaired and repainted and made suitable for brigade use.

In 1934 the brigade moved into new premises which backed onto the police station. They had been converted from the redundant laundry of the Falcon's Nest Hotel with the agreement of the owners, Messrs Manningtons Ltd.

The brigade saw action at two more major fires in 1936, at the Bay Hotel and the Imperial. The new Captain, PC Lace, complained that mains pressure on the lower promenade was poor; at the Bay Hotel fire the hoses could not even reach the windows on the second floor. The Commissioners had been considering improvements to the brigade appliances and these fires prompted the immediate installation of alarm bells. They also discussed the acquisition of a new motor tender.

At the same rime Port St Mary Commissioners suggested the two authorities should form a joint brigade, but Port Erin

The fire at the Laxey Flour Mills in 1921 showing the extent of the fire damage to the roof and upper floors of the mill building. The Laxey Brigade are on the left of the picture while the Douglas Brigade were tackling the blaze at the rear but the delay in getting their horse-drawn engine to Laxey meant there was little that could be done to save the building. *(Manx Museum)*

Chapter 4 DEFENCE OF THE REALM

deemed the approach premature. PC Lace was transferred to St John's in due course. Following a well-established pattern, PC Arthur Corrin was appointed Captain of the brigade in 1937.

Renewed approaches by the Port St Mary Commissioners coincided with moves by the Local Government Board to introduce new legislation. A number of meetings were held and the Rushen Fire Protection Order, 1938, made by the Local Government Board, saw the amalgamation of the two village districts and parish of Rushen for the purposes of fire protection.

The Rushen Joint Fire Protection Board was established under the chairmanship of Mr J Keggin, by an order approved by Tynwald in January 1939. It was financed by a rate levy of 1½d in the £1.

The brigade at Port Erin continued under PC Cowin, but with only the old wheeled escape and hand-cart. Port St Mary still had the canvas fire hose in the box at the police station, and a hand-cart that had been bought in 1922 along with standpipes and hose.

Port St Mary appears to have shared Port Erin's difficulties in raising a fire brigade, and was the last important community on the Island to do so. In 1935 the Commissioners' Fire Committee, comprising Messrs Maddrell, Quayle and Kneen were informed that James Cubbon, the Superintendent, was finding it difficult to hold practices. By November 1936, however, things had improved and James Crebbin had become Superintendent of a newly-formed six-strong brigade, comprising also W L Kinley, W Kneen, James Hislop, C Faragher and James Oliver.

The last time the Port St Mary Brigade attended a fire was Easter 1937 at a property in High Street, owned by a Mr Roberts of Glendown. It was obvious that new equipment was needed for the area. It was not surprising that the new Joint Board made application to Tynwald in March 1939 to borrow £700 for a new motor appliance in the south of the Island.

THE PALACE BLAZE

The new legislation had not affected Douglas: the town had an efficient brigade and operated a reel-cart, ladder-cart, manual engine, several wheeled escapes and the steam engine, yet on 13th July 1920 the brigade were tested to their limit by another major fire at the Palace Ballroom. The ballroom had been rebuilt after a fire in 1902 and was now one of the finest in Europe. It had a beautiful parquet floor, and a large stage with dressing rooms and orchestra accommodation. It was connected by a corridor and vestibules to the Palace Coliseum and Opera House.

The alarm was first raised when a seal-keeper at the Coliseum was woken at about 3am by the barking of his seals. The fire had started in the band-room at the rear of the ballroom and had a firm grip before the alarm was given. When the brigade arrived, shortly before 4am, the whole of the building was on fire and flames were breaking through the roof. It was clear the ballroom could not be saved and the brigade concentrated on stopping the fire spreading. The men demolished the connecting corridors between the ballroom and the Coliseum and brought hoses through to contain the fire. The roof collapsed and sent flames and burning embers 150ft in the air, threatening property in Palace Road. By 6am the fire was under control, but the Palace was completely gutted. The brigade stayed in

Ramsey Fire Brigade pictured outside the Town Hall with their new Merryweather 30hp appliance which was the second motor-driven appliance to arrive on the Island. It was named Richdale after the Chairman of the Town Commissioners Mr J N Richdale who is in the centre of the photograph on the front row with Mr J Smith, the Brigade's Chief Officer. *(IOMF&RS)*

The Ramsey Fire Brigade's motor-driven Merryweather fire engine Richdale. It was chain-driven by a 30hp petrol engine which also drove the Merryweather Hatfield 400 gallons per minute pump which could deliver through two branches at 140 pounds per square inch. Water could be drawn from the mains or from a water source by 4 inch suction. *(IOMF&RS)*

attendance all day, putting out the smouldering remains. Damage was estimated at £50,000 with no more than two gables and some sidewalls left standing. The Coliseum had suffered only minor damage and most of that was from leaking couplings on the hoses that had been run through to stop the fire spreading.

The Island felt the loss of this splendid tourist amenity very deeply. Although the Douglas Brigade were praised for their efforts, the men felt frustrated that it had taken an hour from the receipt of the first call to get to the scene of the fire, a distance of just one and a half miles.

The station was manned at night during the summer season and W Pickett was employed full-time as Brigade Captain. His responsibilities included the upkeep of the appliances and weekly tests on the street alarms and call-bells. He was conscious of these responsibilities in a town whose population more than doubled in the holiday season. He felt the need for a quicker response, and so urged the Council to consider permanent horsing for the appliances. The matter was debated at great length but in the end the Council resolved that horses would be provided from the Corporation Works Department in Lake Road, more than half a mile from the station. This hardly represented an improvement on existing arrangements.

To overcome the inevitable delay in turnout time, the brigade had developed the practice of using a motor car from the Athol Garage, which was close to the station, and sending four or five men to a fire, ahead of the appliances (as in the case of the Laxey Glen Pavilion blaze). Very often these men had extinguished the fire before the arrival of the horse-drawn pumps.

A fire requiring major pumping facilities outside the town limits was an even bigger problem, as the brigade again found at Laxey on 5th January 1921 when fire broke out at J. Corlett & Sons' flour mill. The fire started shortly after noon and developed amazingly quickly. The company clerk, George Quayle, had to leave without the books or the contents of the safe. Men had to run from the building as the fire spread up the natural flues provided by the wooden grain chutes which passed between the floors.

There was modern fire-fighting equipment on the premises and workmen connected their hoses to hydrants fed from the cistern on top of the building. They made a brave attempt to fight the fire but were quickly beaten back by the heat. The Laxey Fire Brigade, which had only recently been formed, were soon on the scene. However, they only had hose and branches, relying entirely on hydrant pressure. The men were powerless to do anything — the whole mill was on fire and the roof collapsed shortly after their arrival, sending flames higher than the mill chimney.

At 1pm word was sent to Douglas for urgent assistance. Mr Pickett obtained a car from the Athol Garage, throwing in

Chapter 4 DEFENCE OF THE REALM

The Douglas Corporation 90hp Merryweather petrol-engined Major Pump appliance based on an Albion chassis photographed when new in 1936. It carried 40 gallons of water and a first-aid hose reel, a 45ft extension ladder and a 400 gallons per minute Merryweather Hatfield pump. *(Author's collection)*

several lengths of hose and other equipment before setting off with some of the brigade. They arrived within twenty minutes, by which time it was obvious that the mill could not be saved. They turned their attention to the burning roof of the adjoining screen house. Their efforts undoubtedly saved this building from destruction.

The Laxey men continued to play water on the main mill building until the steam fire engine arrived from Douglas. No time had been lost in procuring two horses, but it was fifteen minutes before they were harnessed up and under way with six firemen. The horses were worked hard and it took an hour and a quarter to travel the seven hilly miles to Laxey. They arrived at 2.30pm and steam was raised in twenty minutes. There was some difficulty at first with the suction valve and there was a deep lift from the river. After a few minutes full suction was obtained and a considerable quantity of water was thrown onto the fire, which had by this time been burning for more than two hours. The engine was later moved to the rear of the mill and the firemen prevented the fire spreading to the engine house. The fire in the main building was brought under control shortly afterwards.

The roof and all the floors of the main building had collapsed, together with machinery. As men from the mill attempted to clear away the debris, smouldering timber continued to flare up. The Laxey Brigade stayed in attendance damping down for 22 days.

The building was insured with the Norwich Union Insurance Co. and the damage amounted to £60,000 of which only £20,000 was insured, making it almost certainly the largest fire loss on the Island up to that date. The charges for the Douglas Brigade amounted to £22-19s and for the Laxey Brigade £79-1s.

The Laxey Brigade had been formed on 7th January 1920 with Mr F B Holroyd as Captain. Their equipment consisted of a small hose-cart, acquired from J Blakeborough & Sons Ltd of Brighouse, Yorkshire, and several lengths of hose, a standpipe and branches. All this equipment was kept beneath the Commissioners' office, which opened at the rear onto Lower Rencell Hill.

The Highways Committee of Douglas Corporation had meanwhile taken note of their brigade's earlier representations and considered specifications of motor appliances. After hearing Mr Pickett's views they recommended that a Leyland Motor Fire Combination, complete with all accessories, should be ordered without delay. The position of motorman and station keeper was advertised as a full-time job at a weekly wage of £3-10s in anticipation of the arrival of the new appliance. Matthias H. Cannell who had some previous experience in the Manchester Fire Brigade was appointed on 1st November 1920.

The 65hp Leyland arrived in January 1921. It carried a

500 gallons per minute pump with two deliveries and 4" suction. The unladen weight of the vehicle was 10 tons and it was mounted on solid tyres. A standard wooden Bayley 50ft wheeled escape was carried; among the ancillary equipment were two Proto breathing sets and a smoke helmet with hose and bellows. The vehicle was the first motor-driven fire appliance on the Island. It was registered as MN 1233 and was lettered "Douglas Corporation Motor Fire Engine No 1" on each side. The whole vehicle was supplied for £1,897 10s. Had this machine arrived three weeks earlier, the outcome of the Laxey flour mill story might have been rather different.

The new motor appliance necessitated the reappraisal of the whole brigade. A full report was submitted by Mr H A Bridge, the Borough Surveyor. The result was the appointment of Mr W J Pickett as Superintendent, a position which had not been filled since Mr O'Hara's death. Mr Stephen Caugherty was appointed as Second Officer and Mr J. Kermode appointed Assistant Motorman but as a retained member.

A revised scale of charges was approved, fixing the rate for the new appliance at £5-5s per hour, plus £1 for each additional hour within the Borough. Outside the town the charge was £10-10s per hour, plus £1 per mile beyond a five-mile radius of Douglas, with the same charge of £1 for each additional hour. The retaining fees and other charges were also revised,

In March 1921 the brigade establishment comprised the Superintendent, Captain (Second Officer), Motorman and sixteen men. In addition to the motor appliance, the brigade still had the steam fire engine, a hose-cart, five large wheeled escapes, two small wheeled escapes and a tower ladder. There was no mention of the manual engine.

Eleven members of the brigade were connected to the station by call-bells, maintained by the Post Office Telephone Company. Seven street alarms were incorporated in the system, located at the Villiers, Broadway, Crescent, Rosemount, Market, Gas Works and Douglas Bridge. The Borough Surveyor and the brigade were pressing for additional alarms at Murrays Road, Tennis Road, Victoria Road and Derby Castle.

There was a serious fire in Douglas on Monday 12th January 1925 at George Wilding's Hardware and General Dealers' store in Duke Street. At about 7.45pm James Richardson of Dukes Lane whose premises backed onto Mr Wilding's discovered the fire and raised the alarm and the brigade were quickly in attendance. The fire was at first confined to a long cellar under the property and a number of hoses were brought into use. Other buildings surrounded the premises and access was difficult. The brigade brought hoses into the rear of the property through adjoining premises, the Crown Inn and also a house in Muckles Gate.

Just when it appeared that the fire was under control a flashover occurred. It was a phenomenon that the brigade were familiar with but as yet didn't understand. The fire broke through into the shop above and spread rapidly, despite the efforts of the brigade. Police moved people out of their houses in nearby Muckles Gate and, after the roof collapsed, the firemen concentrated their efforts on preventing the fire spreading. By 10.30pm the building was gutted and all that could be done was to damp down the remains. The fire broke out again on Tuesday afternoon and again on Wednesday but the brigade remained in attendance and these outbreaks were dealt with effectively.

The well-equipped Douglas Brigade continued to deal with out-of-town fires and were able to prevent major outbreaks developing. A fire at the Halfway House Hotel, Crosby, which started in a timber lintel in a rear lavatory, would almost certainly have resulted in a major blaze ten years previously, but the brigade arrived twenty minutes after the fire was discovered and quickly extinguished it.

In August 1928 fire was discovered again at the Laxey Glen Mills. The outbreak started on the third floor and the alarm was immediately raised. Many members of the Laxey Fire Brigade worked at the mill and they, together with Mr Thomas, the manager, got to work with a hose. They tried to confine the fire until the arrival of the Douglas Brigade, which had been sent for at the outset. The fire suddenly broke out in the upper section, having travelled up an elevator, and set light to the rafters. The Douglas Brigade had not yet arrived and an urgent call to the station confirmed that it had left half an hour earlier. The fire was now assuming serious proportions but the Laxey men stood their ground inside the building and continued to confine the fire.

The Douglas appliance eventually arrived, having been delayed with a broken valve spring in Onchan. The firemen went to work quickly with additional jets from their motor pump and soon brought the fire under control. The Douglas men stripped the roof and left the Laxey Brigade to damp down and clear up. There was a further slight outbreak the following day and four firemen were despatched by car from Douglas to assist with extinguishing it. This time the damage only amounted to £2,000.

Whenever the new motor fire engine was attending an out-of-town fire, only the old steamer was left to cover any subsequent calls in Douglas. The brigade were not satisfied with this arrangement; representations had been made on a number of occasions suggesting that the Council should provide an additional motor appliance. This latest fire in Laxey served to underline the problem. In September 1928 the Highways Committee recommended the Council to buy a 14hp Bean fire tender and two 30-gallon chemical extinguishers at a cost of £550.

In 1929 the responsibility for the fire brigade was transferred to the Works Committee. Their first job was to recruit younger men for the brigade as many were over the retirement age specified in brigade rules. The Superintendent himself, Mr W J Pickett, was two years over the limit at the age of 67. He retired in March having held the position for eight years. The Committee appointed Mr S J Caugherty as his successor and Mr A J O'Hara became Captain; Stephen A Caugherty took over as brigade secretary.

The new tender arrived in June and Douglas was now in a much better position to answer calls for assistance outside the Borough. It was Laxey yet again which tested the brigade with a series of fires over a two-year period. The largest was a fire discovered in the Manx Electric Railway Company's rolling stock shed on Saturday 5th April 1930 at

Chapter 4 DEFENCE OF THE REALM

On 6th September 1938 a fire broke out in Brown's Gentlemen's Outfitters on South Quay, Douglas. Fifteen firemen attended the blaze under the direction of Chief Officer Stephen Caugherty. It was the scene of the first fatality to a fireman on the Island when Robert Kenna was accidentally electrocuted in the course of duty. The incident led to regulations concerning the placing of external isolating switches for the use of firemen. *(Author's collection)*

10.40pm. It had been locked shortly after mid-day when the electric car bringing workmen back to Laxey from the Dhoon Quarry had been put away. The Captain of the Laxey Brigade, Mr Holroyd, realised on arrival that he had a major incident on his hands and immediately called for assistance from Douglas. The Laxey firemen had trouble finding the hydrant in the main road because it had been covered with tar.

The shed, 240ft long and 36ft wide, was full of rolling stock. The fire had obviously been burning for some time before it was discovered. The hydrant pressure was poor and the efforts of the firemen were to little effect. Company employees rushed to the shed and tried to save the contents. Due to the intense heat, only two trailer cars were saved and one, trailer No 60, was on fire as it was rolled out. Once the doors had been opened, the fire increased in intensity. It was almost 11.30pm when the Douglas Brigade arrived with the Leyland appliance.

Water was scarce and the mains supply inadequate. The Douglas men dammed the river below the shed and pumped water up to the fire. By this time the shed was completely engulfed. The overhead electricity supply had been turned off for safety. The firemen still could not get near enough to be effective, even though they had three jets in operation from the Leyland, and the Laxey Brigade still had a jet running from the mains. The fire was being fed by the timberwork of the cars and the galvanised iron sheeting of

the shed was glowing white-hot. The heat shattered the glass roof-lights, allowing flames to shoot high into the air. Soon the houses backing onto the shed were threatened and timberwork around windows and eaves ignited from the radiated heat. The firemen had to leave the shed to burn itself out and concentrate on saving the houses and other nearby properties. The Leyland pumped continuously for three hours and the brigade were still there at 6am. The Leyland returned to Douglas and four firemen were left on watch until the Manx Electric's breakdown gang arrived from Douglas at 9.30am.

All that was left was a twisted mass of metal. Four motor tramcars, seven trailers and works equipment were lost in the fire.

The following year saw a similar fire in Douglas, this time involving charabancs rather than trams. The fire broke out in W H Shimmin's garage on the Promenade. The garage was built between two blocks of boarding-houses and behind the house occupied by the proprietor. The alarm had been raised by PC Quayle who also woke Mr Shimmin. With the help of some early-rising visitors, they pulled out six charabancs and seven motor cars from a new garage which adjoined the burning building. Captain O'Hara arrived on the Bean tender shortly before 7am. The garage at the rear was a sea of flames, but the fire was to some extent contained by a galvanised roof of steel sheet. The brigade hauled out a burning vehicle and extinguished the fire in the bodywork.

The men then set to work on the fire in the garage, bringing it under control by 8.30am and leaving the scene by 11am. Five cars and two motorcycles were destroyed.

In June 1933 Douglas Brigade had a full turnout to a fire in Walpole Avenue at Victoria House, a large boarding house. Passers-by saw flames coming from the roof and raised the alarm. Constables Quine and Gelling were first on the scene and they evacuated the building. They then attempted to check the fire from the top of the staircase using buckets of water. The brigade arrived with the Bean tender, followed very shortly by the Leyland. Supt Caugherty and Captain O'Hara found the whole of the roof space above the attic bedrooms to be on fire. The firemen set about tackling the blaze from below, working from the top landing. The centre of the roof collapsed without warning and crashed down the stairwell. The firemen had a narrow escape, but had to withdraw and extinguish the fire that had now broken out within the building.

The Bean was sent back to the station to tow the 65ft escape back to the scene. It was pitched with difficulty but the firemen could not use it because of the danger from falling slates. Eventually they got onto adjoining roofs and were able to tackle the fire from above, bringing it under control an hour and a half later.

This incident illustrated the problems facing the brigade when tackling fires in buildings more than four storeys high. The Superintendent made strong representation to the Committee and, in due course, consideration was given to the provision of further equipment, including a turntable ladder.

After visits to various towns in England, and to Merryweather & Sons to view fire-fighting equipment, an order for three appliances was placed on 7th August 1935. The first was a 100ft Merryweather turntable fire escape on a purpose-built chassis powered by a 115hp six-cylinder Dorman engine, complete with an integral two-stage turbine pump delivering 500gpm at low pressure and 300gpm at high pressure. A monitor nozzle for the head of the ladder, telephones, searchlight and electric siren were all included in the quoted price of £3,565. The second was a 90hp Merryweather petrol motor fire engine on an Albion chassis, complete with a Hatfield reciprocating pump rated at 400gpm. A 40-gallon water tank and first-aid reel with 120ft of hose were included, together with a 45ft extension ladder. The appliance also carried a patent foam generator worked off the engine exhaust — all at a cost of £1,725. The third item was a Merryweather Hatfield 22hp reciprocating trailer pump with a capacity of 165gpm. This appliance was the first to arrive, within weeks of the order being placed. The brigade laid on a demonstration of its pumping ability on 28th August. Water was pumped from a dam at Tromode a distance of 1,500ft to Ballanard Road, some 175ft above the dam, at a pressure of 65 pounds per square inch. It was then relayed to Highton, a large house nearby where a ¾" jet delivered water at 260psi. The Committee were suitably impressed.

Douglas was expanding rapidly and there were attempts by the Borough to extend its boundaries, in particular by absorbing the village district of Onchan.

It was revealed by the committee of Tynwald, which had been set up to consider the proposals for extension of the boundary, that the village had only limited fire-fighting cover from a volunteer brigade which had originally been formed in 1911 with Mr J T Skillicom as the Captain. The six members of the brigade had a hand-cart, hoses, ladders and small tools and their equipment was kept in Coupe's stables in Queen's Road and, later, at the Commissioners' yard. Since 1930 Mr E Quiggin had been the Captain and he and the brigade had received training from Mr Caugherty of the Douglas Brigade.

At the time of the inquiry the Onchan Village Commissioners were considering the purchase of a fire engine, but for any major fire their reliance was still almost entirely on Douglas.

The new Douglas appliances arrived on 3rd April 1936. The turntable ladder was driven on a trial run through Onchan to the Liverpool Arms Hotel and back. The Albion was taken on a similar run to St John's. On 6th April a demonstration of the new vehicles was staged for the Works Committee at the Villiers Hotel; further demonstrations were held at Peel, Port Erin and the Ballamona Mental Hospital. These demonstrations, at most of the Island's tall buildings, culminated in a grand display of fire-fighting staged jointly by Merryweather & Sons and Douglas Corporation, in Peveril Square, which included the four motor-driven appliances, the steamer and the hose-cart.

Shortly after 12.45pm on 6th September 1938 the brigade received a call that Brown's menswear shop on North Quay was on fire. The Albion was dispatched with fifteen men under the direction of Chief Officer Stephen Caugherty. The shop was well ablaze when they arrived and the manager informed him that staff at the shop had made an unsuccessful attempt to extinguish the fire, which had started in the basement, before the alarm was raised.

When the first hose was played on the fire the firemen immediately told the chief that they had felt an electric shock. He then entered the building and tripped all the electrical switches that the manager could identify. Caugherty himself and another fireman felt further electrical shocks and he ordered the water to be cut off and the first-floor floorboards to be lifted to get to the main electrical intake. Fireman Kenna, who was on the first floor, walked over towards a window and stumbled on some debris. He reached out and caught hold of a hanging wire and let out a cry. Caugherty was behind him and, quickly realising what had happened, pulled the sleeves of his tunic over his hands and pulled Kenna away by the shoulders. Sadly, the fireman had been electrocuted. He became the first fireman on the Island to die in the course of duty.

Following the inquest, various recommendations were made to the electrical undertakers concerning the placing of firemen's switches in accessible places in both public and domestic buildings.

RAMSEY REORGANISATION

Meanwhile, in 1916, the Ramsey Brigade were still operating their hose-cart, manual engine and 60ft wheeled escape under the control of the Stables and Stores

Committee. The first effect of the new legislation was a complete reorganisation at Ramsey, with new annual retaining fees and charges. A new rulebook outlined the duties of the officers and members and it became effective from 1st July 1918.

During all this activity William Boyde, the brigade's Superintendent and longest-serving member, retired and the duties of the various officers were redefined. The principal officers of the brigade now were: First Officer directly responsible to the Committee for the conduct of the brigade, the Captain, recognised as the Second Officer and Firemaster, and the Station Officer responsible for maintaining the station, appliances and all equipment. He was in addition clearly instructed to remain in charge of the station whenever the brigade were called out and to clean all the appliances and apparatus on their return to station. The duties of the firemen were clearly defined, but branch-pipe men were set apart and given additional responsibilities, as was the Turncock. To qualify for the annual retaining fee, the men were required to attend ten practices each year.

By 1928, the brigade's call-out time was slightly longer than before the turn of the century; nevertheless it was still efficient. The appliances were, however, becoming obsolete and the Commissioners resolved in August to buy a motor-driven appliance. A petition was presented to the Local Government Board for permission to borrow £1,000. The new appliance was registered on 20th September 1928. It was a 30hp petrol-engined Merryweather Hatfield with a Braidwood body and a 400gpm pump delivering water at 145psi and a single first-aid hose-reel. It was formally handed over six days later to J N Richdale, Chairman of the Commissioners, and a demonstration was held at Albert Road School under the direction of Mr F W Frear of Merryweather & Company. Water was thrown to a height of 180ft on the smallest jet and a delivery pressure of 140psi was a tremendous improvement on hydrant pressure in the town mains which averaged a mere 40psi.

The brigade strength was increased by three to nineteen and Robert Cain was appointed driver of the motor engine. In November, at the request of the brigade members, the Town Commissioners agreed to name the new appliance Richdale.

The Commissioners informed the Local Government Board that they were now in a position to allow their brigade to attend fires outside the town boundary without restriction.

The manual engine, now obsolete, was offered for sale the following year. Hose was purchased as the new appliance continued to split the old hoses which could not stand the pressure of the motor-driven pump. The call-bell system operated by the telephone company was also obsolete, and consideration was being given to its replacement or the installation of a Smith's Patent Fire Alarm of the siren type.

However, all was not well with the Richdale. The brigade had experienced difficulty climbing some of the steep hills in the Mayhill and Ballure areas of the town. The matter was taken up with Merryweather's, who solved the problem at the company's own expense by changing the rear chain-drive sprockets from seventeen to fourteen teeth. This solved the hill-climbing problem — but only at the expense of its top speed. During the year there had been eleven fire calls three of which were outside the town limits.

LACKING AT LAXEY

Following the fire at the Manx Electric Railway Shed in Laxey there had been concern about the efficiency of the local fire brigade. A public meeting was called and as a result the brigade was reorganised; on 4th June 1930 the Commissioners appointed Mr D Williamson as superintendent of the brigade with Mr J Beck as his deputy and the brigade strength was fixed at twenty.

Almost two years later, on Sunday 3rd April 1932, a bus employee noticed the Dhoon Glen Hotel on fire; he raised the alarm when he got to Laxey. Williamson summoned the brigade at 7.45pm by maroon and had his men ready within six minutes. Although the hotel was outside their area they decided to respond to the call. They obtained Mr Faragher's van and set off. The Ramsey Brigade had also been called out. The Laxey Brigade got there first, but could do very little with their equipment. The hotel, forty years old and built of pitch pine, was completely engulfed in flames. The Ramsey men arrived soon afterwards and set up their motor pump by the river some distance away. Both brigades set about fighting the fire, although their work was hampered by the presence of a 300-gallon petrol tank in front of the hotel. The road had to be closed after the building collapsed; burning embers flew across the entrance to the glen, threatening the trees. The licensee and his wife returned home at 10pm to find nothing left.

Meanwhile at Ramsey, as the brigade became more familiar with the new appliance, it was apparent that the brigade strength could be reduced and, on the recommendation of the Chief Officer, Mr J Smith, it was brought down by five, to fourteen.

On Thursday 1st February 1934 Mr Harry Crennell was driving through Andreas Village when he noticed a stack of straw on fire at Balleigh farm. He immediately told Mr Wilfred Teare, the owner, and PC Mylcraine. Word was sent to Ramsey and the brigade left the station shortly before 1am under the charge of Chief Officer Smith. The brigade were delayed in getting to the fire due to a severe engine misfire. On arrival they were able to stop the fire spreading but the original stack was destroyed.

The brigade were again delayed returning to station with engine problems with the Richdale. More mechanical problems were encountered later in the year when the brigade were called to a fire in a cottage at Sulby. By the time they arrived the thatch on the cottage was well alight. Hampered by a poor water supply there was little they could do to save the property.

The brigade was clearly efficient but the motor-driven appliance was now unreliable particularly when responding to calls outside the town. The Commissioners had cause for concern in this regard as the agreement with the northern parishes did not include the two largest, Lezayre and Maughold, and as a consequence were not obliged to respond to calls in those areas. If they did there was no guarantee that their charges would be met.

Around this time the Ramsey Brigade were called to a fire in the town at a bakehouse belonging to Mrs W L Corlett, of Wattleworth's Cafe. Harry Martin whose father had a grocery warehouse adjoining the bakehouse discovered the blaze. On the other side of the bakehouse was a large grain warehouse. The fire was difficult to get to and potentially dangerous. A large crowd had gathered in the early evening and saw William Corlett drive the engine at speed round the corner of East Street with the brigade holding on to the grab-rails on the open body. The firemen arrived within five minutes of receiving the call: a remarkably quick turnout. The fire was effectively dealt with and confined to the bakehouse though not without difficulty.

The motor-driven appliance was still giving cause for concern, and the Commissioners sought help from Messrs Merryweather & Company who sent a mechanic, Mr Dunkley, to inspect it. He reported that the crankcase was cracked and that there was also a bad crack in the cylinder bore which would necessitate the engine being returned to England for repair. He found the clutch and brakes worn and defective, though the pump was in good order.

Merryweather & Company were invited to quote for three alternative solutions to the problem. These were the replacement of the defective engine, its repair, or the replacement of the appliance utilising the old pump. In the meantime the Commissioners sent a deputation to Douglas to enquire from the Local Government Board when the new fire tender and trailer pump would be supplied to them under the proposed co-ordinated fire-fighting scheme. To some extent they were anticipating the forthcoming Local Government (Fires) Act, but their position left them with no alternative. A suggestion was made that as a temporary measure a Hatfield trailer pump should be purchased and a Bedford tender be obtained through a local agent but this came to nothing.

Following advice from Messrs Merryweather the Commissioners agreed, at a special meeting held on 27th June 1939, to purchase a new 25hp Merryweather Automobile Fire Tender based on a Morris two-ton short-wheelbase chassis, fitted with a 45ft extension ladder and first-aid hose-reel, at a cost of £575. A Hatfield trailer pump had been ordered; it arrived the same month at a cost of £460.

Kirk Michael Commissioners did not form a fire brigade until 1933, although Government Office had reminded them of their obligations on a number of occasions since 1919. They were preoccupied with installing a drainage system in 1925, and this was followed by involvement in a water supply system that was not completed until 1932. On 27th May 1931, however, the Commissioners did resolve to buy some fire-extinguishing apparatus at a cost of £25 and an application was made to the Local Government Board for the necessary borrowing powers. It was to be two years before a fire brigade was formed, with Mr F W Cowin as its Superintendent and Mr R S Quayle as his assistant, their appointments taking effect from 9th September 1933.

The Douglas Corporation's 100ft Dorman Merryweather turntable ladder photographed opposite the No.2 Station in Lord Street Douglas in July 1950 on the occasion of the visit of Mr H M Smith, Chief Inspector of Fire Services to the Home Office. *(Author's collection)*

Chapter 5 WAR THREATENS

WAR **THREATENS**
The Local Government (Fires) Act 1940

WITH THE THREAT of war looming once again, the UK Parliament was taking precautions which included the Fire Brigades Act of 1938. This gave the Government powers to take over areas not providing adequate means of fire-fighting and to co-ordinate the whole fire service if the need arose.

The Isle of Man was taking its own precautions and in May 1938 a Central Air Raids Precautions Committee was appointed under the chairmanship of Deemster Farrant. The Committee fully investigated all aspects of training for air raid wardens, police, fire and local authorities and submitted their report to Tynwald in November. Recommendations were made to increase the number of fire-fighting personnel and to provide more equipment. Early in 1939 came their final report, which recommended the setting up of a district ARP organisation and made reference to the Local Government Board report on the all-Island scheme to co-ordinate the fire service.

This heralded the first reading of the Local Government (Fires) Bill in May 1939, which outlined requirements for the various districts, for standardising equipment and for making special provision for the Douglas Fire Brigade to operate over the whole Island.

Douglas Corporation were concerned that, having spent £6,979 on new appliances between 1935 and 1937 (plus the £2,725 a year it took to run the brigade), they were not going to get sufficient financial aid from the proposed legislation. They were worried enough to engage counsel, Edwyn Kneen, to represent them at the bar of the legislative chamber. The Act was passed in October and became law in February 1940, but already the war was six months old.

The Act defined seven fire authorities — Douglas, Ramsey, Castletown, Peel, Laxey, Kirk Michael and Rushen — with the Council and Local Commissioners administering all but the Rushen area, which was to continue under the control of the Rushen Joint Fire Protection Board appointed in November 1938. It also specified that there should be mutual assistance between the various authorities.

A fire fund was raised from a penny rate and administered by the Local Government Board. Douglas and Ramsey were to receive set grants of £550 and £120 per annum respectively; the other areas had to keep accounts and submit annual estimates, together with applications for grant aid. Onchan Village Commissioners were the only exception, being covered under the Douglas Fire Authority Area, and were required to pay the Douglas Corporation £100 per annum towards the cost of maintaining their brigade.

The Island Government set up a War Emergency Committee in August 1939, directly responsible to the Governor. This was reconstituted the following November as the War Committee of Tynwald, under the chairmanship of Deemster W P Cowley. They dealt with all the problems of the war, in an executive capacity, until November 1945.

As in the First World War, the Island was commandeered for the internment of aliens. Most hotels and boarding-houses were used for this purpose, or for the billeting and training of military personnel. Soon the Island would be packed to capacity: a daunting prospect for its fire brigade whose deficiencies had been recognised in the Act. The Government lost no time in allocating over £5,000 to the various fire authorities to enable new equipment to be purchased.

Ramsey and the Rushen Joint Fire Protection Board had, out of necessity, ordered new appliances in anticipation of the Act. During November 1939 Ramsey took delivery of a 24hp Merryweather appliance with a Braidwood-type body built on a Morris chassis. It came complete with a Coventry Climax trailer pump. The Ramsey Commissioners also bought an additional 25hp Merryweather appliance in March 1940, at a cost of £870, by which time the Commissioners were able to take full advantage of the grant aid.

The Act proved effective in its first year: two motor fire tenders and five trailer pumps were distributed, with their cost defrayed by Insular Revenue.

In August 1940 Mr A R Corlett OBE was appointed Inspector of Equipment; he had previously been Chief Officer of the Manchester Fire Brigade. His new brief was to visit the Island twice a year to inspect all the equipment and prepare reports on the state of the various brigades for consideration by the Board.

An Auxiliary Fire Services Scheme was introduced during the year at the request of the War Committee of Tynwald. It was prepared by the Chief Constable and the Chief Officer of the Douglas Fire Brigade under the direction of the Local Government Board. The long list of fire-fighting equipment was approved, with £6,018 being made available from Central Government to set up an Auxiliary Fire Service.

The Civil Defence Commission recommended that the Local Government Board Chief Inspector, Mr W E Quayle, should oversee the training of all the fire brigades and auxiliary fire forces. With the co-operation of the Chief Officer of the Douglas Brigade, a suitable training programme was formulated.

Internment camps and military training units occupied the whole of the Douglas promenade and the central area of the town as well as part of Onchan. In July, Douglas Brigade had their first call to one of these camps. At the Central

In June 1941 the Douglas Corporation acquired a 30hp Fordson open-bodied Towing Vehicle and trailer pump as part of the additional cover required for the Second World War. The appliance is photographed in the public car park on Lord Street in Douglas. On the front row left to right are Jim Sloane (full-time driver and mechanic), Bert Kenna (Sergeant), Chief Officer Mr S A Caugherty and Fred Courtie (Second Officer). Those standing on the appliance were all retained firemen. *(Author's collection)*

Internment Camp they first experienced security problems with prisoners, which made fire-fighting even more difficult.

The Island learned many lessons from its first air raid warning, at 2.50pm on 31st July 1940. No central fire control or Auxiliary Fire Service stations had yet been established and, had the raid materialised, the Island would have been found wanting.

Meanwhile, Douglas Brigade dealt with fires at the Palace, Hutchinson Square and Sefton Internment Camps. The fire at the 'Hydro' in the Palace Camp proved the most serious, requiring the attendance of Douglas No. 2 and No. 4 appliances.

On 9th August 1940 the first AFS practice was arranged and 21 members of the AFS turned out with the Douglas Brigade. Subsequently there were several drills each week. The war dictated many such changes; Onchan Village Commissioners surrendered their equipment to Douglas in September and effectively ceased to operate as a village brigade. In reality the members of the brigade joined the AFS and continued to function, training regularly with the Douglas Brigade and the Bean tender.

During February 1941 fire-posts were established in Douglas at Corlett Sons & Cowley's warehouse, Greeba Works in Market Street, McKibbin's Yard in Circular Road, Crown Bakery in Woodbourne Lane, the Corporation Bus Depot on York Road, the Corporation Deck-Chair Store at the Esplanade, Pulrose Manor, Emmetts Garage on Woodside Terrace and Clifton House, St Ninian's. Local tradesmen provided lorries, which were supplied with special badges. With the addition of Onchan, Strang and Crosby, a total of twelve fire-posts had been established in the Douglas Fire Authority Area by the end of the year. These posts were fully equipped and all personnel, both regular and auxiliary, were issued with steel helmets. Military guards at the various camps trained regularly with the AFS and part-time firemen.

Continuing the modernisation directed by the new Act, Douglas, Castletown and Peel acquired new appliances. Douglas took delivery of a 30hp Fordson towing vehicle and trailer pump on 14th June 1941. The appliance had an open body with locker space and a closed forward control cab. This released the Bean, dating from 1929, which was sold to the Castletown Commissioners.

At the outbreak of war Peel still only had its horse-drawn manual fire engine and hand-cart. Large areas of the town had been commandeered for use as internment camps, and the need for a modern fire appliance was urgent. The Commissioners ordered a 20hp Commer fire tender with an open Braidwood-type body and a Merryweather Hatfield trailer pump. They arrived on 19th September and gave Peel a fire-fighting capability, although still falling short of what was considered desirable.

During the year the need for a Central Control and the establishment of a Chief Fire Staff Officer became more

Chapter 5 WAR THREATENS

urgent. The Local Government Board consulted the Chief Fire Advisor to the Home Office and appointed, on his recommendation, Mr C A P Ellis as CFSO. He attended his first drill on 10th May 1942, his skill and enthusiasm soon winning respect from the local brigades.

In the same month the first of four Austin standard Home Office-pattern Auxiliary Towing Vehicles arrived. They were fitted with 35ft extension ladders and 500gpm trailer pumps. These vehicles were obtained by the Manx Government and issued to fire-posts in the Douglas area. Transport for the other fire-posts was still being provided by local hauliers.

By February 1943 ten of these standard towing vehicles had been supplied. In addition to the four supplied to Douglas, two were allocated to Castletown and one each to Ramsey, Peel, Rushen and Laxey. Auxiliary Fire Stations were built in Laxey, Ballasalla, Andreas, Foxdale and Kirk Michael. In addition to the towing vehicles twenty-three trailer pumps and twenty stirrup pumps had been acquired and distributed to the fire-posts.

Training was stepped up to familiarise the crews with the ATVs, and included crews from HMS *Valkyrie* and the RAF who operated similar equipment. Douglas Brigade provided training in the use of escapes and ladders on the practice tower in Lord Street's public car park, using the Merryweather turntable ladder, the Bayley wheeled escape and the Telescale escape ladder.

Large-scale exercises were centred on static water tanks, which had been placed strategically around Douglas, giving the AFS good experience in the use of their trailer pumps. On one occasion an all-Island exercise was staged on the assumption that Douglas had received a major air attack and that the mains water supply had been severed. The whole of the Douglas Brigade and out-of-town AFS were involved in pumping water by relay from Port-e-Chee and the River Glass to the static tank at Waverley Terrace using the small Coventry Climax pumps. The larger Hatfield trailer pumps provided a further relay to the Derby Square static tank. The exercise proved that the fire service could respond if the Island were to suffer a genuine air raid, and draw water from several miles if necessary.

As the Chief Fire Staff Officer Mr Ellis was also the Island Fire Controller and a scheme for mobilising the fire service on an all-Island basis was drawn up and incorporated into the training programme. In addition to the training with the AFS the regular brigades had to contend with the usual number of chimney and roof fires, more important now because of black-out requirements. All this with depleted numbers due to men enlisting for active service.

In February 1940 a fire broke out about 7am at Knottfield in Woodbourne Road. Neighbours were awakened by the screams of servants from the rear of the house and the alarm was raised. Albert Rowell, the owner of the house, received burns rescuing the three maidservants, but all the occupants escaped safely. When the Douglas Brigade arrived, a few minutes later, flames were shooting through the roof at the rear of the mansion. Several members of the brigade escaped serious injury when a gas explosion ripped through the house and engulfed the main staircase. The roof quickly became a mass of flames and, despite water being directed onto the building from the turntable ladder, the house could not be saved. The brigade returned to station eleven hours later.

BLACK-OUT

Because of the air raid precautions, and the need to fulfil black-out regulations, it was also essential that farm and heath fires were extinguished without delay. At 7.10pm on Saturday 24th October 1942, Peel Brigade were called out for a fire at Ballanayre Farm, north of the town. Fifteen minutes later the brigade left Peel, with the new Commer fire tender towing the Hatfield pump. When the men arrived they found all the farm buildings on fire. The police had sent word to Douglas requesting assistance, but the situation was already desperate. The nearest water supply was a quarter of a mile away. The trailer pump was taken to the stream with difficulty and, by 8pm, three jets were playing on the fire. Douglas Brigade arrived soon afterwards, with their Fordson tender, Hatfield trailer pump and fourteen men. They put their pump into the same stream, but found there was not enough water to supply both pumps. Douglas shut theirs down, but stayed at the scene to relieve the Peel men by taking alternate spells at fighting the fire. They eventually returned to station at 1.30am on Sunday, when the fire had been brought under control.

Peel Brigade stayed at the farm until 5am when the fire was out, leaving a watchman until 8am. The buildings were gutted and many tons of hay were lost. The property was insured with the Royal and damage was assessed at £6,.000.

At the end of the month there was an early morning call to a fire at No.11 Beach Street. The occupant was Captain Wallace, a member of the Women's Royal Army Corps, who was woken by choking smoke. She tried to fight her way downstairs, but was beaten back by the fire and smoke. In desperation and choking on the dense smoke she smashed the window, jumped some ten feet into the street and ran to the police station to raise the alarm. The Commer arrived with eight men, who were soon fighting the fierce blaze. However, as the flames were being brought under control it became apparent that the fire was being fed by a gas-pipe burning free under the stairs. The fire had melted a lead pipe, making it essential that the gas supply be turned off. Fireman Bell, later to become Captain of the brigade, crawled into the burning building, located the incoming supply pipe and turned off the gas. The lower storey of the building was completely gutted, and the remainder severely damaged. Mr Ellis, who had by now assumed the duties of CFSO, inspected the scene later in the day and commended the brigade on their work and in particular the action of Fireman Bell in averting an even worse disaster.

The Peel Area had by this time established an Auxiliary Fire Service with fully-equipped posts. A number of full-scale exercises were held in Peel, confirming that in a real emergency the whole town could be covered using water from the harbour by relay pumping, with four light pumps and five heavy ones.

Peel also exercised regularly with Kirk Michael and Ramsey Brigades, and on one occasion with RAF Jurby for

Laxey Brigade photographed in Laxey Glen Gardens with their Austin Towing Vehicle FMN 249. Their trailer pump is on the right of the photograph. The other major trailer pump and personnel belong to the AFS from an unidentified fire-post and the photograph was probably taken on the occasion of a competition in relay pumping judging by the cup being held by the Laxey Station Officer Mr D Williamson. *(Courtesy of Andrew Scarffe)*

familiarisation with aircraft fires. During the war a wheeled escape was stationed in Stanley Road, in full view of the many aliens interned in houses over two storeys high. Its demise was hastened by being stored outdoors; in 1946 it went for scrap. Although unconfirmed it is almost certain that this was probably one of the old Douglas street escapes.

HEATH FIRES RAGE

Perhaps the worst heath fire of the war broke out during May 1943, on South Barrule. The glow could be seen in Douglas and Mr Ellis, on duty at Central Control in John Street, despatched the Fordson tender and trailer pump before the call for assistance came from the Peel Brigade. The ATV and pump from No.2 fire-post were sent soon afterwards. Peel and Castletown Brigades turned out with their appliances, and a full complement of men from the Foxdale fire-post were picked up by the Douglas ATV. The Foxdale fire-post did not receive its ATV until the end of June.

On arrival at Barrule the men found no water supply; they had no alternative but to tackle the fire with beaters and hand extinguishers. The whole operation was directed from the Central Fire Control which had been established in the basement of the Douglas fire station in John Street. Women members of the AFS, of whom sixteen were trained for control room duty, manned the telephones and switchgear.

The Douglas fire-posts were manned by seventy-one members of the AFS. Drills and practices continued on a regular basis, particular emphasis being put on the Central Mobilising Scheme which involved units from all the fire authority areas.

The first all-Island competitions were held in Douglas in August 1943 to boost morale. A trophy for the best hydrant drill was presented by A E Kitto MHK who was Chairman of the Central Executive ARP Committee. Ramsey Johnson, the Chairman of the Civil Defence Commission, presented a similar trophy for the best light trailer pump drill. This trophy was won by Douglas No.12 fire-post, which was the Crosby unit.

The same year a number of standard Home Office canvas dams were supplied to supplement the static tanks. The four ATVs at Douglas were strategically placed to cover the town. FMN 237 was attached to No.1 fire-post, but garaged at E B Christian's garage. Similarly, FMN 280 was attached to No.2 fire-post, but kept in Fayle's garage on Well Road Hill. FMN 238 was garaged at the fire-post in Woodbourne Lane, with FMN 248 at fire-post No.10 in the Onchan Commissioners' Yard. Transport for the remaining trailer pumps was provided by Corlett Sons & Cowley, Douglas Steam Sawmill, Dale & Colvyn, Drennan's coal yard and Messrs Heron & Brearley who provided four wagons to fire-posts 3, 6, 7 and 8.

The Royal Navy operated an ATV and trailer pump from a

Chapter 5 WAR THREATENS

converted shop in Shore Road at the bottom of Broadway. It also had a Gwynne Major pump, which was lorry-mounted on a standard wartime chassis; this was stationed in a converted seaside shelter on the Loch Promenade opposite the Royal Navy shore station, HMS *Valkyrie*.

Fire-fighting teams were attached to other military establishments in the town. The Signals Camp near the Palace had a team of women who regularly drilled with a trailer pump. There were teams at the Officer Cadet Training Unit stationed at the Villiers, HMS *St George* on Loch Promenade operated a fire-fighting party, and there was even a team of aliens at the Port Jack Internment Camp. All these units trained regularly throughout the war with the Douglas Brigade.

Fire-watching was carried out by volunteers from the Loyal Manx Association, which later assumed full Home Guard duties. Some of the larger department stores in Douglas also maintained fire-watching teams; Marks & Spencer were exemplary in this regard.

Under the provisions of the new Act, the Local Government Board allocated a motor tender and trailer pump to Laxey. The appliance was based on a Dodge van that had been converted to a fire tender by Ashton's Garage in Westmoreland Road in Douglas. The vehicle was registered in the Laxey Village Commissioners' name in November 1940; by 4th December it had been delivered by Mr Caugherty and undergone tests in the area. The Laxey Brigade were not satisfied with the performance of the tender and returned it to Douglas for modifications. The fire station under the Commissioners' Office was extended to accommodate it, but the new tender was never successful as a brigade appliance. It lacked power on the steep hills around Laxey, and it was returned to the Local Government Board within a year, to be reallocated to the Harbour Board where it saw service until the end of the war.

The Commissioners preferred to use A R Caine's lorry until they took delivery of an Austin ATV in May 1942. In July the brigade establishment was fixed at eleven men. The Laxey Fire Authority set up an Auxiliary Fire Service with an establishment of twenty-five men, with fire-posts in Laxey and Garwick, all under the direct control of Mr Williamson. They entered the drill competitions and attended the all-Island pumping exercises.

The value of these exercises in relay pumping which Mr Ellis had conducted throughout the Island was illustrated by events at a fire that happened on 6th March 1943 at Ballaragh farm high above Laxey and where no mains water was available. The Laxey Brigade arrived shortly after midnight to find the farm buildings well alight. David Williamson lost no time in calling for assistance from the Douglas Brigade, and at 12.40am the ATV and trailer pump left No.1 fire-post. This was followed shortly after by the Fordson tender towing the Hatfield trailer pump. The fire-post at Onchan was alerted and its men left for Laxey with their ATV and pump. The nearest water supply was over a mile way at Gretch Vooar. The firemen set about damming the stream, then relayed the water more than 7,000ft to the fire using three major pumps and two light trailer pumps.

Late on a Friday afternoon in July 1944, Police Sgt Godfrey, who was outside the police station at Laxey, became aware of the high-pitched note of an aircraft engine. Looking up he saw a 'plane on fire, diving out of control over

In 1942 Kirk Michael Commissioners obtained their first motor appliance when they acquired from Castletown Commissioners the 14hp Bean which had first been purchased by Douglas Corporation in 1929. The driver and Brigade mechanic was Edmund Quayle and the appliance is photographed outside the Mitre Hotel. *(IOMF&RS)*

the village. It disappeared over South Cape; almost immediately there was an explosion and a pall of smoke. Sgt Godfrey called the fire brigade and set off to the scene of the crash. Wreckage was strewn over a two-mile radius on the Grawe farm; the crew of nine all perished.

Part of the wreckage fell on a house at Fairy Cottage and set it on fire. The occupants all received burns and a young child died later from extensive burns. First on the scene were three members of the South Cape AFS post, who rescued the five people from the house and were fighting the fire by the time the brigade arrived from the village. It was one of the most difficult incidents faced by the brigade during the war, although they were called to another aircraft crash at Ballaragh.

The Laxey Brigade was the only one on the Island to be called by a maroon, a procedure that was discontinued during the war; afterwards Laxey fell into line with other towns and villages and used an air-raid siren. David Williamson resigned as Chief 'Officer of the brigade in 1947, and Mr W J Bridson succeeded him.

The Kirk Michael Brigade were by this time operating as an efficient unit. However, it had started out at the beginning of the war with the minimum of equipment and a hand-cart kept in a lean-to shed at the rear of the Commissioners' offices. The brigade had been summoned as required by word of mouth. The Water and Stores Committee had drawn up new rules for the brigade, which were approved in June 1940. The following month a full ARP plan was put into operation in Kirk Michael and an Auxiliary Fire Service formed. Mr S Keig was appointed Superintendent of the AFS, with Mr L Lowe as his deputy. Fire-posts were established and stirrup pumps issued; the first practice was called for 26th July.

On their way back from keeping watch on the hill above the village on 3rd August, members of the Local Volunteer Defence Corps saw flames coming from a shed in Kelly Brothers' yard. They raised the alarm in the village; by 5.30am the brigade were at the scene and soon had water on the fire. Ramsey Brigade arrived shortly before 6am. The two brigades had the fire under control by 9am and by noon it was out. Damage was considerable, with most of the buildings and engineering plant destroyed for the second time.

In November the Kirk Michael Commissioners agreed on a five-year lease of J D Kelly's premises in Main Road for their fire station. Alterations were completed by February. During 1941 Mr F W Cowin retired as the brigade's Superintendent and was succeeded by PC G W A Kinrade, as Chief Officer. In February 1942 Mr Ellis delivered a Gwynne trailer pump to Kirk Michael, giving the brigade their first mechanical pump. In June the Commissioners purchased the Bean tender from Castletown; it was the village's first motorised appliance. It would not fit in the existing fire station, and so it was housed in Quayle's Garage until a new fire station could be built next to the Mitre Hotel. Edmund Quayle was appointed brigade mechanic and put in charge of the appliance.

Early in 1943 the new station was completed and the motor tender and pump installed. The Bean was replaced in April 1946 by a 20hp Austin towing vehicle acquired from the Peel Commissioners. It was used with the Coventry Climax trailer pump which had been previously used by the Kirk Michael AFS, the Gwynne pump having been loaned to the Sulby AFS fire-post.

CHANGES IN THE NORTH

Ramsey had been well equipped at the outbreak of war and trained regularly under the direction of Chief Officer Mr J Smith. The brigade used the Longworth escape on the new pump escape carrier and the old Shand Mason escape was put in store. It did not stay there long, however, once the North Promenade houses had been requisitioned to form the Mooragh Internment Camp. It was painted and repaired and it became operational again, being stationed in the Commissioners' Yard at the Mooragh. The brigade took delivery of an 'X-aust' suds generator at the same time, to give it a foam-making capability.

In 1941 the brigade strength was increased to twenty, and the AFS establishment stayed at the same figure. Fire-posts were established in the Ramsey area, as elsewhere, and supplied with manual pumps, although the Sulby post, at the rear of the Sulby Glen Hotel, had a major pump at a later date. In June 1942 one of the Austin ATVs and a trailer pump were allocated to Ramsey, being temporarily housed in the railway station yard.

The war saw the building of military aerodromes at Jurby and Andreas; suddenly the remote country areas to the north of the Island came alive with personnel, aircraft and fuel stores with their attendant fire risks.

Andreas village and the new RAF training station came within the Ramsey Fire Authority Area, and Chief Officer Smith of the Ramsey Brigade visited the aerodrome at the request of the Station Fire Prevention Officer during January 1942. He found that the military hydrants, standpipes and couplings were of a different pattern to those used elsewhere on the Island. The only help that the brigade could offer in the event of a fire was skilled personnel.

An auxiliary fire-post was established in the Andreas village. During 1943 one of the five new stations being built in the Island was commissioned there and the Ramsey ATV and trailer pump transferred. A similar situation had existed within the Castletown Area, and another of the new fire stations was built in Ballasalla with an ATV and trailer pump being transferred from Castletown.

There were also military establishments within the Peel Fire Authority Area; in addition to the fire-posts in the town at Market Place, Peveril Road and Stanley Road, there were remote posts at St John's, Foxdale and Glenmaye.

The presence of an RAF radio station at Dalby and a camp with living quarters at Glenmaye made it a vulnerable area, particularly as water was always scarce. A static tank was built on the station with a 6,000-gallon capacity and a Service trailer pump was provided. The Captain of the Peel Brigade undertook the training of the service personnel, together with the members of the AFS from the Glenmaye fire-post who operated a light trailer pump.

On 21st June 1943 another of the five new stations was completed at the Foxdale fire-post; shortly afterwards the

Chapter 5 WAR THREATENS

ATV and Gwynne trailer pump were transferred from Peel.

The Peel area had to deal with most of the heath fires during the war. Each one had to be extinguished, often under extremely difficult conditions, because of the stringent emergency regulations. Unfortunately, agricultural land could not be insured against fire damage, which meant that the Authority could make no claim for its services and the firemen did not get paid for such services. Understandably, loyalty was stretched almost to the point of rebellion. Eventually, after representation was made by their Chief Officer, the men received ten shillings each for attending heath fires. The cost was met by the Town Commissioners and this set the pattern for other fire authority areas.

Castletown was ill-equipped at the outbreak of war, with just the disused manual engine and a ladder-cart. The brigade had only one fire call between 1934 and 1940, but the influx of military personnel billeted in the town soon changed that and during the next three years there were eleven calls.

As a result of the new Act, Castletown Commissioners administered the Castletown Fire Area, forming a Fire-Fighting Executive sub-committee for the purpose. They set about reorganising the brigade yet again. New regulations were drawn up by September 1940, the old brigade was disbanded and a new one came into being. T Corkill remained as Captain of the retained brigade and at the same time an Auxiliary Fire Service was formed.

In July 1941 the Bean motor tender was purchased from Douglas for £100, giving the town its first motor-driven fire appliance. A Merryweather Hatfield trailer pump was acquired and the brigade were able to function as a reasonably efficient unit.

The following year an Austin ATV, FMN 259, was allocated to Castletown and the Bean sold to Kirk Michael Fire Authority. In February 1943 a second Austin ATV and light trailer pump were stationed at Castletown until the fire station at the Ballasalla fire-post could be built, after which they were transferred to provide cover for the military establishments in that area.

AFS posts were established within the Castletown Area at Ballasalla, Colby, Ballabeg and St Mark's, with Derbyhaven following later. All the posts were supplied with two-man manual pumps except for Ballasalla, which had the ATV, FMN 451, and pump, and Ballabeg, which had a four-man manual pump.

Mr D C McGowan was appointed Leading Fireman in the AFS. The Captain of the regular brigade assisted by Sub-Captain J W Oates supervised monthly drills. In 1942 Mr Ellis undertook much of the training, achieving a high degree of efficiency with the limited equipment available. Thomas Corkill had resigned in May 1942, and J W Oates was appointed Captain of the Brigade. F L Kennaugh filled the post of Sub-Captain until 1944 when he in turn became Captain.

During 1943 a total of twenty-nine men from the Castletown Area were engaged over a period of several days fighting heath fires on South Barrule. The question of pay for attending such fires was now raised by Castletown, eventually resulting in the same fee as had been agreed at Peel. It was fortunate that the matter was resolved because they fought another heath fire on Barrule in March 1944, the men being engaged for days with beaters owing to the lack of water and water tenders.

Three months later they were called to a fire in the naval administration camp at Janet's Corner which the brigade were able to deal with quickly using the trailer pump and two jets.

Major Young, the ARP Controller, wrote to Port Erin Commissioners in September 1940 reminding them of their obligation to establish an AFS to participate in the Island's ARP fire-fighting scheme. They wrote back to say that the matter was being dealt with by the Rushen Joint Protection Board.

The Rushen Brigade had an establishment of ten men; eight were stationed at Port Erin under PC Cowin and two at Port St Mary with John Hyslop in charge. The new Merryweather motor appliance and trailer pump, which had been ordered earlier, arrived at Douglas late in 1939. Built on a 25hp Morris chassis, it carried a 50ft wartime version of the Bayley escape. Mr S A Caugherty, Chief Officer of the Douglas Brigade, delivered it to Port Erin and undertook to train the Rushen Brigade to use the new appliance that was housed at the premises in the Falcon's Nest yard.

The requisitioning of the boarding-houses and hotels in Port Erin and Port St Mary for internees soon found the area in need of additional fire-fighting equipment. In June 1942 an Austin towing and trailer pump was delivered to Rushen and allocated to Port St Mary. A shed in the Commissioners' yard was converted to accommodate the new appliance. The hoses and equipment were transferred from the hand-cart, which was then taken out of service. PC Cowin had been transferred to St John's in 1941; Mr J R Costain replaced him as Captain, a position he held until 1947.

During the war the Rushen Brigade trained regularly with Douglas and Peel Brigades and also participated in the all-Island relay pumping exercises. John Hyslop, who had been in charge of the Port St Mary sub-station since 1939, was appointed Captain of the Rushen Brigade in 1947.

Difficulties had been experienced by the Local Government Board in carrying out some of the statutory requirements of the 1940 Act, To remedy this an amending bill was prepared and placed before the Legislative Council on 2nd November 1943.

The Fire Brigades Act 1938 in the United Kingdom incorporated recommendations of the Riverdale Committee which had been appointed two years earlier by the Home Secretary, It consolidated and amended the law relating to fire brigades in England. The Manx Act of 1940 set out to do the same thing. There were a number of differences, however; the principal one was that in the Isle of Man it remained the liability of the owner or occupier of a property to pay for the services of the brigade attending at a fire. This point had come into contention in respect of fires on heaths and agricultural land where it was not the general practice to insure against fire. The amending bill attempted to solve some of these problems by altering the areas covered by the various fire authorities. To ease the burden of cost on the authorities it proposed increasing the 1d rate to 2d in the

Peel Brigade with their new 20hp Commer Braidwood-bodied Fire Tender and Merryweather Hatfield trailer pump delivered in 1941. This was the first motorised appliance for Peel. All fire-fighting equipment was carried in lockers in the bodywork and the men rode in the open on the back of the appliance. *(Author's collection)*

pound. Its third major point was to free the owner or occupier of such land from the obligation to pay for the services of the fire brigade. The bill received its third reading in November and then passed to the House of Keys for its first reading in December. It had a stormy passage and at its second reading Douglas Corporation were represented by counsel who objected to certain sections. The whole matter was referred to a committee of the House of Keys under the chairmanship of James Clinton MHK; their report and recommendations were published on 1st August 1944.

On the same day the Peel Brigade were called to a fire at Ballakilmurray farm. The Commer and Hatfield pump were dispatched shortly after 9.30am with three members of the brigade and three helpers; three more brigade members followed later by car. On arrival they found the stables burnt out and the roof collapsed. They confined the fire and had it extinguished by noon. Damage amounted to £900 and the property was insured with the Commercial Union.

The Peel men had to contend with many farm fires but the difficulty of getting water, particularly at the last fire, prompted Robert Kneen, the Captain of the brigade, to write in his report:

"I am concerned at the frequency of these farm fires and the shortage of water in every case, and the attention of Government Office might be drawn to this fact with the object of making it compulsory for all farms to provide a static water tank for use in case of fire". He was not alone; other brigades were voicing similar concerns.

There was another farm fire near Peel during January 1945, this time at Ballanayre farm. The brigade found that the stables adjoining the dwelling and packed with straw were well on fire. The men had the same problem with water and it was almost an hour before they were able to tackle the fire. The straw was packed so tightly that the water had no effect; instead the bales had to be manhandled into the yard, turned over and extinguished in the open. It was six hours before the fire was put out. The fire had been started by the careless use of a blowlamp being used to thaw out frozen water pipes.

The AFS ceased to function shortly after the end of the war, in May 1945. The equipment was collected from the fire-posts and put into Central Fire Stores. All posts were closed down except for Foxdale, Andreas and Sulby. Six of the Austin ATVs were retained, eventually being stationed at Rushen, Laxey, Castletown, Douglas, Andreas and Foxdale. The other four were sold locally within a few months although all the trailer pumps were retained.

The War Committee of Tynwald recognised the valuable work that Mr Ellis had done during the emergency as Chief Fire Staff Officer and suggested that his services be retained by transfer from the Civil Defence Commission to the Local Government Board. The following month he took up his duties as Inspector of Equipment under the Local Government (Fires) Act 1940.

Meanwhile in the United Kingdom the Fire Services Act 1947 had been introduced. Its main effect was to wind up the National Fire Service and abolish the role of Municipal Borough Councils, Urban District Councils and Joint Fire Boards as Fire Authorities. It also laid down certain standards of attendance at fires in respect of appliances,

Chapter 5 WAR THREATENS

time and personnel. The Island's politicians considered the introduction of similar legislation, but what started out as a seemingly simple piece of legislation soon developed into something quite different.

For the Island's brigades it was business as usual, although one incident in June 1947 was relevant to some of the arguments being raised by the legislators concerning the boundaries of the various fire authorities and the need for a central fire control.

A fire was discovered in a cottage at Santon by the son of the family who lived there. He had just lit a fire in the hearth and walked out of the cottage to talk to a neighbour. They were soon both alarmed to see smoke coming from the building. The Douglas and Castletown Police were notified immediately and they informed the Castletown Brigade. Mr Kennaugh, Captain of the Brigade, knew the property and that it was outside the Castletown Fire Authority Area. He told the police he would attend the fire if the Douglas Brigade were not prepared to do so, though he needed their permission.

A police constable and a sergeant left Castletown for the fire; meanwhile Douglas Brigade were unsure of the location of the property, or if it was in their area. The result was that neither fire brigade turned out; the fire raged unchecked and the cottage was gutted. This predicament was one faced by the owners of many such properties situated on the limits of adjacent fire authority areas. This, with the question of payment for services, was among questions addressed in the proposed legislation.

The following year, on 27th August, a tragic fire occurred at a lodging-house, at No.2 Mona Terrace, Douglas, in which four people lost their lives. It was the most serious fire recorded up to this time in the Island. The fire had started in a back sitting room on the ground floor. The tenant, a 55-year-old widow, discovered the fire at about 5am. She smelled smoke and went downstairs to investigate. When she opened the door to the back room, the fire flashed over and engulfed the staircase. Nevertheless, she was able to raise the alarm and warn the others in the house before she was overcome by smoke. With the staircase ablaze, all the occupants were marooned on the upper floors. The woman's son made his escape to the property next door by edging along a narrow ledge on the front of the building. The husband of a couple living at the rear of the house jumped from a bedroom window some 24 feet into the back yard. He urged his wife to follow but was then unable to break her fall. She was taken to hospital by taxi but died later from her injuries.

The police were first on the scene, at 5.15am. As PC Curphey was getting a ladder from a nearby builders' yard, the fire brigade arrived under the direction of Alfie O'Hara, the Chief Officer. A full crew of seven men had arrived at the station within four minutes of the call. They immediately set to work and by 6.45am the fire was under control, but two people had died in the fire in addition to the woman who jumped. The tenant died the following day from her injuries. These two events had a profound effect on the discussions, which were taking place on the introduction of the new legislation.

Top: Peel Austin Towing Vehicle FMN 404 and the Coventry Climax trailer pump which was allocated to Peel in 1942. **Middle:** Competitions were an essential part of training with the AFS. This certificate relates to a competition won by fire-post No.10 in 1943 for major blue trailer pump drill. **Above:** Members of Douglas fire-post No.12 which was the Crosby unit with their trailer pump and Kitto Trophy for the best light trailer pump drill. *(Author's collection)*

TOWARDS ONE SERVICE
The Local Government (Fire Services) Act 1950

THE BILL, which had been introduced to amend the 1940 Act, got no further than its second reading. Debate had been heated and, as a result, the House of Keys appointed a committee to consider the Local Government (Fires) Act 1944. Their report was published in August 1944 but the recommendations were never implemented.

In an attempt to resolve the matter a Fire Service Commission was appointed by the Governor under the chairmanship of Ramsey G Johnson. The Commission were instructed to consider the establishment of a single Insular Fire Brigade or, if this were found to be inadvisable, to recommend changes in the existing system. They deliberated for several years, eventually publishing their report in November 1948. Not surprisingly, many of the issues raised in the now dormant Bill of 1944 came under review. The vexed question of the boundaries between adjacent fire authority areas was also very carefully considered. The Commission eventually concluded that the Island should keep the existing system of fire brigades maintained by local authorities, but under the overall direction of the Local Government Board. They did, however, agree to the boundary alterations called for in the 1944 Bill and further recommended that Foxdale, which at the time of the inquiry fell within three fire authority areas, should be placed in one area. It also recommended the abolition of payment for the services of a fire brigade, subject to certain interim measures. Finally it was recommended that the Local Government Board should appoint a Chief Fire Staff Officer.

As a result of the fire at No.2 Mona Terrace, the Lieutenant Governor also directed the Commission to inquire into the provision of means of escape in case of fire for people staying in boarding-houses or hotels. Under existing legislation such buildings were only required to provide proper means of escape in case of fire if the height of the building exceeded 40ft. As No.2 Mona Terrace was below this height, the provisions of the relevant Acts did not apply and no external fire escape had been provided.

The Commission recommended the introduction of legislation requiring all flats, tenements or public buildings exceeding two storeys to be provided with a proper means of internal or external escape. A Fire Services Bill was introduced to the Legislature by Deemster Johnson in February 1949. It had a stormy passage, the stumbling block being the appointment of a Chief Fire Staff Officer with the Douglas Members being of the opinion that the Chief Officer of the Douglas Brigade could perform the duties; also in contention was Clause 20 relating to the abolition of

Fire broke out at F W Woolworth's store in Douglas on 11th April 1951 during alterations to an adjacent building to extend the store. It was a major fire and the new Merryweather Marquis Pump Escape was in attendance in Howard Street along with the Albion which can be seen in Strand Street. *(Author's collection)*

payments to local authorities for services rendered at fires. It eventually led to an adjournment to allow for re-drafting of the Bill. It was reintroduced in May but there was still disagreement about the same points, the Bill being rejected at its third reading. The Fire Escapes Bill, however, succeeded at its first reading, becoming law in April 1950.

The Fire Escapes Act gave the Local Government Board wide powers to require owners and occupiers of certain buildings to provide proper means of escape in the case of fire and to impose penalties for non-compliance. It also made provision for loan advancement to enable owners of buildings to comply with the regulations.

In October 1951, before the regulations had been

Chapter 6 TOWARDS ONE SERVICE

Douglas Fire Brigade acquired this Limousine type AEC Merryweather Marquis Major Pump Wheeled Escape in 1951 only days before the Woolworth's fire. The outcome of that fire would have been very different without it. The saving grace was the pumping capacity it provided through its 1,000 gallons per minute pump with a capacity to supply eight branches. It is photographed climbing Prospect Hill in Douglas. *(Author)*

introduced, a disastrous fire completely gutted a shop and the flat above. The fire emphasised the importance of the Act and the need for an alternative means of escape in certain types of premises.

Shortly before 4am on Thursday 6th October 1951 Walter Howarth, the proprietor of the Waterloo Hotel in Strand Street, was wakened by people shouting and the noise of breaking glass. He was told that the premises next door, above Hotchkiss' shop, were on fire. His wife telephoned the fire brigade at 3.55am, while he and his son-in-law tried to force an entry through the rear of the premises. They were joined by John Burns, a neighbour, who managed to climb onto an outhouse roof and rescue a fourteen-year-old girl who had been pushed through a window by her twenty-one-year-old sister, Peggy. The fire beat the rescuers back, however, and Peggy and another younger sister died in the fire.

Having been unable to reach the children for the smoke and flames, their mother had managed to climb out of a first-floor window at the front of the building. A policeman helped her down from the ledge above the shop front. A lodger in the house climbed from the window of his room on the same floor and then tried to pull himself up to the second-floor window where he knew that Peggy was sleeping. He managed to pull himself up to the window ledge and break the glass, but he saw that the room was empty. She had gone to her sister's room at the rear of the house.

The fire brigade arrived, under the direction of Chief Officer Courtie, seven minutes after getting the call. This was an exceptionally good turnout, but on arrival the men found the building completely engulfed by fire. While Fireman Quirk was laying on two jets, Mr Courtie learned that two people were unaccounted for. Two firemen wearing Proto sets entered the building, with little regard for their own safety, but they were too late. The fire had been caused by a wireless set not having been switched off at the wall socket.

The Fire Services Bill was presented yet again in November 1949 and was eventually passed by Tynwald on 31st January 1950.

The Local Government (Fire Services) Act 1950 became law on 16th May. As required by its provisions, the Local Government Board elected a Fire Services Committee with representation from each fire authority area. All of the local authorities were designated as Fire Authorities, with the Rushen Joint Fire Protection Board restyled as the Rushen Fire Authority.

Douglas Fire Authority Area had been inspected twice a year, by Mr Ellis in his capacity as Inspector of Appliances, under the requirements of Section 20 of the 1940 Act. During an inspection in November 1948 he noted that the Leyland pump escape was not at the station. Further investigation showed it had been loaned to the Isle of Man Airports Board on 11th September and was stationed at Ronaldsway Airport. It was still absent at the next inspection, and Mr Ellis was concerned that Douglas was without a pump escape. In his report to the Local Government Board, he urged that it should be replaced.

HOLIDAY PROPERTIES

Douglas was the fire area with the most multi-storey properties, many of them used as boarding-houses during the holiday season. The Douglas Brigade had the only turntable ladder on the Island — but now had no appliance, apart from the Albion with the Telescala ladder, carrying a wheeled escape. The loss of a major pumping unit was serious, but could be offset against the trailer pumps that were still available.

On 22nd February 1950 the Works Committee of the Borough considered the provision of a escape-carrying appliance, and a deputation led by Alderman J C Fargher went to Merryweather & Sons to inspect the latest types. Mr Ellis had by now left the Island, though he still acted as Inspector of Appliances. He arranged for an inspection and drill during April.

The Local Government Board were required under the terms of the new Act to appoint a Chief Fire Staff Officer. They approached the Douglas Corporation to enquire if any officer they appointed could be seconded part-time to their brigade. A deputation from the Works Committee discussed the matter with the Board, but with five full-time firemen already employed by the Borough, it is not surprising that nothing came from the meeting.

Alfie O'Hara, Chief Officer of the Douglas Brigade, retired on 1st April 1950, having completed an impressive career. He had served forty years as a voluntary fireman before being appointed full-time Second Officer in 1941 and Chief Officer in 1945. He was succeeded by Fred Courtie, and Bert Kenna was promoted from Sergeant to Second Officer.

The deputation returned from Merryweather, made their recommendation to the Works Committee, and an official order for a new pump escape was placed on 5th May 1950.

During July, Mr H M Smith, Chief Inspector of Fire Services to the Home Office, visited the Island to advise the Local Government Board on the selection of a Chief Fire Staff Officer. Mr S J Mayall was appointed early in 1951.

Late in March 1951 Douglas took delivery of its new appliance. It was a Merryweather Marquis pump escape of the very latest type, powered by a 125hp, six-cylinder AEC diesel engine, with a forward-control enclosed limousine-type body. It was fitted with a centrally-mounted major pump of 1,000gpm capacity that could supply eight deliveries and be operated from either side. A 100-gallon water tank supplied two top-mounted first-aid hose-reels. It carried a 50ft Merryweather Telescala wheeled escape together with full emergency equipment in generous locker space. It was soon to prove its worth. Building work on an extension to Woolworth's store in Strand Street, Douglas, was well advanced. At 10.15am on Wednesday 11th April a tarpaulin between the store and the building works caught fire. Mr Bartlett, the manager, raised the alarm and evacuated customers from the store. He then led some of his staff in an ineffective attempt to fight the fire with hand extinguishers. He regrouped his staff on the stairs and formed a bucket chain but they had to retreat due to the heat of the fire, fanned by a strong south-westerly wind.

The fire brigade arrived within minutes of receiving the

In January 1961 fire broke out in the upper floors of the Hotel Metropole on Queen's Promenade in Douglas. Fire damage was confined to the roof area but the hotel suffered water damage throughout. It was the last fire at which the old Dorman Merryweather Turntable Ladder was to attend - it was broken up the following year for scrap. *(Author)*

call, but the building was already well alight. Smoke was belching out of the top-floor windows and part of the roof collapsed before the second appliance arrived. The spread of fire was rapid; flames shot through the roof and threatened adjoining property. The first and second floors collapsed in a shower of burning debris. The turntable ladder was in use as a water tower, directing a jet onto the flames. Firemen had to be withdrawn for a time from Strand Street as masonry was falling into the street. The front wall buckled and swayed as the internal floors and the rest of the roof fell away. Shortly afterwards the whole of the roof collapsed, leaving the front wall unsupported. By this time the fire had jumped a natural gap and the rear of houses in Howard Street was vacated as flames licked roofs and window frames. The brigade had the fire under control by noon, but they remained on duty through Wednesday night, breaking holes through the concrete pavement late in the evening to flood the basement and extinguish the last of the fire.

Shortly after this incident Mr Mayall arrived on the Island to take up his duties as Chief Fire Staff Officer to the Local Government Board. The various fire authorities were requested to prepare details of their establishment, as required under the Act that also made provision for mutual

Chapter 6 TOWARDS ONE SERVICE

In 1967 a fire broke out in part of the Arragon Hotel at Santon; by this time Douglas Brigade now formed part of the all-Island Fire Service and they responded with the Merryweather Pump Escape and the Dennis F28 Pump Water Tender. The fire was quickly extinguished but one occupant was affected by smoke inhalation and had to receive hospital treatment. *(Author)*

aid and pursuing powers. Mr Mayall prepared a reinforcement scheme for circulation to all participating fire authorities. The scheme listed details of personnel and appliances to be made available to assist other fire authorities. Each scheduled appliance had to be complete with all ancillary gear and a minimum of 1,500ft of delivery hose. The reinforcing authority was required to send the appliance in charge of their second senior officer.

Schedule of reinforcing personnel and appliances

Authority	Personnel	Appliances and special apparatus
DOUGLAS	10	Major pump, 4 Proto sets, Tender plus major trailer pump (or turntable ladder if needed).
RAMSEY	10	Tender plus major pump and light trailer pump.
CASTLETOWN	5	Tender plus major trailer pump.
PEEL	5	Tender plus major trailer pump.
LAXEY	5	Tender plus major trailer pump.
MICHAEL	5	Tender plus light trailer pump.
RUSHEN	5	Tender plus light trailer pump with 50ft escape.

All appliances were required to carry foam compound and foam-making branch-pipes. After some minor difficulties agreement was eventually reached between the participating authorities, and the Fire Reinforcement Scheme 1953 was submitted to Tynwald and approved on 24th July.

Close liaison was maintained with RAF Jurby, and the Chief Fire Staff Officer could call on a trained body of men if required. Following the introduction of the reinforcement scheme the Commanding Officer at Jurby ordered an additional water tender to be made available by the station in case the need arose. Mr Mayall advised a programme of replacement, with strong emphasis on the need for pump water tenders.

The districts covered by the fire authorities were mainly rural, often without adequate water supplies. These appliances could be put into action as soon as they arrived at a fire. This advantage was readily grasped by the various brigades and the Local Government Board adopted the Chief Officer's recommendation as a matter of policy.

Although Douglas had opted out of the proposed all-Island scheme, discussions took place with the Douglas Fire Committee on the same subject and agreement was reached for the conversion of the existing Fordson tender. Work was put in hand for a 300-gallon tank to be installed within the bodywork and the light trailer pump to be fitted on the vehicle and permanently connected to a hose-reel.

The Local Government Board lost no time in implementing the replacement programme and two new appliances were ordered for Peel and Castletown.

In February 1953 the CFSO and a fireman driver from Peel took delivery of the first new major pump water tender from Dennis Brothers at Guildford. The Dennis F8 was a self-propelled pump with a limousine-type body fitted with a 300-gallon water tank and a single first-aid hose-reel. The appliance carried delivery and suction hose and had locker space for all ancillary equipment. The Castletown appliance was delivered in June the same year.

The reinforcement scheme was used for the first time on 27th October 1953 when Laxey Brigade were called to assist Douglas at a fire in a four-bay Dutch barn at Pulrose farm.

An important move was made in 1953 by the Local Government Board towards the abolition of charges for brigade services. Negotiations took place between the Board and the Fire Officers' Committee representing the various insurance companies. Redemption money amounting to a sum of £32,500 was eventually agreed and Sections 19 and 20 of the 1950 Act were repealed and amended by the Local Government (Fire Services) Act 1954. This abolished payment to fire authorities and became effective from 19th October 1954.

A technical committee had been appointed in 1951 to look into the drafting of regulations under the Fire Escapes Act of 1950. These regulations were approved by the Local Government Board in November 1952 and passed by Tynwald the following month.

In March 1953 the Douglas Brigade were called to a fire at a five-storey boarding-house in Palace Road which once again underlined the need for such regulations. The alarm was raised shortly after 3am. When the brigade arrived, the fire had rapidly spread from the kitchen to the first and second floors. Damage to the main staircase had cut off the occupants of the upstairs rooms. They escaped through windows onto ladders placed by neighbours. The brigade found that the fire had a serious hold on the property, and was only contained with great difficulty. If a fire had occurred in the height of the summer season the consequences could have been disastrous.

Ramsey Brigade had a call during the same month, in the early hours of the morning, to a serious fire at Ballure Mount in which a man died. The property was occupied by a 78-year-old man living on his own. When the brigade arrived, the four-storey building was on fire from the basement to the third floor. It had obviously been burning for some time before the alarm was raised. The fire was brought under control more than twelve hours later. The occupier's body was found in the debris during damping-down operations, underlining the hazards of open fires and elderly people living alone.

The brigade were again called out, in October, this time to the Ramsey Gas Works, where the tar plant was found to be on fire. Faced with a very difficult and dangerous task, the brigade eventually extinguished the fire using the new foam-making apparatus. The plant was severely damaged and a large gas main was cracked by the heat. The fire illustrated a

A fire shortly before morning service at Finch Hill Methodist Church saw a full turnout from the Douglas Station, the newly acquired AEC Merryweather Turntable Ladder was used to tackle an outbreak in the roof. The Commer van which Douglas used as a Personnel Carrier and Emergency Tender was also in attendance along with the Dennis F28 PWT. *(Trevor Owen)*

Chapter 6 TOWARDS ONE SERVICE

weakness in the fire service and their ability to make foam in any great quantity.

All the old wartime appliances which were surplus to requirements were taken into store by the Civil Defence Commission. A peacetime Auxiliary Fire Service was started, with an establishment of seventy-five men.

At the request of the Isle of Man Airports Board Mr Mayall arranged 72 training sessions during 1954 for the airport crash crews. By the start of 1955 the airport had a well-trained crew. Most of the Island's firemen had also been familiarised with the aircraft currently in use and the specialised fire-fighting equipment operated by the Airport Fire Service.

The Island reinforcing scheme was again put into operation in 1954 when fire broke out at King William's College. At 9.45pm on 11th May smoke was seen coming from the roof of Dixon House. The College fire alarm was immediately sounded and the Castletown Brigade notified. Staff evacuated the dormitories on the first and second floors and the College fire brigade moved into action with a light pump connected to a hydrant in the quadrangle. They held the fire in check until the Castletown Brigade arrived shortly afterwards, reinforced by units from Rushen and Douglas. The fire was under control by 10.30pm but the brigade stayed until 5am the following morning.

The fire had started in the roof space used as a storeroom for suitcases and books. Although the fire had broken through the roof, damage was confined to the roof and roof space. This fire proved again the potential of an all-Island scheme and the need for a central fire control. This was to be a repeated request of successive Chief Fire Staff Officers, a request not granted until Douglas joined the all-Island scheme.

Continuing the programme of modernisation, a number of featherweight pumps were bought to replace the obsolete trailer pumps. The Rushen Fire Authority continued to provide a service covering the southern parishes and the two village districts of Port Erin and Port St Mary. The Authority still operated two stations, one in each village, with the escape carrier and trailer pump in Port Erin and the Austin towing vehicle and trailer pump in Port St Mary.

In 1951 the Authority embarked on the mammoth task of converting all the ball hydrants in their area. At the same time the Austin was converted to enable additional hose to be carried. Both stations were condemned as obsolete in 1955 and the Authority applied themselves to providing a new central station.

The need for additional foam-making equipment had been worrying the CFSO for some time. To solve the problem he set about converting old trailer pump chassis into foam trailer units carrying 100 gallons of foam compound and two foam-making branch-pipes. The first of these entered service in 1955; three were produced by the fire service's own staff.

Ramsey Brigade's appliances were now becoming obsolete and a further Dennis F8 was delivered to Ramsey in April 1955. With the arrival of the new appliance the sixteen-year-old Merryweather self-propelled pump was transferred to Laxey as a temporary measure to replace the wartime

This fire in October 1964 in a garage at the rear of Princes Street illustrates one drawback to the Merryweather PE which had difficulty in accessing some of the narrow lanes in Douglas. The fire had drawn the usual crowd of onlookers - now Health and Safety requirements would see the whole street cordoned off! *(Author)*

tender and trailer pump.

Later in the year the Austin towing vehicle kept by the Rushen Fire Authority at Port St Mary sub-station was sold to the Civil Defence Commission for £125. An Austin A30 van, complete with hose-racks, was bought and stationed at Port Erin in the Falcon's Nest yard, along with the escape carrier. The sub-station was closed down.

A site for the Rushen Brigade's new fire station had been agreed with the Port Erin Commissioners, situated on their car park adjoining Droghadfayle Road. It was completed in 1957 and opened on 18th January the following year by Mr A Moore of Port St Mary, who had been a member of the Rushen Fire Authority since its inception. The new station had a two-bay appliance room with lecture facilities.

During 1957 a joint police and fire radio communication scheme came into operation. Two sets were allocated to the fire service, one being installed in the Chief Fire Staff Officer's car and the other in the Ramsey first-call appliance. With Douglas still outside the Island Fire Service, Ramsey was considered the main station. An additional set was acquired the following year and fitted to the Peel appliance.

In July 1958 a fire at Gretch Vane, Lonan, further emphasised the value of water tenders as means of getting water onto a fire quickly. Laxey Brigade were called to a fire

On 9th June 1968 a fire had been burning in a tack room at the rear of Parkfield House, Douglas for some time before it was discovered. Douglas Station responded and quickly had the blaze extinguished but not before the annex was gutted and the main house smoke logged. It was the last attendance of the Merryweather Marquis Pump Escape before disposal and it is now in preservation. *(Author)*

in the outbuildings of the farm; the appliance was the old Merryweather from Ramsey, now stationed at Laxey. Although it had a major pump and a portable ultra-lightweight pump, it did not carry water. The nearest water supply was from a stream a quarter of a mile away. However, there was a water trough in the farmyard fed by a one-inch domestic supply. The ultra-lightweight pump was set up and the brigade were able to get two jets working immediately. The major pump was set up at the stream to relay water and supplement the supply to the trough. This kept the two jets in action, which was sufficient to bring the fire under control. This was the first time that a portable lightweight pump had been used at a fire, and only the Rushen Brigade remained without one.

BOY DIES

The tragic death of a boy led to a warning from the fire service that would anticipate requirements which would later appear in byelaws. Late in the afternoon of Saturday 23rd January 1959, a neighbour ran to John Hyslop's home in Port St Mary and told him that smoke was pouring out of a house nearby. He called the brigade and arrived at the house just before the appliance and the rest of the brigade. They entered the building which was heavily smoke-logged and searched for the seat of the fire. They found no obvious source and the house appeared to be empty. It was vented and only then was smoke found to be issuing from a cupboard under the stairs. Some smouldering paper and toys were easily extinguished. As they were clearing this rubbish the firemen were astonished to find a young boy in the cupboard, overcome by smoke. Unsuccessful attempts were made at reviving him. He had, it appeared, gone into the cupboard to look for toys by the light of a piece of burning paper. By some twist of fate the cupboard door had shut behind him.

The incident was a sad reminder of points that had been previously made in public by the fire service. Mr Mayall stressed again the importance of not leaving children on their own. He also cautioned against the use of door-latches that could only be operated from one side, anticipating requirements which would appear in byelaws years later.

On 16th September 1959, the Rushen Fire Authority took delivery of a new Austin Gypsy self-propelled pump with four-wheel drive and a front-mounted 600gpm pump. It was Mr Mayall's intention to have one of these as a supporting appliance at each of the country stations because of the high risk of heath and gorse fires in these areas and the need to get a pump to difficult locations.

On the very day of delivery to the Rushen Brigade it was called to a fire on Cronk ny Iree Laa which was threatening hundreds of acres of valuable grazing land. It was the only appliance that could get near to the fire ground which was two miles from the nearest water supply and several hundred feet above it. A road tanker was borrowed from

Chapter 6 TOWARDS ONE SERVICE

The former Palais de Dance in Strand Street had several reincarnations during its life. On 13th February 1967 while it was being used by the Maypole fire broke out, causing severe damage. Appliances from Douglas, Laxey and Peel responded and it was a particularly difficult fire to contain due to a false ceiling finished with polystyrene suspended tiles which allowed the fire to travel undetected, resulting in a flashover. *(Author)*

Fire gutted the stage area and dance hall at the Douglas Holiday Centre in the summer of 1972, the night after Duke Ellington and his Band had appeared, and valuable music scores were lost in the blaze. The Douglas AEC Merryweather TL was in attendance and is seen in this photo tackling the fire in the proscenium. *(Author)*

Manx Petroleum and used to carry water to a point near the fire where it was relayed to the Gypsy, which was then able to provide pressure for two jets at the fire, in this way proving its worth beyond doubt.

The dry summer of 1959 caused all attendance records to be broken, with a year total of 382. The worst fire occurred in Archallagan Plantation; it destroyed fourteen acres of trees and required a water relay of nearly a mile.

The six fire authorities outside Douglas amalgamated into one on 1st January 1960 and this marked a great step forward for the fire service in the Island. A new committee was set up as the Fire Services Committee of the Local Government Board under the chairmanship of Lieutenant J L Quine MHK, and with representation from the old fire authority areas.

The establishment of the retained brigades on amalgamation stood at 105 but the actual number was only 94. The CFSO expressed his concern over this and other issues, principal amongst which was a plea for the establishment of a central control preferably based on Douglas station despite it being outside the all-Island scheme.

There remained a political impasse on the Douglas issue but nonetheless Mr Mayall reported to the Fire Services Committee that the appliances at Douglas should be replaced, in particular the self-propelled pump and the turntable ladder. A decision on this was deferred pending an independent report from Mr T C A Shirling, the Home Office Fire Service Senior Engineering Inspector.

Meanwhile PC Kinrade had left Kirk Michael, being replaced by PC Moyer in 1951. He was approached by the Commissioners to take charge of the fire brigade; he accepted, having obtained the usual approvals. In October 1952, however, the Government Secretary notified the Village Commissioners that PC Moyer would no longer be able to continue as Chief Officer of the brigade due to a change of Government policy. After considering the matter the Commissioners appointed Mr G E Creer as the new Chief Officer of their brigade.

The obsolete Merryweather at Laxey was withdrawn some months before being replaced in June 1960 by a Dennis F28 pump water tender. The old appliance was stripped down by the transport officer and a 300-gallon tank strapped to the chassis. A hose-reel and pump were fitted and the appliance was stationed at Kirk Michael in 1961, giving the village its first, albeit temporary, pump water tender.

On 23rd March 1961 a call was received shortly before midday by John Bell, Chief Officer of the Peel Brigade, to a fire that followed an explosion in one of the diesel engines in Peel Power Station. On arrival he found the generating room heavily smoke-logged and immediately called for assistance from Douglas and Kirk Michael. The Douglas Brigade were delayed at Glenvine by road works and took 25 minutes to

Chapter 6 TOWARDS ONE SERVICE

arrive, by which time their breathing apparatus was desperately needed.

The Chief Officer had been informed at the outset that the crankcase of one of the large diesel engines had exploded, and two workmen were logged as missing. Entry was made and oil was found to be burning under the floor ducting, though all the other generating sets were still working. The injured men, one of whom was severely burnt, were rescued and the engines shut down, though with some difficulty. This left a large part of the Island without electricity. Men in relays, using breathing apparatus, tackled the fire. In the dense black smoke, the metal and concrete duct covers were lifted one at a time and the burning oil smothered with foam. The fire, eventually extinguished by 1pm, completely vindicated the provision of foam-generating equipment.

During the year a fifth foam trailer pump was commissioned at Castletown, leaving only Douglas and Laxey without. A further Dennis F28 with a wheeled escape was ordered for the Rushen Brigade at a cost of £5,500, complete with a two-inch Alcon portable pump.

The previous year, Mr T A Kelly CBE M.I.F.E. Chief Fire Officer of the Liverpool City Fire Brigade, had been commissioned to report on the all-Island scheme which had been under consideration since its preparation in 1956 by Mr Mayall, Now, in June 1961, his report was received. While it proved controversial in some respects, it did substantiate most of what had been said by Mr Mayall. The Douglas Brigade was singled out for special attention due to its unusual ranking system. This was reckoned to be out of line with current practice in the UK and as adopted by the rest of the Island. Attention was also focused on the age of some of its appliances, particularly the turntable ladder which dated from 1936. Douglas Corporation were understandably taken aback by the report and refuted some of the allegations. They defended the choice of chassis for the major pump, which had been quite properly made in relation to the fleet of AEC diesel buses operated and maintained by the Corporation, The Chief Officer also made the point that without a major pump of the size of the Merryweather Marquis, the Woolworth's fire of 1951 might have had a disastrous result. This appliance had taken water from one of nine special suction hydrants on the promenade and had rapidly distributed water to six branches: four at the fire and two at the properties in Howard Street. However, the Corporation accepted criticisms of the age of the Dorman turntable ladder and the Albion Merryweather, and asked Mr Courtie to report on their condition. Considering his recommendations, the Council lost no time in ordering re-placements. An AEC Merryweather 100ft turntable ladder and a Dennis F28 water tender were delivered in 1962.

Mr Mayall resigned in September to become Chief Officer of Breconshire & Radnorshire Joint Fire Brigade, before he could see many of his ideas implemented. The Fire Services Committee made an approach to the Douglas Corporation and Mr Fred Courtie was appointed as acting Chief Fire Staff Officer until Mr Mayall's replacement was selected. There were twenty-two applications for the post and on 28th May 1962 Mr Cyril Pearson was appointed Chief Fire Staff Officer, taking up his position on 1st September 1962. At the request of the Fire Services Committee he prepared a report based on the two previous reports, and incorporated his own observations. Mr Pearson picked out one paragraph of the Kelly report as being vital to the issue: "It is not possible to obtain any reinforcements into the Island within a reasonable time and this is one of the problems which has to be appreciated and adequate fire cover provided within the Island itself...."

His recommendations endorsed much of what had been advocated by his predecessor. They included the provision of a new five-bay fire station at Douglas, with a central control and full-time staff as outlined in the Kelly report. He amplified Mayall's policy of giving each station a second appliance with a cross-country capability but incorporating certain ideas of his own. His priorities were the abolition of parochial boundaries, the establishment of a temporary all-Island fire control in Douglas fire station, and the remote operation of fire-warning devices at retained outstations from that central control.

Kirk Michael station was the first to receive one of the new four-wheel-drive appliances to Mr Pearson's design. It was based on a long-wheelbase Land Rover chassis with forward control, originally designed for military use. A local firm, Shore Garages Ltd, won the contract for supplying the chassis with bodywork provided by Crosbie, Cain & Kennish of Douglas. The appliance was built in the company's premises and incorporated a 100-gallon water tank, pump, hose-reel, locker space and 30ft ladder. It was completed by September 1963 and entered service straight away, with a second going to Peel in February the following year.

At the request of the IOM Airports Board fire cover was provided at Jurby airfield, now in Government ownership, when used for aircraft diverted due to weather. The Ramsey F8 was the designated appliance with Kirk Michael being required to move one appliance and crew to Ramsey. Exercises continued to be held with the Airport Fire Service to maintain familiarisation with equipment and aircraft types.

In June 1963 a fire broke out at Ballaterson Manor, Ballaugh. The large house was gutted despite the efforts of the brigades in attendance, which were hampered by a poor water supply. Prior to the amalgamation the manor would have been on the limit of two fire authority areas, with all the attendant problems. On this occasion there was no confusion, the call being handled by Central Fire Control and appliances being dispatched from Ramsey, Kirk Michael and Peel.

Five farm fires in the south of the Island the following year underlined the advantages of amalgamation, with multiple attendances at each fire by Castletown, Rushen, Peel and Douglas. This had been made possible by the terms of the Fire Authority Order 1959, made by the Local Government Board and approved by all the fire authorities except Douglas, which nonetheless participated under their obligation to the reinforcement scheme.

Tynwald had allocated £10,000 in 1958 for the improvement of water mains throughout the Island. Farmers had been encouraged to provide hydrants through an agricultural holdings grant-aid scheme. Despite these provisions there had been problems with the water supply at

The first purpose-built Emergency Tender was based on a Ford commercial chassis and stationed at Douglas in 1979. Traffic volume on the Island was increasing rapidly and the vehicle was soon in service here at an accident on Glencrutchery Road in Douglas. It was the forerunner of what have now become the most used versatile appliances in the Service. *(Author)*

some farm fires. The situation in town and village areas was much better, but there were still improvements to be made. This was well illustrated by the problems encountered at one of the most difficult fires faced by the Rushen Brigade. In April 1964 they were called to a fire at Mallmore, a boarding-house on Port St Mary promenade. Although the brigade were quickly on the scene, they found the roof already well alight. The men tackled the fire from the front of the building. However, the water main and hydrants were in a narrow lane to the rear which required hoses to be laid round the block to the appliance. This meant a delay in getting water onto the fire. As soon as the pump was primed, the brigade were able to bring the fire under control. It was some time before it was eventually extinguished, however, due to pockets of fire in the roof space.

The implementation of the Fire Escapes Act and its regulations had been slow, but in 1961 Tynwald resolved to enforce Defect Orders under Section 7 of the Act with effect from 21st March. The task facing the Island Fire Service was formidable, but the problem facing Douglas was worse. Douglas had by far the most hotels and boarding-houses. Although 639 buildings had been inspected since the introduction of the Act, 529 still had not been seen. Further, there were 1,500 premises that were still required to register. This work occupied the Chief Fire Officer of the Douglas Brigade virtually full-time. Following the Tynwald resolution, Douglas served defect notices on 186 owners of premises that needed outside escapes. More escapes were needed than had been anticipated, and so requests went back to Tynwald for more money to fulfil the grant provisions of the Act.

The Island lacked a completely unified service only because Douglas Corporation were unwilling to join the amalgamation scheme. This was due partly to civic pride, and partly to the fact that Douglas had the longest-serving brigade and was the only one with full-time personnel. The Corporation thought, perhaps justifiably, that any new system should evolve around their establishment. However, as the unified system was designed to cover the whole Island, it was quite proper that the new fire service should be administered by Central Government.

To bring matters to a head the Local Government Board presented a six-point report to Tynwald for approval, recommending that the Board should be the fire authority for the Douglas area. The recommendations were accepted and on 16th June 1964 Tynwald approved the Fire Authority Order 1964. The Fire Services Committee was reconstituted under the chairmanship of Mr H S Cain MHK, with Mr P Radcliffe MHK, Mr W E Fargher, Mr J J Quilliam and a representative from Douglas Corporation as members. From 1st April 1965 the Island, at last, had a unified fire service.

Chapter 7 UNITY AT LAST

UNITY AT LAST
The all-Island Fire Service and the Summerland disaster

THE FIRST TASK facing the new Fire Services Committee was to reorganise the full-time staff. Within a very short time the new establishment emerged: Chief Fire Service Officer, Mr C Pearson; Assistant Divisional Officer, Mr F Courtie; Station Officer, Mr H B Kenna; Sub-Officers, Mr J Sloane, Mr R S Skinner, Mr J B Cowley, Leading Fireman Mr M Ventre; and three Firemen to be appointed.

The policy of modernisation continued and Castletown's two-bay station opened in the early part of 1965 at Farrant's Way. It replaced the obsolete premises in the Commissioners' Yard. Flashing lights and two-tone horns were fitted to appliances at about the same time as the rest of the UK.

The most important development took place on 1st April when Central Fire Control, manned on a 24-hour watch system, was at last established at Douglas Station. At the same time, work started on a 999 emergency telephone call system.

Later in the year in November there was a small fire in an electrical workshop at the rear of Express Radio in Athol Street. Douglas Brigade responded and the fire was quickly extinguished. During the attendance, however, a fireman collapsed and died. The irony of this isolated incident was that the fireman involved was Station Officer Bert Kenna, whose father had been the only other Island fireman to die in service some 27 years earlier.

The next new appliance to be delivered, in February 1967, was a Dennis F38 with a two-delivery rear-mounted pump and carrying a 50ft steel-wheeled escape. It was commissioned and allocated to Ramsey. The following month the AFS, now administered by the Civil Defence Commission, took delivery of a Bedford 'Green Goddess' Home Office-pattern self-propelled pump designed following wartime AFS experience. The appliance carried a 1,000gpm pump with delivery to four standard outlets with instantaneous couplings. It was the first of four to be delivered over the next year.

The integrated service was now responding to fires more quickly, and multi-brigade attendances were becoming a regular feature at major fires. During 1966 appliances from Ramsey, Laxey and Kirk Michael attended a serious fire at the Crossag farm near Ramsey. In January the following year another fire at Ballamoar, Lonan, required the attendance of appliances from Laxey, Ramsey and Douglas, with emergency lighting provided from an elderly Leyland emergency tender operated by the Civil Defence Commission. This had been acquired by the Commission from the Glasgow City Fire Brigade, mainly for their capacity to provide light at any incident to which their personnel might have been called. The fire service were quick to realise its potential and it was again in use at a fire at the Maypole Supermarket in Strand Street, Douglas, in February 1967. Douglas Station responded to the call, and reinforcements were immediately sent from Laxey and Peel. The fire was difficult to contain, a task made worse by the presence of a false ceiling of polystyrene tiles, These tiles ignited, giving off dense acrid smoke, and fell in burning lumps on the firemen below. Breathing apparatus had to be used; despite this the fire was tackled directly from within despite the firemen being driven back by a flashover in the first instance. The turntable ladder was positioned at the rear of the building in Market Street, and the roof was perforated to assist with ventilation until the fire was brought under control.

Implementation of the Fire Escapes Act still gave concern to the Chief Fire Staff Officer, following the earlier Tynwald resolution to enforce the defect notices. To remedy the situation, Fred Courtie became enforcing officer for the Act, taking up his appointment on 5th April 1966.

In his report for the year ending March 1967, Mr Pearson stressed the need for the urgent replacement of Douglas Station with new premises, incorporating proper headquarters accommodation. The John Street fire station was still the main one for Douglas, with insufficient space for more than one appliance. The Lord Street fire station was still the temporary wooden building dating from 1935, housing three appliances and incorporating the only maintenance bay. The headquarters staff and Fire Prevention Department were housed in an old building in Christian Road, isolated from the rest of the brigade activity. The situation was obviously unsatisfactory.

Nine sites were under review for the location of the new Central Fire Station. Mr Pearson favoured the selection of a site above the town affording choice of access to fire scenes, echoing the principle implemented by Richard O'Hara almost a century earlier. Sites at Glencrutchery Road, Blackberry Lane and Somerset Road were fully investigated together with a site on Peel Road near the Quarter Bridge. Once again advice was sought from the Home Office and on the recommendation of Mr H M Smith, Chief Inspector of Fire Services, the Peel Road site was eventually approved. The site on Peel Road was bought in 1974 for £14,000; building costs were £257,000. Meanwhile, in 1967, £12,000 had also been earmarked for the building of a new fire station at Heathfield Drive for the Peel Brigade.

A Fire Liaison Panel was established the same year,

The Hydraulic Platform is seen in attendance at a fire in 1982 at Douglas Motorcycle Centre. Also in the photograph is the Peel Wheeled Escape and the Dennis F46A Pump Water Tender from Douglas Station. The fire was potentially very dangerous as it was in premises to the rear of the Tiger Tim Petrol Filling Station. Access to the rear was difficult but the fire was quickly contained and brought under control. *(Author)*

following concern at the figures of wastage attributable to fire on the Island. This followed UK practice, when panels were formed at the instigation of the British Insurance Association to promote a better understanding of the consequences of fire and to stimulate better awareness of fire prevention. The Tower Insurance Company took the initiative; with the drive of its manager, Mr G K Owen, a panel was formed from a broad cross-section of the business community.

During 1968 three new appliances were delivered. The first was another locally-built emergency tender, fully equipped with cutting and handling gear, based on a long-wheelbase Land Rover chassis. The second was a Dennis F35 with a side-mounted pump with four deliveries and carrying a Merryweather 50ft wheeled escape. Both were stationed at Douglas, the Dennis replacing the Merryweather escape of 1951.

The third appliance was allocated to Rushen. It was the last of the four-wheel-drive water tenders, based on the Land Rover, to have been built locally. It was slightly different from the others, incorporating modifications born out of operational experience.

The last major incident attended by the old Merryweather Marquis pump escape was a fire at Parkfield, Douglas, in June 1968. The fire started in a harness room at the rear of the house and spread to a bedroom above. There was a full turnout of the Douglas Brigade; the men managed to confine the fire to the rear of the house, but not before considerable damage had been done.

A Dennis F46A water tender with a 500gpm pump and two deliveries, carrying 400 gallons of water, was delivered in April 1971. Stationed at Douglas, it became the first-call appliance, replacing the F28 of 1962 which was transferred to Castletown as part of the continuing policy of updating the Island Service.

One of the Green Goddess Bedford appliances, allocated to the Civil Defence Commission for use by the AFS, was transferred to the regular fire service, painted red and also stationed at Castletown. The station was then equipped with one 500gpm and one 1,000gpm pump, considered essential in view of its proximity to Ronaldsway Airport. In the event of an emergency at the airport, Castletown would be the nearest reinforcing brigade.

The fire station at Ramsey, beneath the Town Hall, had been unsatisfactory for years. It housed two appliances, one behind the other, which caused frequent operational difficulties. When the Town Commissioners announced in 1970 that they intended to demolish the Town Hall, the Fire

Chapter 7 UNITY AT LAST

Top left: The Kirk Michael-based 4x4 Pump Water Tender Land Rover/Pilcher Green stationed inside the course at Ramsey during TT week 1989.

Top right: Photographed at a fire at Crossag farm is DMN 890, the Morris Escape Carrier dating from 1939 originally stationed at Port Erin and was still in service in 1966.

Above: PMN 999 the Dennis R61 Pump Water Tender allocated to Kirk Michael Station between 1987 and 1995, is seen returning to the station which was still at the time behind the Mitre Hotel.

Below: A photograph taken in 1968 at the former Drill Hall in Douglas showing the Douglas Station allocation at that time.

(All photos: Author)

Service Committee had to look for an alternative site. Tynwald approved £25,000 for the provision of a new station with a three-bay appliance room, adjoining lecture room, recreational facilities, practice ground and tower. It was opened on 13th July 1971 by Mr Rawden Brooke who had just recently retired from the brigade after 23 years' service, ending his career as Station Officer. He had led the brigade through a great deal of change, culminating in a modern unit with the most up-to-date station in the Island.

SUMMERLAND

July 1971 saw the opening of the Summerland leisure complex. It was a pioneering development providing a wide variety of entertainment. The building was wonderful in concept, a huge area covered by a transparent cladding of acrylic material. It had been built by the Douglas Corporation and let to Trust House Forte Leisure Ltd. and was capable of accommodating 5,000 people under one roof. The northern part of the building incorporated a multi-level entertainment area, including a marquee show bar, leisure deck and a ground-floor amusement arcade. Families could spend a carefree day here, in the light and airy atmosphere, enjoying the amenities. The leisure area was connected to a solarium by open flying staircases. Many seaside resorts on the UK mainland were planning similar complexes. The Corporation operated the adjoining Aquadrome containing swimming pools and other remedial baths.

Then, on the evening of Thursday 2nd August 1973, three boys playing with matches accidentally set fire to a dismantled kiosk on an outside terrace. The kiosk collapsed against the building and this small fire spread to the main building. The aftermath was to bring dramatic changes to the legislation governing fire safety on the Island, and leave its mark on the whole of the British Isles. It was the worst peacetime disaster involving fire since 1929.

The fire was discovered at 7.40pm on the Mini Golf terrace outside the main building. The alarm was raised at staff level within Summerland and they set about tackling the blaze with hand extinguishers and a hose-reel. Their efforts had little effect. At 8.01pm the Central Fire Control received a telephone call from Duggan's Radio Cabs, via 999, that Summerland was on fire. This was followed by others in quick succession, one via Douglas Harbour Radio from a ship anchored in Douglas Bay. Appliances were dispatched at 8.02pm with Sub-Officer Quayle as the senior officer in the first-call appliance. By 8.08pm he was on the Promenade and could see that the fire was serious. He called by radio for 'pumps five' and the turntable ladder.

The first message from Summerland was not received until the appliances were on their way. The automatic alarm, a two-stage device with a direct link to Douglas Fire Service Station, was not activated until 8.05pm.

The building had eight levels within the external cladding. Sub-Officer Quayle, who arrived in the first appliance, cleared the downstairs and upper downstairs levels but was unable to gain access to the main solarium floor level due to the heat and burning debris falling from the roof. At this time there was extensive fire on all three terraces above the amusement arcade where the fire had entered the building. The transparent cladding had nearly all been enveloped in a rapid surface spread of fire, which gave off asphyxiating and explosive vapours and allowed burning molten plastic to fall on the exposed stairways and floors.

An all-stations alert was made at 8.10pm; fifteen minutes later they were all mobile. Altogether fourteen appliances attended. When the Chief Fire Staff Officer arrived at the fire it was immediately apparent to him that nothing could be done to save the Summerland building. Instead he concentrated efforts on stopping the fire at the southern boundary; this realistic approach meant that the nearby Aquadrome building was unscathed.

Water pressure for fire-fighting purposes was barely adequate, despite the presence of six fire hydrants in the vicinity of the building. Following urgent calls from the fire service, engineers from the water authority were able to improve the situation. By 9.10pm the fire was under control and by 3am the following day most of the supporting brigades had returned to their stations. Later the outstations were recalled to carry out damping-down operations and provide relief for the Douglas men who had been on duty through the night. However, firemen were in attendance at Summerland for three more days. On Saturday 4th, small outbreaks of fire had to be dealt with by the Douglas Brigade. Out-of-town brigades were again in attendance on the Sunday until about 6pm, damping down and clearing up.

When the fire broke out there were 3,000 people in Summerland. Fifty of them died trying to escape. Fire damage to the building approached £1.5m.

On September 3rd, the Lieutenant Governor of the Island appointed a Commission of Inquiry, under the chairmanship of the Hon Mr Justice Cantley OBE, to inquire into and report on the circumstances of the fire. The inquiry lasted until February 1974 and the report was published in May. Three main reasons were found for the large number of deaths: the very rapid development of the fire, the inadequate means of escape, and the evacuation of the building being delayed, unorganised and difficult. Many family members had tried to find one another; this also hindered the evacuation, with tragic consequences.

The outer cladding was Galbestos fabricated from sheet steel, coated with zinc, asbestos, bitumen and polyester resin. The outer coating ignited and because of the high conductivity of the steel the bitumen in the internal void ignited and quickly spread. The absence of any fire-stops either horizontal or vertical between the outer cladding and the inner lining resulted in the rapid spread of the fire. This in turn set fire to the inner fibreboard linings and the interior finishings. The multi-storey part of the building was very quickly engulfed in fire, which in turn ignited the Oroglas translucent covering to the main atrium.

There were twenty break-glass fire alarm points and seven staff points, all directly connected to the Douglas Fire Station and to an internal two-stage alarm system. The Commission found that 25 minutes elapsed before any alarm was actuated and even then no alarm sounded within Summerland itself. It also found shortcomings in the escape routes from the building. The worst instance was a

Chapter 7 UNITY AT LAST

Fifty people died in the Summerland fire which at the time was the worst peacetime fire disaster in the British Isles since 1929. The fire which started outside the building spread by radiation into the cavity between the cladding and internal lining to the side of the building and then to the Oroglas roof covering. The result of the Inquiry into the fire had far reaching consequences for the Island, the UK and the rest of the world for design, building regulations and legislation involving newer plastic materials. *(Dave Wood)*

supposedly protected staircase into which a permanent opening had been made. This allowed smoke to penetrate the area and this, coupled with the failure of the emergency lighting system and the fact that the emergency doors at the bottom of the stairway were bolted, resulted in the death of twelve people.

The Commission concluded with 34 recommendations, many of which had far-reaching consequences. It had much to say about the use of certain types of building materials, particularly plastics, The outcome was that the British Standards Institute set about revising certain codes of practice and technical data. It was recommended that any fire alarm system installed in a public place should always fail to an alarm state and not be capable of being switched off by unauthorised persons.

It was also recommended that architectural training should include a much-extended study of fire protection and fire precautions. This resulted in the Royal Institute of British Architects reviewing their professional code of conduct and, as an interim measure, publishing a booklet the following July entitled Fire and the Architect.

Turning to the Island, the Commission urged the immediate revision of theatre regulations and building byelaws. These two single recommendations drastically changed the whole approach to fire safety, involving the Fire Service to a much greater extent and paving the way for an even more unified service.

The United Kingdom Fire Precautions Act 1971 did not apply to the Isle of Man, but its contents had been under consideration even before the Summerland fire. It was obvious that something had to be done quickly. Urgent legislation was introduced in the form of the Local Government (Fire Services Amendment) Act 1974 which became effective from October. It gave the Fire Services Committee powers to charge for special services, and to enter, inspect and control fire exits. In October 1975 these powers were incorporated in greater detail in the Fire Precautions Act 1975. The Fire Escapes Act 1950 was repealed and new requirements incorporated in the revised legislation. Fire certificates became compulsory for certain premises.

The Act covered public buildings, hotels, boarding-houses and certain types of residential premises, requiring adequate means of escape and specifying other fire precautions. The Local Government Board made a number of enforcing orders; suddenly the full implications of the new Act became apparent.

The Local Government Board had also set about revising their building byelaws, following the recommendation of the Commission, and in April 1976 they took effect. One section of the new byelaw document related entirely to structural fire precautions and means of escape. There was particular emphasis on compartmentalising and the provision of fire-stops; both were lessons learned from the Summerland fire.

Another entertainment complex had been seriously affected one year earlier by a fire but this time with no loss of life. On 22nd July 1972 the fire service received a call to a fire at the Douglas Holiday Centre where a fire had a strong hold on the ballroom area. Six of the Island's brigades were in attendance but despite their best efforts the ballroom, stage, reception area and a supermarket were totally destroyed. Duke Ellington who had performed on stage the night before lost all his music and instruments. The 800 guests at the centre were not affected, as their accommodation was separate from the main admin building. Three firemen were slightly injured at the incident.

FIRE PREVENTION

Mr Pearson's retirement as Chief Fire Staff Officer saw his replacement by Mr J Hinnigan, Member of the Institute of Fire Engineers, on 1st September 1974. Mr Hinnigan had been involved in the discussions with the committee which had drafted the new byelaws, and was thus under no illusions about the work-load that would fall on the Fire Service. A fire prevention department was set up with four Station Officers and one acting Station Officer working under the direction of Assistant Divisional Officer Whiteford, the senior Fire Prevention Officer.

In May 1975 the Fire Service took delivery of an SS220 Simon Snorkel hydraulic platform, based on a 6.5-litre ERF chassis. The platform operated to a height of 22 metres and it could be controlled from the ground or from the platform itself, which carried a monitor with built-in delivery fixed to the booms. The duplicate controls fitted to the base of the platform had an over-ride capability, allowing the ground operator to intervene in case of emergency. The appliance also carried a lightweight portable Godiva pump.

The platform was allocated to Douglas; it could have been housed in John Street station, though its length would have made access difficult. It was too big for the Lord Street station so it was garaged, as a temporary measure, at the Douglas Gas Works Industrial Estate until the completion of the Central Fire Station. It was stationed at John Street on occasions when the turntable ladder was off the run, and it made several calls to Ramsey.

The Service took delivery, at the same time, of a water tender fitted with a 500gpm pump and similarly based on an ERF chassis. It carried 400 gallons of water and was fitted with standard aluminium ladders. The appliance was allocated to Peel, replacing the Dennis F8 of 1953. In the early part of 1980 it was converted to take the steel-wheeled escape from the Dennis F35 pump escape at Douglas, which then became the spare appliance.

An unusual fire occurred on Wednesday 10th December 1975 at St John's that had been allowed to burn for almost two hours before the fire brigade were called. It was Mart day and there were plenty of people about. Scrap metal contractors were removing sections of the disused railway track and used the former railway station area near the Mart as their depot; people in the area were used to seeing smoke from old sleepers that they were burning from time to time and they were not concerned about smoke coming from that area. This time when the smoke became more noticeable and they could see flames it was realised that something was wrong and the brigade were called. On arrival they found that the carriage shed full of coaches, many of which had been purchased for preservation, was well alight. It was late in the afternoon before the fire was extinguished and a second call to a minor outbreak had to be dealt with the following morning. Irreplaceable rolling stock was destroyed and the steel-framed shed destroyed. Careless use of oxy-acetylene burners was blamed for the outbreak.

In the early part of 1977 the Isle of Man Fire Service took possession of the new Peel Road Central Fire Station and Headquarters which are still in use today, although the administrative staff were later housed in separate premises in Elm Tree Road in Onchan. The formal opening of the new station took place on 30th June and was performed by Mr Percy Radcliffe MHK in his capacity as Chairman of the Finance Board.

The station was basically the five-bay station that had been recommended by Mr Mayall some twenty years earlier. The appliance room is served by four of the five doors and, because of its unusual layout, can house seven appliances. The fifth bay was devoted to the service facilities provided by the full-time transport officer and civilian mechanic. To the rear of the appliance room are full stores facilities for all the stations on the Island, along with service and recharging facilities for breathing apparatus. The first floor originally housed the administration staff, with offices for the Chief and Deputy Officers, together with lecture, recreation and canteen facilities. The rest of the ground floor provided accommodation for the Fire Prevention Department, radio equipment and the Control Room, which then became the nerve centre of the Island Fire Service.

The fire control room was at that time continually manned and all 999 calls were directed to it. The control panel afforded the duty firemen full radio contact with all appliances and also to switchboard telephone and recording facilities. An automatic call system activated personal pocket radio alerters and simultaneously set off the respective station sirens. At out-of-town stations, the first retained fireman to arrive answers the telephone; this cancels the siren and he then receives notification of the location of the fire from Central Control.

In the daytime the duty crew would man the first appliance and leave the station within seconds of the call being received; an internal broadcast system to all parts of the station notifies the location and nature of the fire. The off-duty crew and retained men were alerted in the normal way, arriving at the station within minutes to man additional appliances as required. Outside the station a large training ground and practice tower was provided with full circulation round the station.

Shortly after the Fire Services Committee took possession of the new headquarters, a further ERF (similar to the Peel appliance) was delivered and stationed at Castletown. It became the first-call machine and released the other F8, which dated from 1953. This older machine was taken into the central fire station and converted into a foam-carrying hose-layer. It carried 300 gallons of foam compound and 1,500ft of flaked hose ready-coupled and capable of being laid at 10mph. Two Sherpa general-purpose vans were added to the fleet at the same time.

Production of beer at Okell's Glen Falcon Brewery,

Chapter 7 UNITY AT LAST

In March 1983 the Isle of Man Fire Service (as it was still called) responded with a full turnout involving Laxey, Peel, Castletown and Douglas to the Manx Line vessel the *Manx Viking*. The ship had returned to Douglas shortly after departure following the discovery of a fire in the bow thrust motor room. In the event it turned out to be a minor incident and the ship was able to continue her journey to Heysham after clearance from the Fire Service. *(Author)*

Douglas, was interrupted following a fire that broke out near the lift-motor room in the roof space on Thursday 27th October 1977. It completely destroyed part of the roof and the five-storey building was water-damaged. However, firemen, under the direction of Station Officer Whiteford, were able to place salvage sheets over the vats and thus prevent damage to their contents.

Fire appliances from Douglas, Laxey and Peel were in attendance with 30 firemen. The fire was under control in half an hour but the brigade stayed all afternoon to clear up and secure the building, some 25,000 gallons of water having been used in extinguishing the fire, most of it being discharged through the turntable ladder monitor.

A month later another fire broke out at the same brewery, but this time in the bottling store. The fire was deep-seated in plastic crates, which generated great heat and gave off acrid smoke. The fire was tackled from within and contained, the firemen using breathing apparatus and working in relays. Priority was given to venting the store and the turntable ladder was again used to give additional cover from above while venting was taking place. Six appliances attended initially under Station Officer Cain, later joined by the Chief Fire Staff Officer, in view of the suspicious nature of the fire following so close after the earlier one. The fire was, in fact, treated by the police as suspected arson.

Later in the year in December the Service received a call at 5.32am to a fire in Albert Terrace, in which an elderly resident died, that once again emphasised the problems associated with premises converted into flats. The fire started in the ground floor flat and spread through the building up the staircase. Four residents in the upstairs flat were rescued, three from a front balcony, the fourth having got out of the building and raisied the alarm. Five appliances were in attendance with 25 firefighters, three jets and the Turntable Ladder in use, indicating the severity of the fire.

Continuing its programme of modernisation, the Fire Service took delivery of a new water tender in May 1978. This was a Dennis R61 carrying 400 gallons of water and fitted with a 500gpm pump. It was allocated to Kirk Michael, reflecting the area's population growth and allowing the Land Rover to be transferred to Ramsey. As a temporary measure the new appliance was housed together with the Austin Gypsy in the old station, a relic of the wartime AFS measures, until the new station was completed in the former railway goods shed off Station Road. A second R61 was delivered in February 1979 and allocated to Ramsey, replacing the Dennis F8 dating from 1955.

All stations except Laxey now had two appliances, at least one of which was a major pumping unit. The brigade had full radio communication with all appliances operating through Central Control. All personnel were equipped with personal radio alerters; they could justifiably be described as an efficient brigade functioning as a single unit. The old boundaries had disappeared; from now on the nearest appliance to the fire was turned out, with automatic reinforcement from adjoining stations.

LODGING HOUSE FIRE

The system was put to the test on 17th March 1979, at a major fire in a Douglas lodging-house. The fire was almost certainly first noticed by two policemen on motor patrol in the lower part of the town; Sgt McHarrie and PC Corlett saw smoke at about 3.15am and set about investigating its source. They soon traced it to No.19 Belmont Terrace, which was found to be on fire with smoke and flames belching from the front door. Entry was impossible and they immediately radioed for fire brigade and police assistance. People in the house were wakened by the noise of the fire and one of the lodgers screaming. The noise woke a next-door neighbour, Mr Corris; he was unsure what was happening until he saw black smoke coming into his room through the party-wall. He telephoned the fire service at 3.24am and left the building.

The radio alerters were operated and within five minutes the first appliance had left the station, in the charge of Leading Fireman Counsel. Two minutes later the water tender, in the charge of Sub-Officer Christian, had been despatched. The first appliance arrived at the fire ground at 3.32am, at the same time as the duty officer, Assistant Divisional Officer Cain. Meanwhile, some of the house's eleven occupants had made use of the fire escape at the rear, although access to it was severely hampered by dense black smoke and heat.

Officer Cain was informed by the police that six people were unaccounted for. Three jets were immediately brought into use, but entry was impossible from the front due to intense heat and flame. At 3.39am a message, "make pumps five", was sent, and the duty watch-keeper activated Peel, Castletown and Laxey alerters. The turntable ladder was pitched at the front of the building and Fireman Cunningham manned the monitor to direct water on the fire at second-floor level.

Deputy Chief Officer Hopkin took charge at the front of the building, with Divisional Officer Ventre taking charge of a party to prevent spread of fire to the adjacent properties. With men from Douglas and Laxey, Officer Cain gained entry at the rear and rescued the owner and his wife; they were taken to hospital where the woman was found to be dead through suffocation.

The Chief Fire Officer arrived shortly before 4am and took overall control. With Peel and Castletown in attendance, seven jets were in use but little impression was being made on the fire. At 4.20am the Chief sent the message "make pumps eight" and Ramsey and Kirk Michael were alerted. At 5.50am the fire, which had also broken into No.18, was surrounded; by 6.30am it was effectively out. Three bodies were found in the debris.

The inquest found, after studying forensic evidence, that the fire had been started by a carelessly dropped cigarette,

The 4x4 Austin Gypsy 601 MN Light Pump and the 4x4 Land Rover FMN 999 Pump Water Tender were both stationed at Kirk Michael between 1968 and 1978 and are seen outside their Station behind the Mitre Hotel. *(Author)*

which had set fire to soft furnishings. The foam-filled padding had created heat and dense smoke. The heat had caused the gas cylinder in a room heater to blow a relief valve, thus avoiding a potentially catastrophic explosion, but the free flow of gas instantly ignited and fuelled the fire, causing excessive heat at the seat of the fire.

Despite the deaths, the response to the fire clearly illustrated the efficiency of the Island Fire Service. As with all serious fires, the Service were quick to analyse their performance and learn from it. One of the outcomes resulted in the drawing-up of clear and concise control room procedures with predetermined attendances of appliances for classes and zones of premises.

In June a new Ford A-Series emergency tender was delivered and stationed at Douglas. The appliance was built by Cheshire Fire Engineering and was complete with air lifting-bags, full electric and air-operated cutting gear and jacking. It also carried a large cluster floodlight mounted on an extending telescopic mast, powered by a built-in 2½ kW electric generator. This generator also provided power for the tools and portable lighting. Additional equipment included a portable 2kW generator set, lighting set and a small three-section ladder. It quickly proved its worth in dealing with the increasing number of road traffic accidents, and was a revolutionary tool at night-time fires. It was not surprising that the Service were quick to incorporate a number of its features in one of the Leyland Sherpa vans, stationed at Ramsey, creating another emergency tender fitted with a stalk light and cutting gear.

The Fire Service took delivery in May 1980 of a Dennis RS61 water tender to replace the pump escape at Douglas, which then became the reserve appliance. The new vehicle was fitted with a 1,000gpm pump with four deliveries and carried 400 gallons of water. Its most unusual feature, as far as the Island was concerned, was that it carried a 45ft Angus 464 extending ladder instead of a wheeled escape.

Chapter 7 UNITY AT LAST

The appliance filled the need for a large-capacity pump to power the trailer-mounted Jetmaster Foam Monitor. This was an extremely important consideration in view of the large quantities of liquid petroleum gas and fuel oils stored in the vicinity of Douglas harbour. Operational orders were drawn up and code-named Operation Oil Fire, and exercises were mounted.

Despite the presence of large quantities of water, tidal conditions often made it impossible to take suction from the sea to feed the drencher installations. The Local Government Board provided a static water tank with a capacity of 250,000 gallons in the Harbour Board yard for fire-fighting purposes.

New works at Douglas harbour in connection with a breakwater extension included a 1.33-acre reclamation area for additional liquid petroleum gas storage facilities. The Fire Service requested that a buried seawater pumping chamber be incorporated in the new works to overcome the surge problem encountered elsewhere in the harbour.

The two new appliances attended their first major fire at about 11pm on Friday 5th December 1980 at the Peveril Hotel, Douglas, which was one of the Island's largest and oldest hotels. All the guests and staff were evacuated before the arrival of the first appliance. The fire broke out in the east wing; fanned by a stiff breeze it soon engulfed the top floors. The hotel occupied almost two sides of a square, had restricted access at the rear and a petrol station also abutted the building. This proved to be a difficult fire to attack. It was fought from above by monitors on the turntable ladder situated on the promenade, and the hydraulic platform in Peveril Square. Firemen were also able to use hoses on the rear of the building and managed to confine the fire to the east wing. Wearing breathing apparatus, they also tackled the fire from within the building.

Altogether eleven fire appliances attended; at one time eight pumps were in use. Fifty firemen fought the fire and brought it under control by 3am on Saturday. Twenty sets of breathing apparatus were used. Having broken through the roof, the fire completely destroyed the upper floors of the east wing. The rest of the building was affected by water and smoke, with damage being caused to curtains and decorations. The Fire Service were in attendance on Saturday and Sunday, damping down and making the building safe.

There is no doubt that the Fire Service had undergone more changes in the years since 1975 than at any other time in its history. The amount of legislation passed by Tynwald, and Orders made by the Local Government Board, bear witness to this. The emphasis is on safety to the public in places of entertainment, hotels and boarding-houses.

The effects of the Fire Precautions (Hotel and Boarding Houses) Order 1976 and the Housing (Flats) Regulations 1979, made under the Housing (Miscellaneous Provisions) Act, are perhaps the most noticeable to the public. Premises were required to be registered; adequate means of escape and separate access to individual flats have to be provided. Emergency lighting, smoke-detecting equipment and automatic fire alarms must be fitted. Compartmentalising is also required, with the provision of smoke doors, ventilated lobbies and self-closing doors within flats and similar accommodation.

Hidden in this mass of legislation was one extremely important Act which set out to establish a Civil Aid Services Planning Committee to co-operate in case of a major emergency on the Island. Included in its terms of reference was a brief to make advance planning for the control, co-ordination and administration of all emergency services. This was incorporated in the Civil Aid Services (Planning) Act 1976. However, in practical terms difficulties were encountered over areas of responsibility between the Civil Aid Committee and the Civil Defence Commission. Nonetheless the Committee was set up under the chairmanship of Mr M Ward MHK with the Chief Constable, Chief Fire Staff Officer and the Civil Defence Officer as members. Consultations were undertaken with water, gas, electricity, harbour and lighting authorities and emergency plans drawn up for oil and gas fires, air disasters and oil pollution.

On 24th April 1981 an incident occurred which had not been anticipated in any emergency planning procedures. A family were driving, in severe snow conditions, over the Snaefell mountain road from Douglas to Ramsey. They had ignored the "Road Closed" signs erected earlier in the day. The car became stuck in a drift near the Bungalow at about 3pm. The driver found his way with difficulty to the Creg ny Baa Hotel two miles away and raised the alarm, being concerned for the safety of the car's occupants which included an elderly person and a young child. The police and highway authority were notified, and snowploughs were sent from Douglas, Ramsey and Sulby. They made little progress, however, in what were now blizzard conditions. The Highway Board Northern Supervising Foreman had managed to reach the mountain road in his four-wheel drive vehicle by late afternoon but could see no sign of any stranded vehicle in the limited visibility and got out of his vehicle just as the visibility closed in. He turned and could not see his vehicle with its headlights and flashing warning lights and had to retrace his footsteps on his knees in the snow to find it. He returned to Sulby to direct operations from lower down the hill.

It became known that two telephone engineers who had been working on the mountain road were also stranded nearby and the family had been taken into their van where they had warmth and some facilities for making tea. Contact was made later by police officers who had travelled part of the way by the Snaefell Mountain Railway in the Civil Aviation Authority tram and then walked the rest of the way along the railway track.

By 6.10pm it was realised that very little progress was being made by the snowploughs; indeed one had become firmly stuck. The Fire Service offered two of their four-wheel-drive appliances to assist the Highway Board staff in their attempt to reach the stranded people by way of Tholt y Will. A large tracked excavator from the nearby Sulby dam construction site was eventually used, and contact with the stranded people was made shortly after 11pm. They were brought part of the way down by the excavator and then transferred to the Fire Service all-terrain vehicles for the rest

As part of the continuing improvement programme in the 1960s Ramsey Station received one of the Dennis F8 Pump Water Tenders, TMN 424, in 1960 and seven years later a Dennis F38 Pump Escape, 999 GMN. Both are photographed in 1967 at the Mooragh Park when the F38 was first on station. *(Author)*

of the trip. It was the first time that the highway authority had sat in Fire Control to ensure close liaison between those involved. The upshot of this has been the setting up of a mountain rescue team made up from police and fire service personnel, using existing equipment and vehicles.

Earlier in the year the Local Government (Fire Services) Act 1981 was passed; it abolished the fire service rate and the fire fund with effect from May 1980. The Service became completely funded from Central Government from that date. At about the same time a new Control Room Procedure was introduced into the brigade operational orders. It dealt with numerous control room procedures in respect of the Multitone Alerter radio system and the Automatic Fire Alarm Panel. Its most important features were to revise the specified predetermined first attendance for various classes of high-risk property. Public buildings and residential property required three major pumps, the emergency tender and turntable ladder. In the Douglas area this required an automatic turnout of appliances from Laxey, Peel or Castletown, depending on the exact location of the fire. This efficient brigade radio scheme when introduced operated on both VHF and UHF frequencies. It meant that the officer-in-charge of a fire ground could mobilise full brigade resources through the central control room within seconds of arrival.

The predetermined attendance orders work on the principle that each fire is a major incident. The senior officer can assess the situation on arrival and can, if necessary, recall any appliance not required. The advantage of this system is that valuable minutes are saved on call-out and attendance time if a fire turns out to be major.

A further four-wheel-drive appliance, based by Pilcher-Creen on the Land Rover chassis, entered service in June 1981. Fitted with an integral rear-mounted pump it carried a single hose-reel, 100 gallons of water and a small extension ladder. It was attached to Kirk Michael station, allowing the Austin Gypsy to be transferred to Laxey, thus giving the station a second appliance for the first time.

With only Douglas and Castletown still without a four-wheel-drive appliance, the opportunity was taken at the same time to acquire two Austin Gypsy vehicles from the Civil Defence Commission that were surplus to requirements. Altered and adapted for fire service use in the brigade workshops, they entered service towards the end of 1981 at Castletown and at Douglas early in 1982, completing the policy introduced by Mr Mayall in 1959.

In December a new Dennis DS Series pump water tender entered service, with a 500gpm pump and carrying 400 gallons of water. It was allocated to Laxey and replaced the Dennis F28, which was transferred to the Civil Defence Commission for AFS use.

Just as the Isle of Man Fire Service had reached the pinnacle of its development it found itself at yet another crossroads. The Home Affairs Board Bill 1981 was presented to the House of Keys in June 1981, and the future of the Fire Service was very much tied up in the Bill. Its object was to establish one single Board of Tynwald to take over certain functions relating to the Fire Service. The Bill was signed at a sitting of Tynwald on 13th October 1981. Following a General Election held in November, a new Home Affairs Board was established under the chairmanship of Mr R G Anderson MHK.

Chapter 8 THE SERVICE THROUGH THE 1980S

THE SERVICE THROUGH THE 1980S
Formation of the Isle of Man Fire & Rescue Service

THE YEAR 1982 was a hectic one for the Service; a number of major fires occurred from which, as always, lessons were learnt. A 999 call at 6.12pm on 6th March reported a fire in a building in Bucks Road, Douglas, occupied by Neil Kelly's motorcycle showroom. The first appliance arrived six minutes later and sent the call, "make pumps four". Peel and Laxey stations were alerted to provide additional support. The fire started in the workshop at the rear of the showroom, when a spark ignited the gas from batteries that were being recharged. It spread quickly to the showroom, engulfing motorcycles and tyres. The proprietor re-entered the building wearing a nylon shop coat and attempted to extinguish the flames himself and remove some of the stock. He was overcome and detained in hospital for a week suffering from burns and the effects of smoke inhalation. The fire was intense; at its peak it required four jets and breathing apparatus to be used.

ADO Whiteford sent the stop call at 6.41pm; by 9.35pm fire-fighting had finished and adjoining properties had been made secure. Nothing was left of the showroom, and the motorcycles were reduced to piles of molten metal. It highlighted the care that must be taken when charging batteries, and emphasised the golden rule of fire safety: never re-enter a building after discovering fire.

An incident six days later involved the IOM Steam Packet Company's vessel *NF Jaguar* on which a container had fallen onto a trailer of propane cylinders. On arrival the fire officer in charge found nitram fertilizer in the container: a potentially disastrous cocktail because adjacent cargo included a heated tanker of bitumen. It took two hours to retrieve the container and check the propane cylinders, during which time Douglas Brigade had two jets and two ground monitors in place as a precaution. It illustrated the need to take care when loading vessels, having regard to the interaction between differing cargoes, especially those where potentially explosive situations could develop. Both the shipping company and the Fire Service learnt these lessons from this incident.

For the emergency services public safety was an important consideration. In this incident the harbour was a comparatively secure location and public access limited. It might not have been so easy if a similar situation had developed from a road traffic accident within a residential area.

In April, Laxey Glen Gardens cafe and associated buildings were gutted by fire in the middle of the night, requiring attendance from Laxey and Douglas Brigades. At the height of the blaze, five jets were in use and it was four hours before the fire service was stood down.

One of the most unusual 999 calls came from the Ramsey Coastguard at 9.27am on Friday 6th August, reporting a fire at Snaefell Summit Hotel. Laxey and Ramsey Brigades were alerted. There is no road to the summit which is 621 metres (2,037ft) above sea level. The Laxey Brigade got to the top the same way that thousands of tourists do every year; an electric tramcar from the Snaefell Mountain Railway was requisitioned and the firemen made off for the summit with a wagon carrying 300 gallons of water. At 10.12am, Station Officer Boyd reported to Douglas Fire Control that the Summit Hotel was burnt out. The fire had probably burned all night after the building had been vacated. Although only about three miles in a direct line from the Laxey fire station, it had taken the crew 45 minutes to reach the summit. They were in attendance until 6pm damping down and securing the premises.

It was to Laxey later in the year that the Chairman of the Home Affairs Board came, to open the new two-bay fire station. It was on a new site in Mines Road, not far from the old wartime station, completing the Island-wide programme of modernisation begun in 1965 with the new Castletown station and Port Erin station, which had been modernised earlier while still under the Rushen Fire Authority.

As part of the continuing process of modernisation, another Dennis/Hestair DS appliance was purchased in 1983 at a cost of £42,500, and allocated to Port Erin. These short-wheelbase appliances proved invaluable in both rural and urban areas, their small turning circle allowing them access to areas where larger appliances could not venture. This appliance was believed to be the only Dennis DS supplied to any brigade in the British Isles fitted with a 50ft wheeled escape. Because of the extra equipment being carried on a chassis limited to an 8.5 tons gross vehicle weight, the water carried was limited to 200 gallons. Otherwise the vehicle carried all the usual equipment of a DS, including a 500gpm pump with two deliveries and two standard first-aid hose-reels.

A further DS appliance was delivered the following year and allocated to Castletown, replacing the F28 that had originally belonged to the Douglas Brigade. This older appliance was retained, becoming the foam tender/hose-layer and replacing the older Dennis F8 at Douglas.

At 3.50pm on Sunday 1st May 1983 a call was received that the Queen's Hotel in Ramsey was on fire. Ramsey responded with two appliances and confronted with a major incident immediately called for back-up. Altogether eight appliances attended involving Ramsey, Laxey, Kirk Michael and Douglas and with 45 firefighters. Hotel staff safely

Two fires occurred at Okell's Brewrey in 1977: the first, seen here, in October started in the drying room at the top of the brewery and the second a month later started in the bottling store both were subsequently found to be arson. Appliances from Peel, Laxey and Douglas were in attendance with Castletown brought in to Douglas to provide cover. *(Author)*

evacuated fourteen guests before the arrival of the Fire Service. The fire travelled through the building and internal floors collapsed, leaving the building structurally unsafe. It further illustrated shortcomings in regulations relating to hotels and guest-houses.

The matter was already in hand and the Fire Services Act 1984 repealed all the earlier Local Government (Fire Services) Acts and consolidated the provisions, vesting authority in the Home Affairs Board. One outcome of the Act was the re-designation of the chief officer of the brigade as the Chief Fire Officer and it clarified that no charge should be made by the brigade for fire-fighting purposes.

AIR-SEA RESCUE

The years of training with helicopters from RAF Valley in Anglesey for incidents at sea were put to good use in 1985, though not for fire-fighting purposes. The Fire Service received a call from Noble's Hospital just before noon on 17th April and were instructed to prepare the landing site at King George V Park (adjacent to the fire station) for a helicopter which was to land shortly with an injured seaman on board. This was followed by a message from Ramsey Coastguard that fire brigade personnel might be needed to release a man trapped in a winch on the fishing vessel *Wendy Anne*. The brigade mobilised to await further instructions and at 12.45pm ADO Cain, Sub-Officer Simpson and Leading Fireman Warriner were lifted to the fishing vessel. A doctor was already on board. Work proceeded on cutting cables and other gear while the vessel made for Douglas. She berthed at 1.15pm at the Victoria Pier, where the emergency tender was used to power hydraulic spreaders to remove the winch drum. Fifteen minutes later the man was released, having sustained severe injuries. He was transferred to Noble's Hospital for emergency surgery and the winchman was returned by fire personnel to the helicopter at the landing site.

Another fire in November 1985 presented difficult problems for the Fire Service and could have changed the face of Laxey for ever. A 999 call was received at control in Douglas from a Mr Cowin at 2.40am, reporting a fire near the famous Laxey Wheel. Four minutes later Station Officer Boyde acknowledged the call from Laxey fire station — having seen the glow in the sky he requested "pumps three"; an additional pump was despatched from Douglas before anyone had reached the fire. On arrival it was found that the Wheel Cafe, a timber-framed building, was totally engulfed in the fire. Radiated heat was threatening the world's largest water wheel, built to serve the lead and silver mines of Laxey. At 3.06am, a request was made for an additional pump appliance for water relay purposes in order to protect the wheel, which was largely built of timber. Several minutes later the building collapsed and radiated heat ignited a car parked nearby. The fire remained seated in the basement of the brick-built building. It was almost four hours before the Fire Service could pack up and return to the station. At the height of the blaze there were four jets and one ground monitor in use. Although the pretty cafe, resembling a Swiss chalet, was lost, the Fire Service were able to contain the fire. The Laxey Wheel, which had been threatened by the flames fanned by a strong easterly wind, was saved.

A fire at Linden Grove in Douglas was a reminder to the

Chapter 8 THE SERVICE THROUGH THE 1980S

Top left: Introduced in 1992, 999 GMN was a purpose built Rescue Vehicle built for the IOMF&RS by Carmichael on a Volvo FL614 chassis and is photographed during fitting out at Douglas Station.

Top right: Another bespoke appliance was MAN 999B, a Foam Tender/Hose Carrier on a Volvo FL10 chassis and built by Nova Scotia. It was the brain-child of CFO Godfrey Cain who is seen on the photograph.

Above: The Hydraulic Platform built by Simon Engineering on an ERF chassis was introduced in 1975. It suffered with problems of engine overheating which led to it being re-chassised by Simon onto a Volvo FL617 chassis and is now in service in Romania.

Bottom: In 1988 the IOMF&RS replaced the AEC Merryweather TL with a 30m Metz Turntable Ladder on a Volvo FL6 chassis. It is photographed at Douglas Station.

(All photos: Author)

Chief Fire Officer about the problems that could still be encountered in old properties, where there are common roof spaces above individual properties. The incident was also a timely reminder for firemen to take care over the spread of fire. This same point was further illustrated in March 1987, at Bretney Estate in Jurby, this time involving modern houses built to current byelaw standards. The area is some distance, in Isle of Man terms, from the nearest fire station and nearly equidistant from Ramsey and Kirk Michael. A 999 call reported a fire in a two-storey house on the estate at 10.10pm. Ramsey and Kirk Michael Brigades were alerted and the first Ramsey appliance arrived twelve minutes later. They quickly got to work with one jet and firemen wearing breathing apparatus; both hose-reels were in use. The occupant had been overcome by smoke but neighbours had rescued her before the brigade arrived. The ground floor of the house was well alight on arrival; even with the Kirk Michael R61 in attendance, and three jets in use, the fire could not be contained.

ADO Cain arrived from Douglas and as the senior officer took charge, immediately requesting "pumps four". Laxey was alerted and a Douglas appliance on its way to Ramsey to provide cover was diverted when the request was increased to "pumps five" and the hydraulic platform, as three houses were now involved in the fire. Shortly after 11pm, the roof of No.15, where the blaze had started, partially collapsed, and flames spread to the roof of the second house. The fire was eventually stopped in the roof of the third house, having been surrounded by five jets and three hose-reels, with appliances from Ramsey, Kirk Michael, Douglas, Laxey and Peel in attendance. A Kirk Michael fireman received an injury to his hand that required hospital treatment, and the occupant of the house where the fire started was admitted to Ramsey Cottage Hospital suffering from shock and smoke inhalation. The Salvation Army gave help to those who had been evacuated.

The stop call came from ADO Cain just before midnight, almost two hours after the first call, though the brigade were actually in attendance for nine hours. Three houses out of a terrace of six had been involved, and the fire had spread un-checked at roof level. There was smoke damage to the remaining properties due to percolation through the roof void.

The Fire Service, like many other Government Departments, had been swept up in reorganisation with the introduction of a system of ministerial government on the Island. From 1st April 1986, the Fire Service found itself part of the Department of Home Affairs which was also responsible for the police. The Hon E G Lowey MLC was appointed Minister for the Department and he appointed Mr AC Duggan MHK as Chairman of the Fire Services Committee, with delegated powers. The other member of the Committee was Councillor Fred Watterson. Their first task was to review the appliance replacement programme and then examine the full-time manning levels of the brigade.

In 1987 the Service acquired the first of a new breed of all-terrain appliances: a Fulton & Wylie appliance on a Mercedes 1300L Unimog chassis. A far cry from the early 4x4 vehicles, it carried a crew of six, 300 gallons of water, a front-mounted twin-delivery pump, four sets of breathing apparatus and a 10.5 metre Angus/Sarol ladder in addition to the usual small tools and ancillary items. After full evaluation and acceptance trials at Brigade Headquarters, the appliance was allocated to Laxey.

There were a number of fires in the lower part of Peel later the same year, culminating in a fire on 21st October at No.7 Charles Street. This intense fire occurred after midnight; access was difficult due to cars parked in the narrow streets nearby. Attending the blaze were two appliances from Peel and one from Douglas. Firemen wearing breathing apparatus rescued three people, two of whom were removed to hospital after receiving medical treatment at the scene. Questions were asked subsequently regarding access for emergency vehicles and the need to enforce parking restrictions.

Gas leaks at various times during the previous decade eventually led to additional legislation. The Fire Services (Amendment) Act 1990 gave the power to evacuate property, in the event of an emergency, to any constable or member of the fire brigade of Leading Fireman rank or above. This piece of legislation was unique in the British Isles at the time and followed on from the lessons learnt at two incidents.

The first occurred on 21st September 1983 when men employed by the Douglas Gas Light Company were working on a main at the South Quay near to the entrance to the gasworks. The work involved the use of a grinding wheel and sparks from the work ignited gas in a pipe, causing an explosion in the pump house that damaged a large spade valve. Appliances from Douglas, Castletown, Peel and Ramsey were mobilised. The fire was quickly extinguished, but a major gas leak occurred because the damaged valve could not be closed. About 11am, twenty-five minutes after the first incident, DCO Hopkins confirmed that the major incident plan should be put into operation.

The police requested people to evacuate property on the South Quay and spray jets were placed in strategic positions. Other out-of-town stations were alerted and placed on stand-by. By noon 44 firemen were at the scene. The leak had been partly sealed but it was not until 3.30pm that the damaged valves were removed and the pipes blanked off. The escaping gas had been able to vent safely within the harbour, which had been closed to shipping. The wind direction had blown the gas towards the mouth of the harbour, away from the town. The fire service stood down at 5.15pm and most of the population of Douglas had been unaware how close they had come to a major explosion.

In 1988 there was a different gas problem. For three years, complaints had been made about alleged gas leaks around Granville Street. All had been investigated by the gas company, and nothing found. During March there had been a significant increase in complaints, particularly in the cellars of the Rio Hotel which fronted the Promenade but also adjoined Granville Street. The fire brigade made several attendances and eventually found flammable gas using portable detection equipment.

On Saturday 26th March, Douglas Corporation officials investigated the pump chambers of a sewage ejector station

Chapter 8 THE SERVICE THROUGH THE 1980S

The scene at Belmont Terrace, Douglas in March 1979 at first light following a major fire in one of the houses which was divided into flats. At its height appliances from Peel, Castletown, Laxey, Ramsey, Kirk Michael and Douglas were in attendance. The fire was fuelled by a free-burning gas cylinder at the source of the fire, making it extremely intense. Tragically three persons lost their lives in the fire. *(Author)*

in Granville Street. They broke up the footway adjoining the Rio Hotel to release trapped gas under the highway. Gas readings continued to rise on the Sunday, and so electricity and gas supplies were disconnected to the Rio and the El Cortez hotels to minimise the risk of explosion. Tests on the gas main in Granville Street detected nothing. During Monday the street was sealed and drainage engineers from the Department of Highways, Ports and Properties used closed-circuit TV equipment and found damage in a pipe leading from the pneumatic sewage ejector. The underground ejector chamber was again entered; disused ejectors were inspected and found to contain old raw sewage, which had generated biological methane. The gas had found its way through damaged pipes into the surrounding ground and into the basements of the properties. Natural ventilation relieved the immediate problem but the remedial work was to take many weeks. The fire brigade attended on and off for more than a week, in particular during the following Saturday and Sunday. With flammable gas readings of 80% in the basements of the hotels, and 100% in the manholes in the back yards, the fire brigade had recommended evacuation. The owners were reluctant to leave; this presented a dilemma for the fire service and the police, who lacked at that time any statutory powers. In the event, evacuation was completed by Sunday night.

In May 1988 a severe fire occurred in premises at Merton Bank occupied by BP Joinery. Two calls were received at Control, the first from the proprietor of La Cuchina restaurant and the second from Harbour Control at the Sea Terminal, both around midnight on 7th May. Five pumps and the turntable ladder were quickly in attendance with six jets, with the turntable ladder monitor and ground monitor in use. Sub-Officer Cliffe and Fireman Howland were the first to enter the building. They were progressing to the seat of the fire with a branch when a flashover occurred, forcing their immediate withdrawal and resulting in the whole building, a former church hall, being engulfed in fire.

An old people's home in Demesne Road backed onto the fire ground; radiated heat broke glass in rear windows and activated smoke alarms, which led to the safe evacuation of fourteen residents who were temporarily accommodated in the Salvation Army hostel in Lord Street. The point of interest was that the smoke detectors responded to a fire outside the building, once again underlining their value.

A number of fires towards the end of 1990 involved elderly people, with regrettably tragic consequences. In one incident in Castletown, a passer-by heard the alarm going off inside a building. He called the brigade, but it was too late to save the elderly person inside. The incident did, however, emphasise the value of smoke detectors, particularly for elderly persons living alone. They can attract the attention of neighbours in the event of fire. These instances led to the Chief Fire Officer, John Hinnigan, issuing a Christmas message: "Hear smoke with a smoke detector".

Douglas had operated a foam tender/hose-carrier for a number of years, starting with a Green Goddess transferred from Castletown to Douglas in 1977 and carrying foam in drums. This was followed by an F8, also formerly stationed at Castletown, which carried foam in the water tank. Finally there was an F28, originally stationed in Douglas but at Castletown from 1984, and converted in the brigade workshops to a foam tender/specialised appliance in 1988.

With the increased storage of fuel and gas at Douglas, it was time to consider a purpose-built appliance to meet the various demands of the Service. The new appliance arrived in the summer of 1988, built by Nova Scotia of Blackburn on a three-axle Volvo FL10 chassis. It carried thirty lengths of hose, which could be laid on the run, and an independently Fiat-powered 900gpm Coventry Climax pump which enabled the vehicle to discharge 1,200gpm of foam through a centrally-mounted Kerr monitor on the run. The same pump could, if necessary, be used for relay pumping in remote rural areas. It was designed to carry 1,000 gallons of water, 300 gallons of high expansion foam and 300 gallons of low-expansion foam. Foam generation was through an Ess mixer with a 400-gallon water capacity, giving a total generated capacity of 2,400gpm of foam. This enabled full delivery through the monitor and two branches, through a variety of discharge methods. Although large, the appliance proved very versatile. Largely the brainchild of ADO Cain, it was designed to deal with everything involving flammable liquids from storage facilities to road traffic accidents, ship engine room fires, hose-laying, relay pumping and additional cover for airport back-up. It was at the time of its introduction the only appliance of its type operated in the British Isles. The thinking behind it was prompted by the lack of back-up available from other brigades.

Later in the same year, the old turntable ladder was replaced by a 30-metre four-section Metz ladder supplied by Angloco on a Volvo FL6 chassis. The ladder was the first on the Island capable of working to 17 degrees below the horizontal and with a maximum elevation of 75 degrees. The head of the ladder was fitted for cage operation; this allowed the fireman at the head of the ladder to operate the monitor from above the source of fire, giving him protection from radiated heat. The appliance was supplied with a 500gpm pump and the usual equipment, at a cost of £247,620.

The turntable ladder turned out to its first call at a fire on a demolition site at the former Douglas Bay Hotel. The hose-laying vehicle was also used, as water had to be relayed at this area notorious for poor water pressure. The fire was severe but did not endanger any other property. Nevertheless, five pumps were required and three ground monitors were also used, in addition to the monitors on the turntable ladder and hydraulic platform.

In the early hours of the morning of Thursday 4th February 1988 the Isle of Man Fire Service was called to Mooragh House, Mooragh Promenade, Ramsey. Douglas and Ramsey were mobilised and on arrival the first fire crew were confronted by a severe fire. The fire soon took hold of the building and shortly after the arrival of the Fire Service the whole of the building was engulfed in flames. Although unoccupied at the time, it did illustrate the need for improving compartmentation of old properties to prevent the rapid spread of fire. For the Fire Service there is always the ever present chance that vagrants may be

During the demolition of the former Regal Cinema in 1984 an unsupervised fire left by the demolition contractor got out of control and threatened other properties. This was one of many such fires that gave concern to the IOMF&RS at the time. *(Author)*

dossing in properties such as these, which of course adds to the need for care and to control and extinguish the fire as quickly as possible. The post fire investigation discovered that a plumber had been sweating joints in pipes in the floor space above the ballroom and sawdust packing between the joists, used for sound deadening in the original construction, had, unnoticed, started to smoulder. Time and air circulation led to the fire taking hold before being discovered.

The brigade became concerned at this time about the number of fires carelessly started on demolition sites. There had been serious fires to contend with at the Peveril Hotel site and the Regal Cinema site where adjoining property was put at risk. These incidents and those that had occurred at Ramsey, where building work resulted in the spread of fire and the eventual demolition of the properties involved led to the Fire Prevention Department, in conjunction with the Health and Safety Inspectorate, insisting on proper precautions being taken by demolition contractors.

During 1988 the Service was renamed The Isle of Man Fire and Rescue Service. In accordance with Government policy, this name appeared on a number of appliances in Manx Gaelic as well as English.

In 1989, following extensive evaluation of numerous all-terrain vehicles, the first of a new breed of appliances was introduced to replace the ageing Land Rovers at the outstations. The requirement was for a small, compact vehicle capable of getting up narrow country and farm lanes,

Chapter 8 THE SERVICE THROUGH THE 1980S

A 999 call was received in November 1985 at Fire Control in Douglas at 2.40am, reporting a fire near the famous Laxey Wheel. Four minutes later Station Officer Boyde acknowledged the call from Laxey Fire Station and immediately called for back-up as he could see that the fire was serious and his immediate concern was for the safety of the Laxey Wheel. The fire gutted the adjacent timber Swiss chalet-style cafe but the wheel was unscathed. *(Andrew Scarffe)*

which also had good road speed, could carry its own water and be able to service the town and village districts. The appliance that arrived did all that the old Land Rovers did and more. Built by Saxon on the Steyr Daimler Puch Pinzgauer 6x6 chassis, and powered by a 2.3 litre turbo-diesel engine, it carried a five-man crew, three breathing sets, 200 gallons of water, a 350gpm Godiva pump with two deliveries also capable of being removed from the vehicle, a standard hose-reel and a 10.5 metre Angus/Saro triple-extension ladder. After further trials by full-time personnel it was allocated to Peel, replacing the 1964 Land Rover. Two more of these appliances were immediately ordered. The first was stationed at Ramsey during 1990 and the second, manufactured by Mountain Ranger, was stationed at Castletown, replacing the Austin Gypsy.

On 28th August 1989, the Island lost another of its traditional timber-built cafes left over from the Victorian era. At 4.22am a call was received at fire control reporting that the Waterfall Cafe at Glenmaye was on fire. Peel Brigade were alerted and had their first appliance at Glenmaye ten minutes later, followed by the Douglas appliances some eight minutes after that, manned by the full-time duty crew. That was eighteen minutes from the call being logged to arrival at the fire ground, almost ten miles from Douglas: a very creditable performance. Even so, they were still too late to save the cafe. The timber building was gutted and severely damaged, eventually having to be demolished. The stop call came only twenty minutes after arrival, three jets and breathing apparatus having been used on the fire.

The end of the decade saw yet more appliances being delivered as part of the progressive modernisation programme. Early in 1990 a Fulton-Wylie-built water tender ladder on a Volvo FL614 chassis was delivered to become the first-call appliance for Douglas. Narrower than the Dennis it replaced, it had a six-man crew cab, a 1,000gpm Godiva pump with four deliveries, carried 400 gallons of water, 200 litres of high-expansion foam, two high-pressure hose-reels, a selection of ladders (the longest being a 15m Angus/Sarol ladder) and all the usual hand tools, including a Black Hawk hydraulic cutter, reflecting once again the increasing number of road accidents to which the brigade were having to respond.

Despite being a narrow appliance, it still had difficulty getting to the scene of a serious fire in Castle Mona Avenue on 3rd March 1990. A call was received shortly before 3am, reporting a fire in the Aston Ville, a residential hotel, with people trapped on upper floors. The cul-de-sac behind Central Promenade is notorious for parked vehicles. The first appliance collided with a parked car and was slightly damaged. The fire was serious and the call was for "pumps four" and the turntable ladder. Twenty-one people were reported as being resident in the hotel, and access to the three-storey rear outlet was difficult. Laxey, Castletown, Peel and Kirk Michael Brigades were alerted; at the height of the fire, six pumps and the turntable ladder were in use and ten breathing sets used by the firemen. Eleven people were rescued by ladder from the front and rear of the building; one was taken to hospital suffering cuts, burns and smoke inhalation. The problems of access caused by indiscriminate parking in residential areas remained a problem for the brigade, despite meetings involving the police and others.

Another 4x4 appliance was delivered later in the year and allocated to Douglas, giving the station a modern, purpose-built all-wheel-drive vehicle. It was supplied by Carmichael on a Mercedes 917 chassis with a six-man crew cab. It carried 300 gallons of water and 100 litres of foam, delivery being through a 500gpm pump. In addition to the usual hand equipment, it carried a 10.5m triple Angus/Sarol ladder, four breathing sets and a high-pressure hose reel. It was bigger than those at the outstations.

Over the last decade the Fire Service substituted, or added, fifteen new appliances to their fleet, together with van and car replacements. The manning level of the brigade had increased by twenty and the Fire Prevention Section was also increased to enable the requirements of the Fire Precautions Act 1975 and its subsequent orders and regulations to be enforced, including the inspection of all plans submitted for planning approval.

MANN ABLAZE

INTO THE 21ST CENTURY
Preventing, Protecting & Responding

IN 1989 AFTER trialling a 4x4 Unimog-based appliance, which had been in service for two years stationed at Laxey, against a 6x6 Pinzgauer the latter was seen as the ideal replacement for the remaining Austin Gypsy vehicles and ageing Land Rovers. The replacement programme saw a total of ten Pinzgauer eventually being purchased for all-terrain duty, the latest being powered by 2.5 litre 5-cylinder Volkswagen engines. These vehicles have proved their multi-purpose role by not only attending domestic fires but also in tackling heath fires on otherwise inaccessible uplands where walking long distances to the fire carrying beaters was the order of the day.

Two years later a larger 4x4 WTL based on a Mercedes 917 AF chassis with bodywork by Carmichael was introduced and stationed at Douglas for further evaluation. Whereas the Pinzgauer was primarily an off-road vehicle with a road-going capability, the Mercedes was a road-going vehicle with an off-road-going capability and much heavier. Both had their good points and when it came to upland heath fires and access into plantations the Pinzgauer still scored.

A second vehicle of this type on a Mercedes 112.4 AF 4x4 chassis also by Carmichael was acquired in 1995 and allocated to Kirk Michael. It carried 300 gallons of water and a 300gpm pump with two deliveries, Two high-pressure hose reels and a portable 50hp Honda-powered portable pump. As well as all the usual equipment it carried 100 litres of foam and a 10.5m ladder. The vehicle is the second oldest appliance still in service. The earlier Mercedes has gone to Romania as described later in this chapter.

At Douglas station the first of a completely new concept in rescue vehicles arrived in 1992; based on a Volvo short-wheelbase FL614, it carried a full range of emergency equipment and carried a Paflinger hydraulic crane. It was a very compact vehicle. Its role had expanded from dealing just with road traffic accidents to a more versatile vehicle capable of providing support at other incidents in line with the recent change of title of IOMFS to the Isle of Man Fire & Rescue Service in 1988 but it did not carry fire-fighting

Introduced in 2006, this is the Enhanced Rescue Vehicle 999 GMN based on a Volvo FL6H chassis and with bodywork by Angloco. Photographed outside the Douglas Fire Station. it gives an indication of the amount of equipment that this specialised vehicle carries. *(Author)*

Chapter 9 INTO THE 21ST CENTURY

A chimney fire on Gas Works Hill in Douglas with one of the Bronto Skylift Aerial Ladder Platform appliances in attendance. Based on a Volvo FLE18A chassis these appliances are also manufactured by Angloco. This photograph shows the appliance positioned facing downhill, as mentioned in the text. *(Leading Firefighter Justin Mc Mullin)*

media.

By the end of the twentieth century the population of the Island was estimated at 80,000 with more than 53,000 vehicles registered. This has seen an inevitable increase in road traffic accidents that has resulted in the fire and rescue service having to increase its response capability. The aim of previous Chief Fire Officers had always been to provide each of the outstations with a capability of dealing with such accidents and this had pretty well been achieved. The impact of Health and Safety legislation did necessitate an urgent reappraisal of these requirements, resulting in the provision of specialised and dedicated appliances at a number of stations. These were initially incorporated into the existing Pinzgauer appliances and other all-terrain vehicles.

The ultimate development of this philosophy for the outstations was the Emergency Tender stationed at Ramsey in 1994 that was designed around a 6x6 Pinzgauer military ambulance with bodywork conversion by Bedwas. The original configuration of the body allowed for a greater amount of locker space, providing a versatile emergency tender for the north of the Island.

By 2006 the role of the emergency tender had been further expanded into an appliance capable of tackling any emergency and by necessity carrying considerably more equipment. The evolution was an Enhanced Rescue Vehicle (ERV) constructed by Angloco on a Volvo FLE chassis. When the decision was taken, personnel from the IOM Fire Service and Angloco visited Greater Manchester to view their ERV and with their consent a vehicle for the IOM was designed based on their experience using the vehicle. The principal differences are that the IOM vehicle has only a two-man cab allowing for more locker space and smaller wheels, giving greater stability. It is powered by a 250hp 6-cylinder diesel engine with Allison automatic transmission and limited to a top speed of 65mph. It carries a full selection of Holmatro cutting and spreading gear, Paratech stabilising gear for shoring purposes and airbags along with a considerable array of tools and has retractable full-length awnings both sides. It carries two Night Owl floodlights but doesn't carry a pump nor any fire-fighting media or hoses. The only ladder it carries is a small folding ladder for access in confined spaces. It has come a long way from the Ford Series A of 1979!

The Community Fire Safety Department and the work that they undertake have perhaps represented the greatest change in the role of the Fire Service over the last two decades. In 1991 it did not exist; now it spreads the word about fire safety in the home to children in schools. It uses an interactive presentation involving a MINI car, donated by Zurich Insurance in 2008, to capture the imagination of primary school children. Newly-qualified drivers on the Island are required (as in Northern Ireland) to display a red R plate for the first year of driving. The emergency services have been concerned at the number of R plate drivers involved in road traffic collisions, particularly the young, and so the MINI has also been taken to schools and colleges for presentations to educate those recently qualified to drive and so reduce the incidence of road traffic collisions involving R drivers as part of the "drive safe live long" campaign.

In July 2003 the Department took delivery of a new community fire safety demonstration vehicle. It is used to demonstrate the effects of a chip-pan fire and the different methods of extinguishing it and is a means of getting the fire safety message across at agricultural shows and other public events. They also offer home fire safety checks and all within the three main tenets of the Service – prevention, protection and responding. The vehicle was ingeniously designed to make the most of the available space and its other function is to operate as a forward control unit.

In 2004 the 30m Metz turntable ladder was withdrawn from service, sold to Lothian & Borders Fire and Rescue Service and replaced by the first of two Bronto Aerial Ladder Platform (ALP) appliances. Like all new appliances there are pros and cons; firstly they have not as much outreach as the extending ladder due to the inherent weight of the telescopic boom but they are able to reach up and over obstacles and allow hands-free operation of the monitor which is permanently coupled to an extending supply built into the boom and fed from the base of the ladder. The two-man cage or the ladder attached to the boom can be used for evacuation purposes with, of course, weight limitations within certain parameters.

The ALP has a maximum working height of 32m and is also able to reach 5m below ground level. It owes much of its development to the crane industry and its associated technology. Boom weight reduces its operating parameters at lower angles and safety is ensured through overriding limit switches to avoid operator error. The all-up weight of the vehicle at 18 tonnes also presents access problems in certain locations and when pitched on a hill it has to be positioned facing downhill. Fitted with a two-man crew cab and having no pumping facility, it has to be accompanied to a confirmed fire by a major pumping unit. One advantage that the ALP has over the HP is that the operators no longer have to look over their shoulder as well as in front as there is no back-swing of the articulated boom when working in congested locations. The appliance can be controlled either from the cage or from the turntable at the base of the boom. The second ALP was introduced in 2007 and replaced the Hydraulic Platform dating from 1975.

These points were well illustrated at a chimney fire on Gas Works Hill in Douglas where the ALP in attendance had to be positioned facing down the hill in order that the self-levelling jacks could operate properly. In this case had the fire prevented the appliance getting past the fire scene in order to turn and face in the correct position. as there is no alternative means of approach, then reversing up the hill would have had to have been considered. This appliance has also been fitted with a state-of-the-art camera that has a facility for changing between normal, thermal image and infra-red views. The images from this camera can be viewed

Photographed outside Laxey Fire Station is the short-wheelbase Water Tender Ladder MAN 999B introduced in 1998. Built by Saxon on a MAN 10.224F chassis it carries a 500gpm pump with two deliveries and first-aid hose reels each side, a 10.5m triple extension ladder and a small ladder is roof mounted together with some emergency rescue equipment. The appliance has proved its worth in negotiating some of the narrow streets in lower Laxey. *(Author)*

Chapter 9 INTO THE 21ST CENTURY

Four Water Tender Ladder appliances built by Emergency One on Volvo FL chassis were introduced in 2008 and one was allocated to Castletown Station. It carries 1,800 litres of water and a computer-controlled Godiva high and low pressure pump fitted with two delivery outlets and has two 90m first-aid hose-reels. A selection of ladders is carried with the largest being a 3-section ladder with a maximum reach of 13.5m. A Night Owl stalk light is carried, fitted with two 24v x 500w floodlights. *(Author)*

in a command vehicle from where it can also be remotely controlled. This can remove the need to put a firefighter in harm's way.

2008 saw the introduction of four Water Tender Ladder appliances built by Emergency One on Volvo FL chassis. They carry 1,800 litres of water and have a computer-controlled Godiva high and low pressure pump fitted with two delivery outlets. They also have two 90m hose-reels, which is a departure from previous appliances which have carried 60m reels. This is in the light of experience dealing with fires in rubbish bins in back lanes where access is difficult.

A Night Owl stalk light is carried, fitted with two 24v x 500w floodlights. A selection of ladders is carried with the largest being a 3-section ladder with a maximum reach of 13.5m. It is of interest to note that some of the smaller ladders are manufactured by Bayley who first provided wheeled escapes to the Island in 1921. The new vehicles were allocated to Douglas, Castletown, Peel and Ramsey, upgrading appliances covering the main centres of population. The appliances were officially handed over at a ceremony at the Central Fire Station in Douglas in July 2008. They were designed to specific requirements of the IOMF&RS following a three-year development period to provide appliances which would give service to the communities they serve over their fifteen-year lifespan.

One question that had vexed successive Chief Officers was the lack of availability of back-up in the event of a major incident. It was first identified after the fire at the Woolworth store in 1951 but fortunately the large-capacity Merryweather Marquis that Douglas had not long purchased saved the day. At that time self-sufficiency was the norm in the Island and the decision of the Corporation to purchase such a large pumping appliance was vindicated. The Summerland fire was another that highlighted the problem and stretched the Island Service to the limit.

The advent of the first ro-ro service between the Island and the UK changed the situation and the further introduction of fast craft on the service to Liverpool has made the possibility of back-up from another brigade a reality. It is in effect now only three hours away. The absence of high-volume pumping capability on the Island was identified in the 2007 Inspection Report by Her Majesty's Fire Service Inspectorate (Scotland) but it did acknowledge that there is a Memorandum of Understanding with the Merseyside Fire & Rescue Service for the deployment of high-volume pumping equipment in the event of a major incident.

BEHIND THE SCENES

One aspect of the IOMF&RS not generally appreciated is the involvement in providing cover for motor cycle racing on the world-famous TT Course. During racing which occurs in May/June and August/September almost 38 miles of the Island's roads are closed to traffic and pedestrians. This restricts access to many areas of habitation and the island's principal hospital. Appliances have always been strategically placed inside the course and for houses which front onto the course for which there is no alternative access. A recent development has the strategic crewing of Laxey and Kirk Michael Stations during racing to provide a more timely response during these periods of congestion. A senior officer is now located in the race control tower during practice and race periods to liaise directly with the Clerk of Course who has the power to suspend the racing to allow for emergency services access.

The principal areas affected are Willaston, Governor's Hill, Tromode, The Baldwins, Main Road Crosby, Main Road Kirk Michael and Ramsey although there are other individual properties fronting onto the course for which there are no alternative means of access. During practice week, if a fire occurs in these areas the practice session is stopped to allow access for the emergency services; the course, however, is still closed to vehicular traffic. In 1982 the Friday evening practice was delayed just as it was about to start to allow three appliances to cross the course at St Ninian's to respond to a serious barn fire at Ballamillighan, Mount Rule.

Incidents occur from time to time on the race course related to the racing and, whilst most can be dealt with by race marshals who undergo basic training and who are issued with hand extinguishers, there are others of a more severe nature. One such occurred during a sidecar practice in 2006 when a sidecar outfit driven by Dave Molyneux crashed at high speed at Rhen Cullen. He and his passenger Craig Hallam were both injured and the outfit disintegrated and burst into flames. Race organisers had no alternative other than to cancel the practice and allow the fire service access to deal with the incident, which was too big for marshals to handle.

Normally, during periods of racing, stopping the race would only occur for a major incident and so the Fire Service position appliances inside the course at strategic locations. Douglas when it was an independent fire authority had an appliance stationed inside the course on Greenfield Road opposite the grandstand where personnel were in attendance and later when part of the IOMFS in Ballanard Road. Kirk Michael positioned an appliance on the Orrisdale Loop Road, which although on the outside of the course is inaccessible during racing. Their station was on the inside of the course but now is on the outside and manned during race periods, but in both cases there is no alternative access. Ramsey has always positioned an appliance in Brookfield Avenue near the bus station.

The situation remains much the same now except that the newly-built hospital at the Strang on the outskirts of Douglas is situated inside the course and has the emergency helicopter landing pads located within the grounds. To provide cover during the period that racing takes place a fully-crewed appliance is also stationed at the hospital and provides cover for areas of Glenvine, East and

Ramsey Fire Station with its allocation of appliances in 2009, seen left to right: KMN 999 WTL Volvo FL280/Emergency One, BMN 999R 6x6 WTL Pinzgauer 718K/Angloco, HMN 999 6x6 Emergency Tender Steyr/Pinzgauer/Bedwas and CMN 999D WTL Volvo FL280/Emergency One. It is the second largest station on the Island, serving a large area in the north. *(Author)*

Chapter 9 INTO THE 21ST CENTURY

ROMANIAN INTERLUDE

Top left: One of the appliances operated by the volunteer fire service at Girisu de Cris. *(Firefighter Danny Dooley)*

Top right: The Chief Minister of the Isle of Man, the Hon. Tony Brown MHK, performing the opening ceremony of the new Fire Station at Girisu de Cris. *(ROM-AN-AID)*

Above: The new Fire Station at Girisu de Cris in Romania completed with assistance from Isle of Man-based charities and the Isle of Man Government Overseas Aid Committee, with the two appliances from the Isle of Man Fire & Rescue Service. *(ROM-AN-AID)*

Left: The Girisu de Cris Volunteer Brigade undergoing training with their new appliance and supervised by Island firefighters. *(ROM-AN-AID)*

West Baldwin, Tromode, Willaston and Governor's Hill.

In addition to all of this, the IOMF&RS, I suspect uniquely, have an appliance and crew situated at the TT grandstand during racing, as there are considerable quantities of fuel in refuelling equipment in the pits area. They provide cover during filling and emptying of the equipment and during racing when refuelling of the racing bikes takes place.

One other consequence of roads being closed for racing and compounded by the increase in traffic on the Island has been gridlock at peak times on the Promenade at Douglas for vehicles accessing Onchan and the north. This severely delays fire service response to Onchan and Laxey. To provide the necessary cover one retained crew and an appliance are put on stand-by at Laxey to maintain rapid response to these areas.

Flooding is another instance where it is the fire service to which the public inevitably turn for help in times of emergency. The Island by its very nature is used to gales and its fair share of maritime weather. It is not unusual for the fire service to pump out harbourside properties particularly around the time of the equinoxial gales. Friday 1st February 2002 saw the Island lashed by a full South-Westerly gale and a high tide coupled with a deep low pressure area. The consequence was the highest tide to hit the Island since 1924. Properties and roads in harbour and promenade areas on the east coast were flooded. High tide was predicted for 2pm but one hour before that the fire service received their first calls to a number of minor electrical fires caused by the rising tide shorting out installations. Altogether during the day fourteen appliances were called out to deal with incidents and the subsequent pumping-out of properties and it was 9pm before all were back on station and stood down.

Port Erin was hardly affected because of its relatively sheltered position but the Port Erin crews were turned out to assist Castletown with an electrical fire at Qualtrough's yard. Afterwards they returned to Port St Mary to assist their second appliance with pumping-out. Douglas had five appliances out dealing with incidents and later pumping-out, with perhaps the Empress Hotel on the Central Promenade being the worst affected with plate glass windows to their basement restaurant damaged with subsequent flooding.

OVERSEAS AID

Until comparatively recently, fire-fighting vehicles that had fulfilled their operational and financial usage were advertised for disposal by tender. Following security risk assessments UK-wide, emergency vehicles can no longer be offered for sale out of service to private individuals. This presented problems to the fire service and the Island in particular as very few appliances see further use in other brigades due largely to advances in design and technology.

Fortunately, a number of aid charities are involved in helping countries less fortunate than ours to build their public service infrastructure — this has provided a solution to the problem of disposal.

Operation Florian is a UK Fire Service Humanitarian Charity run entirely by fire service volunteers working to promote the protection of life amongst communities in need, world-wide, by the provision of equipment and training to improve fire-fighting and rescue capabilities, and this provided an outlet for redundant appliances. In the Isle of Man, the Voluntary Service Overseas Committee was set up in 1985 to fund overseas postings of Island VSO volunteers. It has developed and broadened its scope over subsequent years and is now the Overseas Aid Committee of the Council of Ministers under the chairmanship of Mr G H Waft MLC.

In the Island a number of charities have also been established with much the same aims and Isle of Man Fire Service personnel have participated in two of them with some funding provided by the Island Government.

In 2006 Island firefighter Danny Dooley and Carl Hunt from Humberside organised a week-long training programme through Operation Florian UK for firefighters in the Odessa region of the Ukraine in dealing with road traffic collisions and in the use of twenty breathing apparatus sets which they had taken there. It was the start of an association with Balkan countries that is continuing to develop.

The Malawi Mission Projects is an Island-registered charity to which two Dennis pumping appliances were donated in 2006 and they became part of the Malawi Airport Fire Service. Another charity registered in the Island is RO-MAN-AID; established in 1992, it has strong links with Romania. Many of the rural communities in Romania, for example, have no emergency response capability as they often do not have sufficient manpower or equipment to deal with fires. In 2007 the Romanian Central Government in Bucharest recognised the need to establish fire-fighting services in rural areas and charged the Mayor of each region with the task. No funding for uniforms, training or equipment was provided, consequently each region was struggling to provide even the most basic of services; meanwhile the army is still undertaking fire-fighting in major towns.

The ties between Girisu de Cris in the county of Bihor in Romania and the Island, already well established, have become even stronger after the Mayor of the region, Ioan Paca, visited the Isle of Man to thank the people of the Island for all that had been done for them in a number of other significant projects. The Mayor expressed an interest in learning how the fire service worked on the Island, obviously with his new responsibilities in mind.

A meeting was arranged and Bruce Kirkham (formerly the DCFO) was given the task to explain how the Service in the Island was structured and operated. He suggested that it might be possible to donate surplus equipment as they had done previously through the Island's Government Overseas Aid Scheme. Later he went to Girisu de Cris to carry out a strategic assessment and assist with the formation of a fire service. Subsequently the Fire Service have been able to release appliances which for Island purposes were due for replacement having reached the scheduled replacement time and also been superseded by new more up-to-date equipment.

As a consequence, early in April 2008, three appliances, including the hydraulic platform that had spent a short time in reserve, were driven from the Isle of Man to Romania by

Chapter 9 INTO THE 21ST CENTURY

Leading Firefighter Justin McMullin, Firefighter Danny Dooley, Dave Collister (retd. StnO Castletown), John Boyde (retd. StnO Laxey), Steve Brew (a civilian mechanic), Bruce Kirkham and Dave Callow. John Moss, a reporter from Manx Radio, joined the party in Romania. The journey took six days, driving up to nine hours a day in shifts and staying at fire stations on the way! The hydraulic platform went to Oradea and the other two appliances to Girisu de Cris.

The same year Station Officer Tony Varley went to Argentina under the 911 fund, an American charity, of which Danny Dooley is an international advisor, to train firefighters there, all on a voluntary basis and in their own time. Later in October Dannny Dooley, John Boyde, retired Station Officer at Laxey and now Chairman of Florian Isle of Man, Andrew Collard, and Dave Pendlebury delivered another Volvo pump appliance to Oradea in Romania for the City Fire Service.

All of this was done under the ROM-AN-AID and Florian Isle of Man banners and supported by the Isle of Man Government Overseas Aid Committee. The arrival of these appliances and the provision of a new fire station transformed the fire-fighting capability in the area from a horse-drawn manual appliance to a hydraulic platform in one step! Through this work many active and retired firefighters have built up strong relationships with their counterparts in Girisu de Cris. Bruce Kirkham, Dave Collister, Tony Varley and StnO Barry Gelling have made further visits to continue training the Volunteer Rural Fire Service. Cementing the links still further the Chief Minister of the Isle of Man, the Hon Tony Brown MHK, visitied Girisu de Cris to open the new two-bay fire station built to house the two appliances from the Island.

In April 2009 three firefighters from Romania were invited to the Island by the fire service and they undertook training in driving, pump operation, ladder work and breathing apparatus techniques. Another appliance donated by the IOM Fire Service was delivered to Macedonia and local firefighters Ian Alder, Nicky Mulhearn, Dave Pendlebury and Sub Officer Chris Halsall drove the appliance there.

FIRES AND THEIR CONSEQUENCES

Despite the lessons learned in the late 1980s and greater regulation by the Health and Safety Inspectorate, demolition sites and building sites continued to give problems. This was vividly brought to public attention at a major incident at the Delamere Hotel on Mona Drive in Douglas where work on conversion to nine luxury flats was almost complete.

A fire had been burning for some time before the alarm was raised at 5am on Friday 14th March 2003. Shortly after the arrival of the first appliance fire broke through the roof and the whole building became engulfed. It very quickly became a major incident with multiple attendances. Part of the roof eventually collapsed, sending burning embers across Palace Road and setting fire to the roofs of four other hotels on Empire Terrace that required the use of the TL to deal with these additional outbreaks. Thirty people had to be evacuated for their safety and some faced the problems of water and fire damage to their properties on their return.

Most of the shell of the building collapsed and the when the fire had been brought under control the remaining gable was considered unsafe and had to be demolished. This incident, even though it was suspected that it had been started deliberately, gave impetus to regulations already under consideration by the Department of Local Government and the Environment. They were The Construction (Design and Management) Regulations 2003 (CDM Regulations) and The Management of Health and Safety at Work Regulations 2003 which were approved at the January 2004 sitting of Tynwald. In March, the Health and Safety at Work Inspectorate invited the Fire Protection Association to present their training sessions on Fire Risk Assessment in the Workplace to representatives from the building industry to reinforce the message.

There was another major fire in the area two months later on Monday 26th May, which was a Bank Holiday. The alarm was raised at 1pm when fire was discovered at the rear of the Welbeck Hotel in Mona Drive. The fire quickly spread to an oil tank in the back yard which ruptured, allowing burning oil to ignite a gas main.

Station Commander Tim Howland in the first appliance described the scene confronting him on arrival as "Armageddon". Already the flames from the free burning gas supply had set fire to four cars in the roadway, one of which exploded when the fuel tank ignited. They were dealt with by the crew of the Pinzgauer which was the second appliance to arrive. The burning oil from the storage tank ran down the surface water drains from the yard to add to the mayhem as the fire spread down towards the Promenade emerging from road gulleys on the way. Eventually four appliances attended, taking three hours to extginguish the blaze.

The staff from the hotel were all safely evacuated from the hotel by the time the fire service arrived and later accommodated, along with others evacuated from neighbouring properties, in a reception centre at the Sea Terminal set up by Civil Defence volunteers.

You will have read in earlier chapters that gorse and bracken were ever present in the eighteenth and early nineteenth centuries as a fire risk. These were used extensively for fodder, bedding and for domestic fuel. They are still is present on the Island's uplands and other marginal land that to this day is used for sheep grazing and latterly cattle. Burning has traditionally been used as a management tool on these areas with the attendant fire risk. The outbreak of the Second World War saw the introduction of the Heath Burning Act 1939 to prohibit burning for obvious reasons; outbreaks did however occur and following a number of serious fires further regulations were introduced in 1942.

Although better managed, the problem has still continued to present difficulties for the fire service and it was once again drawn into focus by a severe outbreak of fire on Bradda Head above Port Erin. The fire started on Friday 17th October 2003 and the fire service were in attendance for eight days. On Sunday 19th at the height of the fire which was fanned by a strong breeze there were eleven appliances in attendance and seventy firefighters. It was closer than usual to domestic dwellings, involved an area of high scenic beauty and so was very much in the public eye. Ironically the fire started from a garden bonfire near some gorse hedges and spread rapidly to engulf the whole of the

On the occasion of the official hand-over of the four new Volvo/Angloco Water Tender Ladders in 2008. Left to right Castletown StnO Tim Clague, Ramsey StnO Nigel Fairclough, CFO Brian Draper, Minister of Home Affairs Hon Martyn Quayle MHK, Peel StnO Barry Gelling and Douglas Station Commander Mark Christian. *(Author)*

headland. Difficulty of access added to the problems for the fire service personnel together with the lack of water which had to be conveyed by the off-road appliances. Without the Pinzgauer appliances the outcome may have been very different.

The outcome of an inquiry into this fire on Bradda Head, which was under consideration for designation as a conservation area, was the introduction of the Heath Burning Act 2003. This revised the 1939 Act; it extended its powers to include and regulate bonfires on domestic property adjoining heathland and to regulate controlled burning of heathland, giving greater powers of enforcement to the Department of Agriculture, Fisheries and Forestry.

Multi-occupancy buildings have increased considerably in the Island following the redevelopment of many of the boarding-houses on the promenades. Their replacement by apartment blocks has improved the areas considerably but led to much increased work for the fire service in planning and completion inspections. There are still many of the older houses divided into flats and these continue to give the service great cause for concern both for their condition and the provision of adequate means of escape. Coupled with this is the question of access as flat occupants in these older properties have to street-park vehicles and in the process cause difficulty for access by the emergency services.

A fire in a flat at No.44 Demesne Road in Douglas on 13th March 2004 resulted in the death of a tenant. The inquest into the death found that fire precautions were inadequate and that the landlord had ignored the flat regulations. The result was that the landlord was sentenced to fifteen months in prison for the manslaughter of the tenant. His company was fined £8,500 for breach of regulations with costs of £10,000. He was also ordered personally to pay costs of £25,000. It was a stark warning to those owning and letting flats of the requirements of the 1996 Fire Precautions (Flats) Regulations, which are unique to the Isle of Man. Following this, the Chief Fire Officer issued a public warning to flat landlords and tenants that non-compliance with regulations which are in place to prevent injury and death would be rigorously enforced by fire safety officers. Questions in Tynwald (the Island's Parliament) further raised public awareness of the regulations.

These and other associated regulations covering the safety of the public in housing and public places had followed hard lessons learned from incidents like this one and from the earlier Summerland disaster. The importance of fire safety has led to a gradual expansion of the role of the Fire Safety Section, from just one man, Fred Courtie, the former Chief Officer of the Douglas Brigade, in 1966 trying to do everything to the present-day situation where fifteen headquarters staff are devoted primarily to promoting and enforcing fire safety, including three Station Officers and a Sub-Officer in a specialised flats team and a Station Officer, Sub-Officer and Leading Firefighter in the Community Safety Team.

Chapter 9 INTO THE 21ST CENTURY

On Tuesday 8th January 2008 Port Erin Station was called to a house in Maine Road, Port Erin at 7.30am following an explosion that blew the roof off the house and caused extensive structural damage. The four occupants were lucky to escape with their lives although two had to be taken to hospital for treatment. A full-time crew from Douglas joined the Port Erin retained men and the fire was extinguished by mid-morning but the house had been totally destroyed. The suspected reason for the explosion was a gas leak.

Another incident in December 2008 occurred at the new Peel power station forty-seven years after the fire in the old station. The emergency services were alerted at 5pm and responded to a fire which had broken out following a rupture in the fuel supply line to one of the engines. This time, however, there were no casualties and the station's in–built deluge system extinguished the fire before the arrival of the fire service. They entered the building using breathing apparatus, extinguished a number of small residual fires and vented the buiding, handing it back to the station staff at 7.06pm. This fire is an illustration of the advances made in automatic detection and control of outbreaks of fire in industrial buildings since the introduction of safety legislation.

Just after 4am on Sunday 22nd March 2009 the emergency services were notified of a fire at a house — No.19 Demesne Road - that was also divided into flats. Appliances were quickly on scene under the command of SubO Halsall and entry gained although the fire was well established in the hallway and staircase. Occupants of flats not already out of the building were assisted out. An Aerial Ladder Platform was positioned with some difficulty due to parked vehicles and brought into action to contain the fire, which had broken out of the roof having spread rapidly to engulf the top flat. Shortly after 6am the fire was contained but damping-down continued afterwards for some time. The body of the occupant of the top flat was later discovered when fire personnel were able to access the flat.

The fire had been started deliberately along with several other fires in the neighbourhood and the culprit was subsequently charged. Once again the problems associated with flats and access were brought to the attention of the public. Despite all the regulations and inspections, multi-occupancy buildings still constitute a high risk and safe means of escape are paramount as is good housekeeping for tenants.

Another fire in Port Erin in September 2009 further emphasised the need for properly-maintained fire alarms. Three appliances were sent to a house in Edromony Estate at 7.30pm following a chip-pan fire in the kitchen. Firefighters wearing breathing apparatus extinguished the fire but there was fire damage to the kitchen and smoke damage throughout the house. The smoke detectors had not operated and were found to have been switched off. Once again the fire service emphasised the need to maintain detection devices properly and never disconnect them. No matter how many regulations are in place, safety against the risk of fire still remains very much with the individual.

The debate over the value of automatic sprinkler systems has run for years. They are installed by regulation in many public buildings such as hotels, theatres, cinemas and multiple stores and are accepted without question. Installation in a domestic dwelling is another matter, the general misconception being that they would cause unnecessary water damage and are unsightly in a domestic environment. The Fire Service, as part of their ongoing risk management assessment of fire safety, would like to see automatic sprinkler systems fitted to all domestic dwellings. To increase public awareness of the value of sprinkler systems, an impressive demonstration was staged in October 2009 in two houses in the Douglas Corporation housing estate at Pulrose which were scheduled for demolition as part of a refurbishment scheme. Following an introduction by CFO Draper the houses in Hazel Crescent were deliberately set on fire; both were fitted with automatic sprinkler systems but one was switched off. The result was impressive and clearly demonstrated the value of the sprinklers. The unprotected house was engulfed in smoke and flame within five minutes and flashed over at 1,000 degrees C at which point it had to be extinguished by firefighters. There was extensive fire damage to the room at the seat of the fire and smoke damage throughout. The fire in the second house was extinguished quickly when the sprinkler head was activated at 80 degrees C with minimal damage. ADO Murtagh then took the invited representatives from the Council and other Government Departments round the two properties to see for themselves the obvious advantages, particularly with regard to the safety of occupants.

PREPARED FOR THE FUTURE

John Boyde retired in 2002 as the retained Station Officer at Laxey after almost forty years' service, twenty as Station Officer, and was succeeded by Mr M Cleator. John Boyde is one of those who have been heavily involved with Operation Florian. At Ramsey Mr G D Foulis retired as Station Officer and his successor was Nigel Fairclough.

In 2010 the Chief Fire Officer is Mr Brian Draper GIFire E who was appointed in 2004 and succeeded Mr Alan Christian. He is located at Fire Service Headquarters at Elm Tree House in Onchan and is responsible for the strategic management of the Brigade, forward planning, major projects and procurement and the implementation of policy and procedures. His position also requires giving advice to political members of the Home Affairs Department and liaising with other departmental heads.

His Deputy is Mr Kevin Groom who is responsible principally for Finance and Human Resources, procurement of appliances and equipment, interoperability and New Dimension procedures and Health and Safety. He is also located at Headquarters as are the Divisional Officer in charge of Fire Safety and his deputy, who are responsible for the Fire Safety Department, the Community Safety Department and the flats team. There are an additional eleven professional headquarters staff of officer ranking.

The Divisional Officer in charge of Operations and his deputy together with the Operational Support Department are also stationed at Douglas Fire Station. Station Officer Mark Christian is Station Commander at the Central Fire

Station; also located there are the whole-time front-line fire fighting personnel comprising four Sub Officers, four Leading Firefighters and twenty-four Firefighters divided into four watches. There are also nine retained men allocated to Douglas and all are responsible to the Station Commander.

Each watch of the whole-time firefighters rotates with two days 0900 - 1800, two nights 1800 - 0900 and four rest days, the third and fourth of which they are on first call; they will then be on second call between their day and night duties. Whole-time fire-fighters are required to give 84 hours of on-call commitment per week whilst the retained personnel are expected to provide 120 hours per week. Whole-time personnel are still largely trained at Moreton in Marsh and retained personnel trained in-house by the Brigade Training Department with attendance at Chorley with Lancashire County Fire Service for specialised courses.

Three teams with special skills are drawn from all ranks within the personnel. The Hill Search Team is usually mobilised at the specific request of the police to incidents such as missing persons or aircraft. The team is made up from one overall officer-in-charge, currently DCFO Kevin Groom, five team managers and eighteen firefighters, all trained to a high level in the skills required. It was the first of the specialised teams to be formed following the incident on the Snaefell mountain road in 1981 – it has come a long way since then.

The Water Rescue Team is made up from twelve volunteers with a varying range of experience and ranks from Firefighter through to ADO John Murtagh who is currently in overall command. All have been trained in near-water safety and water rescue techniques by the Outreach Organisation in North Wales. Their principal purpose is to support the other functions of the Service at incidents on or near water using a variety of specialist equipment.

CFO Brian Draper, ADO Geoff Quayle and Leading Firefighter Roger Brown were involved in establishing the Line Rescue Team, to deal with rescue from heights and confined spaces; they too trained initially with Outreach. The redevelopment of Douglas saw an increase in the use of tower cranes on building sites and a risk assessment identified the problem of rescuing any crane operator who had suffered injury or heart attack as most were beyond the reach of Aerial appliances. Other risks identified were, amongst others, at grain silos, reservoir tunnels, the incinerator and in the use of rope work rescuing stranded animals from awkward locations.

The Transport Officer and Procurement Officer are also stationed at the Douglas Fire Station. It is also the base for the Training and Operational Support Department.

All of the outstations operate with retained personnel comprising one Station Officer, one Sub-Officer, two Leading Firemen and between twelve and fourteen Firefighters. The total establishment is 167 firefighters of which 56 are full-time and 111 (of whom two are female, one stationed at Laxey and the other at Ramsey) are retained, and in addition there are four civilian staff based at Headquarters and two civilian mechanics based at Douglas. Protective clothing is generally replaced on a ten-year cycle and the present Nomex fire-resistant uniforms will shortly be due for replacement. The Gallet F1 helmets used by the brigade have already been upgraded and personnel are now issued with Rosenbauer Hero-xtreme helmets.

Incidentally, as well as donating time-expired appliances to the Florian charity, the brigade have also donated replaced clothing and other equipment, some of which has seen further use in Paraguay.

On a lighter note and retaining links with the past, Firefighter David Cowley of Red Watch and his wife Kate were driven by colleagues in one of the latest WTLs from St George's Church to their reception at the Mount Murray Hotel on 22nd August 2009. Seventy-nine years earlier Jim Sloane of the Douglas Brigade and his wife were driven, by the Superintendent Mr S J Caugherty, from their wedding to their reception in the open solid-wheeled Leyland appliance. Apart from continuing the tradition, both were blessed with fine sunny weather; perhaps in Jim Sloane's case he really was fortunate!

Fire Control is no longer situated at the Douglas Fire Station. Since 2004 it has been located at the Emergency Services Joint Control Room where a full-time multi-discipline civilian staff of 25 handle all emergency calls for police, fire and ambulance services. It was an essential part of the IOM Government's improved communication system that was introduced by the Island's Communications Department based on Terrestrial Trunked Radio (TETRA). It is a digital trunked mobile radio system developed by the European Telecommunications Standards Institute. It links all the Island's Government Departments and was designed by Motorola to meet the Island's specific needs.

The 2007 Inspection Report carried out for the Department of Home Affairs by HM Fire Services

One of the Ariel Ladder Platforms in attendance at a fire in Demesne Road, Douglas in March 2009. It was a house divided into flats and one of the occupants tragically died in the fire. It highlighted a number of issues which had concerned the IOMF&RS for some time. *(John Davis)*

Chapter 9 INTO THE 21ST CENTURY

Inspectorate (Scotland) reported that – "The service is in the forefront of innovation in regard to its Emergency Services Joint Control Room. UK Fire and Rescue Services can look to the Isle of Man as an example of how to introduce and operate such a system."

TETRA has proved invaluable in major incidents and with nineteen participating Government Departments it really does lead to a "joined-up" response. Interestingly the fire service still uses some UHF handsets with BA for point-to-point communication in fire situations.

In September 2009 the IOMF&RS launched a "Park Smart" campaign supported by the Department of Home Affairs, the police and other emergency services. One of the main thrusts of the campaign asks people who block narrow roads and housing estates to consider that it may be their property that the services are trying to reach. It comes from continuing problems recently highlighted by incidents in Castle Mona Avenue and in Demesne Road where there is a high proportion of flats and was further highlighted by another incident where firemen had to carry equipment and breathing apparatus on foot 100 metres to get to a fire.

Road Traffic Accidents, now referred to as Road Traffic Collisions (to avoid legal presumption of blame), have seen a reduction of 25% in fatalities following a highly effective road safety campaign involving several Government Departments including the Fire Service.

The Department of Home Affairs is responsible for Fire, Police, The Prison Service, Emergency Planning and Civil Defence and the Communications Department. Not surprisingly there is competition between the various sections for the allocation of money. The fire service has had in place, for a number of years now, a vehicle replacement programme the envy of many. It has led to the brigade having a very modern fleet of vehicles fit for purpose both in the operational and reserve fleet and in line with the most

On 17th October 2003 Port Erin attended a fire call to a heath fire to the rear of properties on Bradda Road. It appears innocent enough in this photograph with the Port Erin Pinzgauer/Saxon in attendance but the anxious look of the householder on the left indicates the proximity of the fire to residential property. The fire was to last eight days and involve eleven appliances at its height. *(Fire-fighter Paul Rothwell)*

modern brigades in the UK. The Service handles around two thousand calls per annum but more than half are false alarms mostly caused by defective automatic fire detection systems.

In line with progress in UK legislation and the culture of Health and Safety which has pervaded all aspects of our lives, the Department of Home Affairs have a new Fire and Rescue Service Bill in their legislative programme to consolidate all the existing legislation and bring it up-to-date for the 21st century.

Douglas Fire Station was built in 1974; now, thirty-six years on, its functions have changed somewhat and it has outgrown its present site. Not all of the appliances can be accommodated in the appliance room and some equipment is kept in rented accommodation along with the reserve appliances over a mile from the station. This is no longer like running down Lower Church Street from John Street to turn out additional appliances. Even fire crews making their way to the storage facility have to negotiate very congested busy roads to get there, adding considerably to attendance times. It is inevitable that sooner rather than later the station will have to be replaced on a larger site with a drive-through appliance room and an adequate drill ground. Will the Headquarters staff come back under the same roof again?

Watch this space!

This was one of the points highlighted in the Demesne Road fire in March 2009 concerning indiscriminate car parking impeding access by the emergency services which gave rise to the Park Smart Campaign. The problem had been getting worse over a number of years caused by multi-occupancy of old buildings converted to flats. *(Leading Firefighter Justin Mc Mullin)*

The aftermath of the fire at the Delamere Hotel in Mona Drive, Douglas in March 2003. The roof and floors have collapsed and the dangerous state of the building is clear to see from this angle. Of interest is the use of ground monitors which can be seen bottom right of the photograph. *(SubO Peter Killey)*

Chapter 9 INTO THE 21ST CENTURY

Top left: The line rescue team in training. The IOMF&RS is a multi-discipline service and personnel can perform diverse but integrated tasks. *(Leading Firefighter Roger Brown)*

Top right: The business end of an Aerial Ladder Platform. *(Author)*

Above: Firefighters demonstrating how to extinguish a motorcycle fire to Marshals for the TT motorcycle races. Yet another aspect of the IOMF&RS work. *(Leading Firefighter Roger Brown)*

Left: IOMF&RS personnel undergoing Breathing Apparatus training at the Airport Fire Service training ground for aircraft access familiarisation. *(Author)*

MANN ABLAZE

Top left: The IOMF&RS personnel provide cover for refuelling at the Grandstand and Pits area for motorcycling events held around the famous TT road race circuit *(SubO Peter Killey)*

Top right: The Service is fully equiped with the necessary protective clothing and decontamination showers to deal with chemical or other hazardous substances. *(Firefighter Paul Rothwell)*

Above: The two Volvo FLE18A/Angloco Bronto Skylift Ariel Ladder Platforms pose outside Douglas Fire Station. *(Leading Firefighter Justin Mc Mullin)*

Left: The Hill Search Rescue Team in training *(Leading Firefighter Roger Brown)*

Chapter 10 PRIVATE FIRE BRIGADES

PRIVATE **FIRE BRIGADES**
The Airport Fire Service and others

DETAILS OF THE Island's private fire brigades are scarce. The first was without doubt the Sun Insurance Brigade, which has already been adequately described because of its place in the development of organised fire-fighting within the Island.

The next brigade was formed at King William's College following the destructive fire of 1844. It stemmed from the need for self-preservation and included masters and boys. They acquired second-hand equipment from time to time from the regular brigades. After mains water was installed at the College, the brigade operated with hose and standpipes from the various hydrants within the grounds. At one time two of the old street escapes from Douglas saw service there.

Some years before Castletown had a motor fire engine there was a fire at the College which was first tackled by its own brigade. It was soon joined by the Castletown Brigade, which lost no time in summoning help from Douglas. The Leyland was dispatched and eventually the fire was put out. The Douglas men telephoned Mr Caugherty, their chief, to say that they were returning to station and left the College. Some two hours later he became concerned because his men had not returned. Fearing the worst he set off in search of them. It was a clear moonlit night at Douglas and he could not understand the delay. He met them at the top of Richmond Hill; they were tired, cold and wet. Snow had started to fall shortly after they had left the College and it took them an hour and a half to get up Ballaglonney Hill, manhandling first the appliance and then the trailer pump. For the rest of the time they sat on the outside of the appliance, exposed to the elements.

The College later acquired the Bean engine, which had seen service in various parts of the Island. In the mid-1950s the Civil Defence Commission loaned the 1939 ex-Ramsey Morris to the College brigade, and a garage was built to house it. It remained in use at the College for almost twenty years, being replaced by a Bedford Green Goddess, also on loan from the Commission. It is now disbanded as a private brigade.

James Moore had been agent to the Sun Fire Office in 1801 and had instigated the formation of the local Sun Insurance Brigade. When the Sun withdrew their service, James Moore's son William was the agent. He purchased the small manual fire engine in 1848 for use in his sailcloth works at Tromode. It is known from contemporary reports that William Moore had a number of trained men capable of fire-fighting and operating the fire engine and that it was still in use some ten years later. Details of its use are scant although the factory was large and it had a number of tied workers' cottages at Cronkbourne Village. There was good need for a fire brigade due to its comparatively remote location.

THE MENTAL HOSPITAL

In 1867 a lunatic asylum was completed at the Strang, almost three miles from Douglas. At first it accommodated 76 patients, the number soon increasing three-fold. The asylum had its own gas-producing plant, laundry and steam-pumping arrangements for its water supply, which was taken from wells and underground rain-water tanks. The building represented a high fire risk, notably because of the presence of a system of timber ventilating ducts serving Howorth's Patent Ventilating System.

By 1870 the maintenance staff and the attendants had formed a fire brigade under the charge of the Clerk of Works. In 1876 two L'Extincteur patent fire extinguishers were purchased and the Medical Superintendent, Dr T O Wood, recommended the installation of external hydrants. An outbreak of fire in the female division in 1882 prompted the installation of an external main and hydrants, complete with steam force pumps to pressurise the system.

The asylum fire brigade was in action at 6.45am on 5th February 1891, after an attendant accidentally set fire to the proscenium curtain and staging in the dining room while lighting the gas lamps. The Sun Insurance Company met the repair costs.

Between 1901 and 1902 the Asylum Board renewed all the pillar hydrants and installed internal hydrants with lengths of hose supplied by Wm Rose & Co and incorporating their instantaneous couplings. The asylum had underground water storage of 19,000 gallons, with header tanks of 4,000 gallons' capacity but, even with steam force, the pressure was inadequate for efficient fire-fighting, as it was impossible to throw a jet of water over the highest building. The situation was remedied in 1904 when terms were agreed with Douglas Corporation to take a four-inch supply off the main town supply that had been laid from the new Baldwin Reservoir. This mains water supply was fed into the existing asylum system and the pressure was sufficient to throw a jet over the ridge of the three-storey dormitories. In 1907 the asylum brigade were called to a fire outside the grounds in a cottage at the Strang belonging to a Mrs Corkill. The fire had threatened the stack-yard belonging to the asylum, but was quickly and efficiently extinguished.

The influx of internees to the Island after 1914 and a tremendous increase in the number of inmates presented further problems for the asylum. Accommodation for the

MANN ABLAZE

Top left: A very poor photograph but the only one I have of the first fire appliance at Ronaldsway Airfield attending, I think, a stricken de Haviland Dragon. *(Author's collection)*

Top right: The Fordson WOT1 Crash Tender from Ronaldsway Airport passing through Kirk Michael in 1962 on its way to Jurby Airfield to provide fire cover for diverted aircraft due to fog at Ronaldsway. *(Author)*

Above and left: IOM Harbour Board employees undergoing anti-gas training during the Second World War at the Harbour Board yard and on the Viaduct between the Victoria Pier and the King Edward Pier. *(Author's collection)*

Chapter 10 PRIVATE FIRE BRIGADES

The former Douglas Corporation Leyland Major Pump of 1921 at Ronaldsway Airport stripped of pretty well everything but its pump in 1948. It was the only fire cover until 1951 when all the remaining wartime appliances were acquired by the Airports Board. Sitting next to the driver is Arthur Corlett at that time Chargehand at the airport but later to become SAFO until his retirement in 1970. *(Author's collection)*

poor was built adjoining the asylum, and so there were now some 500 persons under the care of the Asylum Board. Fire prevention had never been more important.

The brigade was completely reorganised in 1917 and a simple set of rules printed. Arrangements were made for Douglas Fire Brigade to give demonstrations and hold regular drills with the asylum brigade.

In 1922 one of the main fire hazards at the asylum, later known as the Mental Hospital, was removed with the installation of an 18hp Crossley oil engine and 18.2 kW dynamo generator and conversion to electric lighting.

The Asylum Board had continued the training of both male and female hospital attendants; regular drills were conducted by the Superintendent of the Douglas Brigade. However, Douglas had now acquired its first motor fire engine and it could be in attendance at the hospital ten minutes after leaving the station. This radically altered the situation at the hospital. In order to meet the demands of the motor pump, one of the rain-water tanks in the basement was connected to the mains supply and used as a static tank. The Leyland engine could then be fed with a good supply of water and a jet thrown over the central tower.

The staff at the hospital continued to drill regularly and provided an efficient first-aid cover. They extinguished many small fires within the hospital and the Home of the Poor, later known as the Mannin Infirmary. In 1935 additional mains and hydrants were provided and extra hose acquired.

During the Second World War a fire party was maintained, despite many of the young nursing staff and maintenance staff serving in the armed forces. A Merryweather Warspite pump powered by a twin Anzani engine was stationed at the hospital for use in the event of a mains failure. The fire party, made up mostly from maintenance and ancillary staff under the direction of the Clerk of Works, was finally disbanded in 1986.

The hospital was still a high-risk building; following the 1975 Fire Precautions Act, heat and smoke detectors were fitted in all the buildings, with a direct link to the Automatic Fire Alarm Panel at Central Fire Control in Douglas.

Mention has been made of the numerous fire parties formed during the Second World War, many loosely falling into the category of private fire brigades. Most were not part of the AFS set-up although they did attend training courses and combined exercises from time to time. Notable examples were the fire parties formed by Marks & Spencer, Boots, the IOM Times office and Noble's Hospital. The branches of the national multiple stores had implemented an overall policy on fire-watching which had become compulsory in the UK following the London blitz. There was, however, no such legal requirement in the Isle of Man.

Some of the military establishments had fire parties mainly made up from civilian personnel. One such party operated at the Royal Naval Sick Quarters at the requisitioned Children's Home on Glencrutchery Road, which was attached to the land-based training establishment HMS *St George* which was housed in Cunningham's Holiday Camp.

FIRE AT SEA

Vessels of the IOM Steam Packet Company, and other shipping companies operating out of the Island, come under the jurisdiction of subordinate legislation of the UK having effect in the Isle of Man. The Merchant Shipping (Fire Appliances) Rules 1965 and their 1974 amendment, lay down stringent safety rules enforced by the Department of Business, Innovation and Skills for UK-registered ships. Manx-registered vessels have similar requirements enforced by the Marine Survey Division of the Manx Department of Trade and Industry under Manx legislation. Each vessel is required to have fire parties and to hold regular drills; inspections are made annually by Marine Surveyors of the Manx Department. They also carry out inspections for other administrations on vessels registered elsewhere but operating in local waters.

The fire prevention equipment they carry varies from ship to ship, although the principle is essentially the same. Car ferries, for example, are fitted with Mather & Platt Grinnel automatic sprinkler systems designed to operate when the temperature under the sprinkler heads reaches 68 degrees C. The vessels are divided into eight drencher sections with central control valves and port and starboard shore connections to supplement the onboard fire-fighting equipment. An automatic fire alarm panel is linked to the system and located in the wheelhouse, together with a smoke detector indicator panel.

Alarm and communication systems are operated from the wheelhouse and emergency procedures to compartment the ship are also indicated there. Fire parties are made up of the engineering staff, crew and the ship's carpenter under the direction of an officer. The vessels have a comprehensive hydrant and hose-reel system and the steam-operated vessels had separate foam boiler-room drench systems. Vessels are also equipped with Siebe Gorman smoke helmets with trailing air lines connected to hand bellows, giving the fire parties limited access to smoke-logged areas. The modern motor ships have a different method of dealing with onboard fires and it is essential that the fire service is familiar with all types.

The Isle of Man Fire Service undergoes familiarisation drills with various vessels to acquaint personnel with ship layout and shore connections. The latest exercises have involved the very latest high-speed vessel *Manannan* which has a totally different layout from the traditional ro-ro vessels. A number of minor outbreaks, mostly confined to ships' lounges, have been dealt with while vessels were berthed overnight at Douglas.

The earliest incident involving a vessel of the IOM Steam Packet Company occurred at Liverpool on 12th June 1847. The ss *King Orry*, berthed at the landing stage, blew a boiler plug and required the attendance of the Liverpool City Fire Brigade. One man was injured in the boiler room. The efforts of the crew and the fire brigade ensured there was no

Jurby Airfield was still operational as a training unit in 1963 when this photograph was taken in the motor transport compound. It shows a Thornycroft/Pyrene Mk V Military Crash Tender. In the background can be seen a Land Rover-based Rapid Intervention Vehicle. There was also a Thornycroft domestic appliance stationed at Jurby at the same time. *(Author)*

Chapter 10 PRIVATE FIRE BRIGADES

permanent damage.

The Douglas Brigade were called to a fire on board the ss *Mona* in May 1928; an account for £19-17s was rendered, but other details are tantalisingly scarce. More recently the fire service were called to a fire in a linen store on board the ss *Manxman*. Fire at sea is possibly the most difficult situation to confront fire-fighting personnel. Responsibility initially rests upon the ship's fire party, but urgent help is a priority if the fire is too large to be contained.

Conscious of its strategic position in the Irish Sea, the Isle of Man Fire Service set up a procedure with the Coastguard and RAF Valley in Anglesey for getting aid to any ship on fire. Regular exercises were held in the 1980s in conjunction with the RNLI. Equipment was pre-loaded into purpose-made canvas bags, enabling it to be handled quickly and easily into helicopters; in addition to personnel they carried suction hose and a lightweight pump. This paid dividends in several incidents involving fishing vessels.

Exercises have also been undertaken with tugs belonging to the Laxey Towing Company. While these vessels are primarily harbour tugs, they do have a reasonable seagoing ability. They also have built-in salvage pumps; in one case a monitor is mounted aft of the funnel. Now supplemented by portable pumps and monitors, the Island Fire Service had an afloat capability. Three jets had been discharged simultaneously from the tug *Union*, reaching a height of 70 feet. However, now because of new regulations in the use of helicopters over the sea the Island Fire Service do not fly to incidents of fire at sea. They do respond to incidents in the harbour and would respond to cruise liners visiting the Island by tender if necessary.

During preparations for the Second World War, the Central Air Raids Precautions Committee were concerned about the effects of gas warfare, and so the Harbour Board introduced anti-gas precautions in 1939. A decontamination squad was set up in each port, with personnel recruited from harbour police and Harbour Masters.

In December 1941 the Harbour Board acquired the Dodge fire tender from the Laxey Fire Authority for decontamination duties and to provide additional fire cover for Douglas harbour. It was parked during the period of the war by the Edward Pier viaduct and manned by the Harbour Board employees as required. At the end of hostilities it was broken up.

Harbours subsequently came under the control of initially the Department of Highways, Ports and Properties following the change in Government to the Ministerial system. They are now the responsibility of the Department of Transport, and following the redevelopment of the outer harbour a drenching system was put in place in 1981 on the fuel discharge berth on the Battery Pier as part of the breakwater extension works. The pumps that were installed then are now at the end of their useful life and with spares no longer available the system is to be replaced in 2010 at a cost of

This photograph was taken in 1962 showing the appliances stationed at Ronaldsway Airport at that time - left to right: TMN 760, the first Thornycroft/Pyrene MkV civilian Foam Tender to be stationed at any airport in the British Isles, GMN 888, a Fordson WOT1 Crash Tender and 1819 MN, an Austin CO2 Tender. *(Author)*

This was the next generation of fire appliances at Ronaldsway to be purchased by the Isle of Man Airports Board for their Aerodrome Fire Service. Photographed left to right on the apron outside the Fire Station: in the distance **Fire 4** 621 BMN, the Bedford/Angus Domestic Water Tender, **Fire 3** MN 4359, the 6x6 Thornycroft/Nubian MkII Foam Tender, and **Fire 2** E526 MAN, the Jet Ramger 2000 Shelvoke & Drewry/Carmichael Foam Tender. *(Author)*

£1.98m with a new system capable of pumping 20,000 litres of water per minute. This will enable the harbour installation to comply with new Oil Depot Regulations following the 2005 Buncefield oil depot fire. Whilst still not strictly a private brigade it is a fire prevention system operated by the staff of another department of Government.

On cessation of hostilities the wartime AFS was disbanded and all equipment not returned to the UK was placed in central stores on Woodbourne Road later the home of the Civil Defence Commission.

Following the report of the Fire Service Commission in 1948 the value of the wartime AFS was recognised as an asset which could be useful in the event of a national emergency. The Civil Defence Commission was established and it inherited all the redundant equipment remaining on the island. A fire-fighting unit was formed from within its volunteer ranks using the old wartime equipment which was held in store by the Commission. Later a number of Green Goddess appliances were purchased from the UK with relay pumping in mind. However, lack of personnel interested in this activity led to the Civil Defence being unable to provide support to the fire service, notwithstanding that they at one time had a female section who regularly carried out pumping drills at Pulrose.

During the winter of 1979/80 the AFS was reconstituted by the Civil Defence Commission. Mr R A Christian was appointed officer in charge of the AFS with a strength of eight and operating the two remaining Bedford Green Goddess appliances. These were due to be supplemented by the Dennis F28 on its replacement by the new DS series Dennis, stationed at Laxey. It was not to be — the Civil Defence Commission was absorbed by the Home Affairs Board under the terms of the Home Affairs Board Act 1981 and later the Department of Home Affairs. Although providing suppoprt to the emergency services in other ways they now no longer provide any AFS personnel.

AIRPORT COVER

Regular air services between the Island and the United Kingdom began in the early 1930s, and the first regular airport was established on fields at Ronaldsway farm in the south of the Island. A service was established by Blackpool & West Coast Air Services Ltd, and regular flights began in June 1933. Soon de Havilland DH84s, and other aircraft, were using the airfield.

On Monday 1st July 1935, a twin-engine de Havilland Dragon, operated for Manx Airways by Railway Air Services, began take-off. At the end of the 700-yard airstrip it became airborne, but as it fought to gain height the undercarriage caught in the wire of the airport boundary fence. The pilot, Captain Pierce, fought to regain control, crossing the field adjacent to the airport, but the aircraft hit the next hedge and nose-dived into a potato field. Two passengers were thrown out on impact; despite being dazed they set about

Chapter 10 PRIVATE FIRE BRIGADES

The Thornycroft/Nubian MkII discharging protein foam through its roof monitor. This type of foam compound had to be discharged at regular intervals due its short shelf-life and so the airport firefighters used the opportunity to practice laying foam carpets which at that time was standard procedure if an aircraft reported undercarriage problems prior to landing. *(Author)*

rescuing the other four passengers and the pilot. The starboard engine had caught fire but the occupants managed to get out before the fire spread to the fabric of the plane. Mr Mason, the airport manager, telephoned for the police and the Fire Brigade. The brigade were despatched from Douglas; though quickly at the scene they were unable to save the plane. The ambulance was also despatched from Noble's Hospital and made two journeys between Ronaldsway and Douglas. Captain Pierce and a passenger, a Mrs Teare from Ballagaraghyn, were detained in hospital. The brigade account for the service was £14.

After an inquiry, by two Inspectors from the Air Ministry, the airfield was required to provide its own fire-fighting cover. The Blackpool & West Coast Company acquired a 12hp Morris van from a Port Erin confectioner and converted it to a fire tender. Their own ground staff carried out the work; they removed the van body and fitted a rack to the chassis to take three Pyrene foam extinguisher bottles, giving Ronaldsway its first airport fire tender.

As an aside to this incident, the ambulance from Noble's Hospital that was used at the crash was acquired for airfield use at Ronaldsway in 1950.

A second airport operated between 1935 and 1937 in the north of the Island, on fields at Close Lake Farm, Andreas. Scant records indicate, however, that the only fire-fighting equipment was a small trolley-mounted portable fire extinguisher.

With the advent of war, Ronaldsway was acquired by the British Government and additional land purchased. Three tarmac runways and associated hangarage were built and, in the winter of 1939-40, Ronaldsway became a Royal Air Force training station.

In 1942 the RAF transferred to a newly-established aerodrome in the north of the Island, and Ronaldsway was handed over to the Admiralty. It established a training station as part of the Fleet Air Arm and named it HMS Urley. The West Coast Company was allowed to operate a restricted service out of Ronaldsway, with fire cover provided by the Royal Naval Air Service. The station operated Barracuda aircraft, fire cover being provided by duty crash-crews using three crash tenders. The principal appliance was a Crossley FE1 6x4 with a 300-gallon water tank and a 28-gallon foam liquid tank. Foam was generated by an air-entraining perforated impeller pump with a single hose delivery. In addition, four carbon dioxide bottles were carried on the side of the vehicle.

The second foam tender was a Fordson WOT 1 standard wartime appliance, also on a 6x4 chassis and carrying 300 gallons of water, but with 100 gallons of foam. Delivery was through two hose sidelines from a pump identical to the Crossley. CO_2 could also be discharged from four 60lb cylinders through 75ft of ¾" hose. The third appliance was a four-wheel conventional-drive Austin fire tender with a 1,000gpm Tangye pump and four deliveries. It also towed a

100gpm trailer pump, all equipped for water only.

In 1939 the RAF began work on a permanent station at Jurby, in the north of the Island. Eventually two tarmac runways were built and hangarage for 70 Anson aircraft, on the condition that RAF Jurby became an air navigation school under Flying Training Command.

Less than five miles away a temporary aerodrome with three runways was opened in August 1941 at Andreas. RAF Andreas was initially a fighter station, its role being the defence of shipping using the North Channel and the ports of Belfast, Liverpool and Glasgow. Later it came under the Flying Training Command as No.11 Air Gunnery School. Martinets, Wellingtons and Spitfires regularly used the airfield.

Both stations had the standard allocation of a Crossley and a Fordson, similar to those at Ronaldsway. The normal procedure was for the crash tenders to be stationed alongside the control tower while the station was operational, returning to the motor transport compound on stand-down.

The worst incident of the war occurred at Jurby; although no lives were lost, the damage was extensive. During May 1945 a Sunderland flying boat with one engine on fire made a forced landing on the airfield. It was carrying eight aerial mines and was successfully brought down. The station had been evacuated of all but essential personnel, because of this dangerous cargo. The crash-crew tried to tackle the fire, which had spread to the wing, but it was too well established. Because of the mines, they were ordered to retreat. The Sunderland blew up and almost every window on the camp was broken. The roofs of the main hangars were severely damaged, and the crash-crew had little else to do but damp down small fires around the airfield.

Later, in September, a fire broke out in the stack-yard at Ballalough Farm, Andreas. The fire was extinguished by the RAF Andreas Fire Section; the men were unable to save the 20-ton stack, but at least they stopped the fire spreading to the adjoining buildings. Shortly after this incident Andreas aerodrome closed down.

Jurby continued after hostilities as a training and operational aerodrome. The Crossley was replaced by a military version of the Thornycroft/Pyrene Mk V, and the Fordson by a Thornycroft dual-purpose tender with a large water-carrying capacity. It served as a back-up vehicle and carried an extension ladder; it had sidelines for domestic fires on airfield property and was part of the all-island reinforcement scheme.

A personnel rescue vehicle was also stationed at Jurby in the late 1950s. It echoed the wartime experience of getting people out of a crashed 'plane quickly where converted Jeeps or similar vehicles had been used for the purpose. Now it was purpose-built, based on a Land Rover chassis and carrying two dry-powder extinguishers discharged by compressed nitrogen through two hose deliveries stowed flaked on side racks. The vehicle also carried a stalk light and other emergency gear.

During 1946 and 1947 the Ministry of Civil Aviation operated Ronaldsway. Then, in March 1948, the airport was purchased by the Isle of Man Government for £11,500, shortly after the Isle of Man Airports Board was formed. The

The driver's eye view of a Viscount aircraft on the apron at Ronaldsway seen from the front seat of one of the crash tenders. *(Author)*

Chapter 10 PRIVATE FIRE BRIGADES

The Jet Ranger 2000 Foam Tender was powered by a 12-litre turbo-charged V8 430hp Detroit diesel engine and was capable of discharging foam through the roof monitor at the rate of 7,000gpm. It is photographed outside the new Fire Station at Ronaldsway Airport in yellow livery and bearing the latest logo for the appliances stationed at Ronaldsway Airport. *(Author)*

fire appliances and the two crash-crews were part of the deal. Each crash tender hand earned £5-4s per week and the one chargehand, Arthur Corlett, £5-9s per week. He was to take charge of the Airport Fire Brigade and stay at Ronaldsway until his retirement in 1971.

Ronaldsway, operating under the new Board, soon found their wartime appliances unable to make long road journeys. This gave the Board a problem as it had obtained permission to use Jurby as a diversionary airport in the event of fog or cross-winds, and a condition of its use was that it should provide its own fire cover. To overcome the problem the old Leyland was loaned to the Airports Board by the Douglas Corporation. Stripped of its wheeled escape and accessories, but still with its pump and hose-reel, it took up its duties on 11th September 1948. The Airport Fire Service was at this time made up on a part-time basis with members of the fire crew working also as baggage-handlers, porters and maintenance staff.

During 1953 Mr Mayall, Chief Fire Staff Officer, was instructed by the Local Government Board at the request of the Airports Board to advise on the Airport Fire Service arrangements and to assist in training. Prior to this, one appliance was housed in a small fire station under the control tower, with the remainder in one of the hangars. The aircraft on regular service were becoming larger; Dakotas predominated, with occasional Elizabethans, Doves and Herons. Mr Mayall could clearly see the need for a drastic re-organisation of the Airport Fire Service. During the following year he undertook 72 lecture sessions, including practical training, on fighting aircraft fires. He also arranged for Castletown and Ramsey Brigades to exercise with the Airport Fire Service.

When a major fault developed in the Austin's foam pump, the Airport Board were left with no alternative but to order a replacement. The new appliance was a 40 hp Thornycroft/Pyrene Mk V foam tender based on the Nubian 4x4 chassis; it entered service in July 1955. For the first time the crew were accommodated within a fully-enclosed cab. The appliance carried 550 gallons of water and 50 gallons of foam compound. Foam could be discharged through a roof monitor with the vehicle stationary and from two four-inch deliveries either side. Water could be discharged through two rear deliveries. It was the first civilian Mk V to be delivered to a civil airport in the British Isles.

During 1958 the Airports Board continued to improve the fire section, adopting International Civil Aviation Regulations. Mr Mayall continued to train the crash-crews, conducting a further series of lectures and exercises with members of Castletown and Ramsey Brigades for appliance familiarisation. Crews at RAF Jurby were joined in similar exercises by Ramsey and Kirk Michael Brigades.

In June, a full-scale exercise was staged, involving all units. Following the lessons learned, a scheme for dealing with a major air crash outside the airport limits was drawn up and code-named Operation Hillsearch.

In September a diesel-engined dual-purpose appliance based on a Ford Thames Trader chassis was introduced. It carried 800 gallons of water and 75 gallons of foam with two side deliveries on each side through a Coventry Climax 600gpm pump, foam being aspirated at the branch.

To bring the airport fire section up to date a rapid intervention vehicle based on an Austin Gypsy was introduced in May 1959. It was fitted with dry-powder cylinders discharged by CO_2 through two 27ft hose deliveries. It carried a full set of electrically-operated cutting tools and a small folding ladder.

In 1960 Vickers Viscount turbo-prop aircraft were introduced on regular service flights to Ronaldsway. Fire section facilities had to be improved.

The section leader, Mr Arthur Corlett, who had been in charge of the crash-crew since 1946, attended the first of many training courses organised through the Civil Aviation Authority Fire School at Rhoose Airport, Cardiff. Mr R W C Corkish was appointed as deputy and he too attended similar courses. After completing basic training, the fire section was reorganised using the same ranking system as in the rest of the UK and Mr Corlett became the Senior Airport Fire Officer.

To provide additional cover a second-hand War Department 30 hp Austin 4x6 CO_2 fire tender was acquired. It carried 24 bottles of CO_2 in four racks, amounting to a total capacity of 1,440 lbs of gas at a pressure of 800psi. Discharge was through two 75ft lengths of ¾- hose and long-handled applicators. The appliance was bought in June 1960 and reconditioned in the airport's own motor transport section; it entered service soon afterwards.

The airport was modernised at the same time. The improvements included a new three-bay station built adjacent to the east apron. The fire station moved into the new premises in March 1961; for the first time the crash-crew and appliances were all housed together adjacent to the main terminal area. All appliances were fitted with radio and put in direct contact with Air Traffic Control.

In 1964 the RAF ceased operations at Jurby; Operation Hillsearch ended with the withdrawal of skilled personnel. The Isle of Man Government bought Jurby to use as a diversionary airport, and extended the main runway to accommodate Viscounts. The Airport Fire Service provided fire cover whenever the airfield was used, usually with the old Fordson and an appliance from the Ramsey Brigade. An additional dual-purpose appliance was bought for Ronaldsway in January 1965. It was based on a Bedford chassis with the same bodywork pump and equipment as the Thames dual-purpose appliance.

Runway extensions were made at Ronaldsway during 1970 to allow for the introduction of BAC 1-11 Series 400 jet aircraft. At the same time the Airport Fire Service took delivery of an 18ft inshore lifeboat powered by a 40hp Evinrude outboard motor. The boat was acquired to comply with international regulations as three of the airport's main

The full line-up of the airport appliances on 21st May 1990 on the occasion of the opening of the new Fire Station at Ronaldsway. **Fire1** and the Bedford are still carrying the old red livery. **Fire I** was a Rapid Intervention Vehicle by Carmichael based on a 6x4 long wheelbase Range Rover. In the background is the new **Fire 4,** the 4x4 Simon Saro Defender. *(Author)*

Chapter 10 PRIVATE FIRE BRIGADES

runway approaches are over the sea. The boat was trailer-mounted and towed by the Gypsy, extending its role as a rapid intervention vehicle.

All fire-crew personnel were now regularly attending courses at the Civil Aviation Authority Fire School, although the training base had moved to Stansted. As part of the continuing need to modernise the service, the Airports Board embarked yet again on a change of equipment. A major foam tender was acquired in January 1973, the largest ever to be introduced in the Island up to that date. It was a Thornycroft Nubian Mk II based on a three-axle chassis powered by a 15-litre 300bhp Cummins V8 engine. Carrying 1,400 gallons of water and 140 gallons of foam, it had an all-up weight of 20 tons. The appliance was the first on the airport capable of discharging foam on the move, through a fully-controllable roof-mounted monitor at a rate of 7,000gpm. In addition to the roof monitor the appliance carried side deliveries for foam and water and a rear-mounted first aid hose-reel. Branches, tools and hose are carried in side lockers and a Bristol reflectorised fire-fighting suit, helmet and boots are carried in the crew cab together with breathing apparatus.

The modernisation programme was completed in 1979 with the addition of two further appliances. At this time the vehicles were numbered and given call-signs and lettered out on the side panels as Ronaldsway Aerodrome Fire Service, all vehicles carrying UHF radio. The first of the two appliances arrived in March. It was a rapid-intervention vehicle built by Carmichael and based on a 6x4 Range Rover chassis. Designed mainly for personnel rescue, it carried 200 gallons of light water premix discharged through a roof monitor and 92kgs of Bromochlorodifluoromethane (BCF) liquid, a halogenated fire-extinguishing agent, through a nitrogen pressurised hose-reel. The appliance was designated Fire 1 and became the first-call appliance, carrying full cutting gear, small ladder and Bristol suit. The total discharge time for the firefighting agents carried was 90 seconds, during which time any rescue had to be effected although the back-up foam equipment would be very close behind. The standard of firemanship of the crew and knowledge of entry into aircraft was to an extremely high standard.

The second appliance arrived in October and cost £80,000. It was a Jet Ranger 2000 major foam unit, also built by Carmichael, on a specialist chassis from Shelvoke & Drewry, powered by a 12-litre turbo-charged V8 Detroit diesel engine of 430 bhp, giving a top speed of 50mph. The appliance carried 1,800 gallons of water and 200 gallons of FP 570 foam compound and, like the Nubian, discharged foam at the rate of 7,000gpm through a controllable roof monitor fed by a 1,200gpm Godiva Mk 14 pump. Side foam deliveries at 1,000gpm are similar to the Nubian, with the hose reel mounted on the offside. The normal crew complement is three, with the driver and monitor operator linked by internal intercom. The operational weight of 22 tons made it the largest appliance on the Island at the time. The Jet Ranger was allocated the call sign Fire 2, the Nubian Fire 3 and the Bedford, dating from 1965, Fire 4. The brigade complement was 14 firemen in two seven-man watches under a Station Officer, Deputy Station Officer and Section Leader. A continuous training programme was undertaken with wet and dry drills, and frequent combined exercises held with the Island Fire Service for appliance familiarisation.

The Airport Fire Service operates under comprehensive operational orders and procedures, with predetermined attendance to all locations on the airport. For a full emergency turnout at Ronaldsway there is a predetermined reinforcement scheme involving the Island Fire & Rescue Service with attendance originally by two major pumps from Castletown, a major pump, hose-carrier and emergency tender from Douglas and a pump escape from Port Erin. Now the PDA is five pumps and a rescue unit on the basis of nearest availability.

Fire 1 and Fire 3 had a complete foam discharge time of just over two minutes each, so that any aircraft fire had to be knocked out and smothered within that time to be effective. Again, this requires a high degree of skill.

To produce foam the major units required a vast amount of water. The airport had no water ring main at this time so the additional manpower and pumping capacity provided by the reinforcement scheme was essential for relay pumping from the five static water tanks, storing 132,000 gallons within the airport boundary. Foam blankets were no longer laid as they were considered to be inefficient.

A reciprocal arrangement was made with Operation Oil Fire, in which Fire 3 would immediately be sent to Douglas as a reinforcing appliance in the event of a fire occurring in the main petroleum fuel storage depot.

The fire section provided cover on the airport apron as required, using portable BCF251b wheeled extinguishers with long-handled applicators.

In 1986 the former Isle of Man Airports Board became part of the Department of Highways, Ports and Properties, with its fire vehicles being maintained at their central plant depot at Crosby. The airport soon embarked on an improvement scheme that was to be phased over a number of years; one of the first problems to be addressed was the fire section. Personnel were increased to 22, made up from one SAFO, Mr David Young, who was appointed in the same year, one Deputy Fire Officer, two Section Leaders and eighteen firemen. A watch consists of one Section Leader and six firemen. A new site was determined for the Airport Fire Station and it was built near to the old barn site on the opposite side of the airfield to the terminal building. From this modem five-bay station, with full messing facilities and a modern control room located at roof level, the duty watchman could now for the first time command a view of the whole airfield. The station was opened on Monday 21st May 1990 by the Chief Minister, the Hon Miles Walker MHK.

The same day saw the DHPP take delivery of a replacement for Fire 4. Just as Ronaldsway had been the first airport to receive a civilian Thornycroft/Pyrene Mk V, so this new appliance was to be an all-time first. Manufactured by Simon Gloster Saro and built on a 4x4 Mercedes Benz 1936 AF-38 chassis, the new airport crash-rescue vehicle was the first of the Defender series. Carrying 4,500 litres of water and 540 litres of foam, delivery was through a roof monitor at a discharge rate of 2,300 litres per minute over a distance of 50m through 135 degrees of rotation. It carried two foam sidelines, two water branches and a first-aid hose-reel. Foam generation was through a centrifugal unit powered by a Godiva UFPX Mk 14 pump. The appliance could also deliver 100kg of Halon 1211 powder through a sideline. For night work, illumination was provided by a Clark TF mast carrying two 1,000 Watt floodlights. The standard Mercedes cab provided accommodation for a crew of five, the appliance being capable of accelerating to 50mph in forty seconds with an all-up weight in excess of 16 tonnes.

The new appliance proved its value in December 1990 when a Manx Airlines British Aerospace Advanced Turbo-Prop careered off the runway after its nose-wheel collapsed on landing. The Airport Fire Service were mobilised immediately and reached the aircraft before the engines were shut down. Fortunately there was no fire and the seventy passengers were evacuated without injury by the aircrew through the front passenger door. Two branch lines were run out from Fire 3 and the aircraft checked for fuel leaks. Appliances from Castletown, Douglas and Port Erin attended the incident but were not required. Retrieval of the aircraft was achieved with some difficulty, illumination and cover being provided by the Airport Fire Service.

Under the DHPP a programme of vehicle replacement and refurbishment began with Fire 5 being replaced by a Toyota 4x4 vehicle from within the Department's vehicle fleet, its normal duties being for inspection, bird-scaring and towing the inshore rescue boat. Fire 3 received a comprehensive refit, extending its useful life by twenty years.

All the airport appliances changed their livery from red to yellow, and during 1990 all appliances adopted the new airport logo "The Airport Isle of Man". Fire 2 was sent to Angloco for a similar refit towards the end of the year, after which the Airport Fire Service had a modern station equipped with completely updated appliances, Graham Winstanley taking over as SAFO on the retirement of his predecessor in 1991.

In 2001 the airport placed an order for a new front-line appliance which was a 6x6 Carmichael Cobra1 fire-fighting vehicle to be designated Fire 1. These appliances were introduced onto the market in 1992 following a two-year development period and were state-of-the-art. It weighed 33,000 kg, was powered by a Caterpillar four-stroke turbo-diesel rated at 710hp and had an overall length of 10.74m. With a roof-mounted foam monitor capable of discharging foam at 4,500 lpm it was a tight squeeze for the appliance room.

In 2001 Ronaldsway became a Category 6 airfield with all its attendant requirements. A second first-line crash tender was ordered from AMDAC-Carmichael. Similar to the first 6x6 it was a Carmichael Cobra2, which was a development of the Cobra1 following experience with similar vehicles supplied to the Ministry of Defence.

At the same time SAFO Mick Rodger retired and in line with the change in category the fire personnel structure was changed and increased to thirty-one in three watches of ten. The total establishnent comprises four Watch Commanders (equivalent to Station Officers) of which one is dedicated as training and development officer, six Crew Commanders

The two largest appliances at the airport are 6x6 Carmichael Cobra2 Foam Tenders. Fire 2, photographed outside the Airport Fire Station, is powered by a Caterpillar four-stroke turbo-diesel rated at 710hp and has an overall length of 10.74m. The roof-mounted foam monitor is capable of discharging foam at 4,500 litres per minute on the run. *(Author)*

Chapter 10 PRIVATE FIRE BRIGADES

(equivalent to Leading Firefighters) and twenty-one Firefighters. Coincident with becoming a Category 6 airport Ronaldsway was required to have a Senior Fire Services Manager as opposed to a SAFO and the post of Rescue and Fire Services Manager was created with Mr Lindsay Armstrong being subsequently appointed.

It is a non-operational position, with overall responsibility for all areas of IOM Airport Rescue and Fire Fighting Services. It involves a higher level of liaison with IOMF&RS and CAA and responsibility for station administration, ensuring regulatory compliance and writing policy documents. All off-Island specialist training is now carried out at Teesside or Durham Tees Valley Airport.

Although outwardly similar, the second Cobra, designated Fire 2, has a number of differences. It is powered by a Detroit two-stroke supercharged engine and it weighs slightly less at 31,800kg. The discharge rate of the monitor and sideline is the same but it carries slightly more Monnex fire-retardant powder and BCF. The water capacity is the same at 10,000 litres and it carries 1,400 litres of Class B foam.

Eventually all the old appliances were replaced and Fire 3, a Simon 4x4, makes up the front-line cover for the airport. This appliance carries 6,100 litres of water and 750 litres of foam; on maximum discharge the monitor delivers slightly less than the other two appliances at 3,200 lpm but the same rate for the sideline at 450 lpm.

Regular exercises are carried out with the Isle of Man Fire & Rescue Service to ensure familiarisation with equipment in the event of a major incident and at present one of the IOMF&RS appliances, a 4x4 Mercedes/Carmichael pump tender JMN 366E, is on loan to the Airport Fire Service as a domestic appliance and relay pump. The airport is still without a complete water ring main and has a hose trailer which can be brought into use for additional supply to any incident.

The Airport Fire Service is completely up-to-date with an impressive fire-fighting capability that is likely to increase if the airport is further uprated on completion of extensive runway extension work, modernisation of the Air Traffic Control Section and the provision of a new control tower.

As a matter of interest and just about qualifying as a private brigade, Thermo Skyships who had started building airships at Jurby airfield had to provide cover for their activities and to enable their use of the airfield. The Austin CO2 tender which the Airport Fire Service acquired in 1960 became surplus to requirements when their new appliances were delivered in 1979. It was quickly snapped up by the new company. The elderly appliance saw several years of service at Jurby before being acquired for preservation in the Imperial War Museum in 1988.

The company, changed their name to the Advanced Airship Corporation Ltd, and continued to expand, with its first flight planned for 1991. It had provided fire cover since 1988 with a Land Rover-based appliance. It could only discharge water through two sidelines and carried 50 gallons of water with a further 200 gallons in a coupled trailer. It was intended to modify the vehicle to carry and discharge foam, being manned by the company workforce.

The company ceased operating in without the airship ever flying.

Fire 3 dates from 1996 and was a replacement for the Simon Saro Defender which was involved in two accidents on the airfield. The appliance is a Simon Protector 4x4 Foam Tender and carries 6,000 litres of water and 720 litres of foam. As well as the roof-mounted monitor it carries one foam-making branch and a BCF discharge lance. *(Author)*

APPENDICES

(i) LOCATION OF FIRE STATIONS

DOUGLAS
1803-1860	Sun Insurance Office, Douglas
1860-1862	Douglas Court House, Church Street
1862-1864	Collister's Yard, Athol Street
1864-1869	Hampton's Yard
1869-1874	Commissioners' Yard, Fort Street
1874-1894	Hill's Brewery, Hill's Estate
1894-1900	Thos Moore's Livery Stable, Circular Road
1900-1977	Municipal Buildings, John Street
1977-	Peel Road

DOUGLAS No 2 STATION
1935-1977	Lord Street (station closed)

PEEL
1885-1895	Rocket Brigade House.
1895-1921	Station Road
1921-1941	Boilley Spittall
1941-1968	Market Square
1968-	Queen's Drive

RAMSEY
1887-1889	The Old Brewery
1889-1971	Town Hall, Parliament Square
1971-	Station Road

CASTLETOWN
1845-1896	Military Barracks, Market Place
1890-1896	Union Hotel Yard, Arbory Street
1896-1898	The former Barracks
1898-1912	Alexandra Road
1912-1965	Commissioners' Yard, The Old Barracks.
1965-	Farrant's Way

PORT ERIN
1897-1934	Commissioners' Yard, Lower Rowan.
1934-1939	Falcon's Nest Yard

PORT ST MARY
1907-1939	Hosebox at Police Station
1921-1939	Harper's Yard (station closed)

ONCHAN
1911-1938	Coupe's Stables, Queen's Road
1938-1940	Commissioners' Yard, School Road (station closed)

LAXEY
1920-1943	Commissioners' Office, New Road
1943-	Mines Road

KIRK MICHAEL
1931-1940	Commissioners' Store, Main Road
1940-1942	Kelly's Yard, Main Road
1942-1942	Quayle's Garage, Main Road
1942-1979	Mitre Hotel Car Park
1979-	Station Road

FOXDALE
1942-1950	Main Road, Upper Foxdale (station closed)

ANDREAS
1942-1950	Andreas Village (station closed)

BALLASALLA
1942-1950	Crossag Road, Ballasalla (station closed)

RUSHEN FIRE AUTHORITY
1939-1958	Falcon's Nest Yard, Port Erin
1942-1955	Commissioners' Yard, Athol St, Port St Mary
1958-	Droghadfayle Road, Port Erin

(ii) LIST OF CAPTAINS OR CHIEF OFFICERS

DOUGLAS
SUN FIRE OFFICE
1811-1848	Mr Clarke (foreman)

DOUGLAS TOWN COMMISSIONERS
1848-1860	High Bailiff (in charge of engine)
1860-1867	Mr C Craine
1867-1871	Mr J Cartwright
1871-1890	Mr W Kewiey
1890-1903	Mr R O'Hara

DOUGLAS TOWN COUNCIL
1903-1916	Mr R O'Hara (Superintendent)
1903-1921	Mr W Pickett (Captain)
1921-1929	Mr S J Caugherty (Captain)
1921-1929	Mr W Pickett (Superintendent)
1929-1935	Mr S J Caugherty (Superintendent)
1929-1935	Mr A J O'Hara (Captain)

1935 BRIGADE STRUCTURE REVISED
1935-1945	Mr S J Caugherty (Chief Officer)
1935- ?	Mr S A Caugherty (Brigade Secretary)
1945-1950	Mr A J O'Hara
1950-1965	Mr F Courtie

TRANSFERRED TO IOM FIRE SERVICE
PEEL
1885-1895	Mr W Kermode
1895-1901	Mr H Quayle

APPENDICES

1901-1933   Mr T E Watterson
1933-1942   Mr E Cowell
1942-1946   Mr R H Kneen
1946-1955   Mr W H Watterson
1955-1960   Mr J Bell

TRANSFERRED TO IOM FIRE SERVICE

RAMSEY

1887-1900   Mr W Boyde (Superintendent)
1887-1900   Mr A Wall (Captain)
1900-1918   Mr W Boyde
1918-1921   Police Inspector King
1921-1928   Police Inspector Fayle
1928-1942   Mr J Smith
1942-1945   Mr J W Sayle
1945-1960   Mr J R Brooke

TRANSFERRED TO IOM FIRE SERVICE

CASTLETOWN

1845-1896   Commanding Officer of the Garrison
1896-1921   Mr J Cubbon
1921-1928   Mr J Kneale
1928-1942   Mr T Corkill
1942-1944   Mr J W Oates
1944-1960   Mr F L Kennaugh

TRANSFERRED TO IOM FIRE SERVICE

PORT ERIN

1897-1915   Mr Wm Harrison (Escape Minder)
1915-1927   Mr Wm Harrison (Captain)
1927-1933   PC A Corris
1933-1937   PC J Lace
1937-1939   PC A Cowin

AMALGAMATED WITH PORT ST MARY AS THE RUSHEN JOINT FIRE PROTECTION BOARD

PORT ST MARY

1907-1912   Police Sgt E.H.Corkill (Hose Minder)
1912-1912   Police Sgt Wm Fargher (Hose Minder)
1935-1936   Mr J Cubbon (Superintendent)
1936-1939   Mr J Crebbin

AMALGAMATED WITH PORT ERIN AS THE RUSHEN JOINT FIRE PROTECTION BOARD

RUSHEN JOINT FIRE PROTECTION BOARD
1939-1941   PC A Cowin
1941-1947   Mr J R Costain
1947-1950   Mr J Hyslop

RECONSTITUTED AS THE RUSHEN FIRE AUTHORITY
RUSHEN FIRE AUTHORITY
1950-1960   Mr J Hyslop

TRANSFERRED TO THE IOM FIRE SERVICE

ONCHAN
1911- ?   Mr J T Skillicorn
? -1940   Mr E Quiggin

DISBANDED UNDER THE TERMS OF THE LOCAL GOVERNMENT (Fires) ACT 1940

LAXEY

1920-1930   Mr F B Holroyd
1930-1947   Mr D Williamson
1947-1960   Mr W J Bridson (Sen)

TRANSFERRED TO IOM FIRE SERVICE

KIRK MICHAEL

1931-1941   Mr F W Cowin
1941-1951   PC G W A Kinrade
1951-1952   PC P Moyer
1952-1960   Mr G E Creer

TRANSFERRED TO IOM FIRE SERVICE

(iii) ISLE OF MAN FIRE SERVICE

CHIEF FIRE STAFF OFFICERS
1941-1950   Mr C A P Ellis
1951-1961   Mr S J Mayall
1961-1962   Mr Fred Courtle (acting)
1962-1974   Mr Cyril Pearson

CHIEF FIRE OFFICER (re-designated 1977)
1974-1990   Mr John Hinnigan
1990-2000   Mr W Godfrey Cain
2000-2004   Mr Alan D Christian
2004-   Mr Brian Draper

DEPUTY CHIEF OFFICERS
1965-1966   Mr F Courtie
1966-1976   Mr S Skinner
1976-1990   Mr R J I Hopkins
1990-1990   Mr W Godfrey Cain
1990-2000   Mr Alan D Christian
2000-2007   Mr Bruce Kirkham
2007-   Mr Kevin Groom

STATION OFFICERS

DOUGLAS STATION

1965-1965   Mr Bert Kenna
1965-1966   Mr R Stan Skinner
1966-1981   Mr Mike M Ventre
1981-1990   Mr W Godfrey Cain
1990-2000   Mr Alan D Christian

LAXEY STATION

1960-1974	Mr W J Bridson (Sen)
1974-1982	Mr W J Bridson (Jun)
1982-2002	Mr J Boyde
2002-2004	Mr G Lawson
2004-	Mr M Cleator

RAMSEY STATION

1960-1968	Mr J R Brooke
1968-1974	Mr G Foulis
1974-1990	Mr P B Quayle
1990-2000	Mr G D Foulis
2000-2001	Mr C Foulis
2001	Mr N F Fairclough

KIRK MICHAEL STATION

1960-1964	Mr C E Creer
1964-1965	Mr L Lowe (Acting)
1965-1967	Mr L Lowe
1967-1974	Mr D Collins
1971-1977	Mr J Lowe
1977-1981	Mr K Telford
1981-1990	Mr L E Teare
2000-2001	Mr D Mayne
2001-2002	Mr D Corlett
2002-	Mr J M Cashen

PEEL STATION

1960-1970	Mr J Bell
1970-1974	Mr J Killey
1974-1991	Mr L Halsall
1991-1994	Mr A Kelly
1994-1997	Mr E Leece
1997-2004	Mr L Armstrong
2004-	Mr B Gelling

CASTLETOWN STATION

1960-1968	Mr F L Kennaugh
1968-1975	Mr A Kelly
1975-1988	Mr A L Sayle
1988-1995	Mr T E Craine
1995-2001	Mr D Collister
2001-2005	Mr T Taubman
2005-	Mr I T Clegg

RUSHEN STATION

1960-1968	Mr J Hyslop
1968-1971	Mr D T Quine
1971-1984	Mr A J Corkish
1984-1986	Mr B T Peyton
1986-1991	Mr N T Gandy
1991-2007	Mr D Woodworth
2007-	Mr J Preston

RONALDSWAY AIRPORT FIRE SERVICE
SENIOR AIRPORT FIRE OFFICERS

1946-1970	Mr A Corlett
1970-1978	Mr R W C Corkill
1978-1986	Mr L Kinrade
1986-1991	Mr D Young
1991-1996	Mr G Winstanley
1996-2001	Mr M Roger

RESCUE AND FIRE SERVICES MANAGER

2001-	Mr L Armstrong

(iv) LIST OF APPLIANCES

DOUGLAS (SUN FIRE OFFICE)

1803-1848	Manual Pump (sold off island)
1808-1848	Manual Pump (sold to A W Moore, Tromode sailcloth works)

DOUGLAS TOWN COMMISSIONERS

1848-1884	Manual Pump "Grampus" – McGhie, Lewthwaite & Teare.. Ladder-Cart
1875- ?	Reel Cart – Shand Mason & Co
1877- ?	50ft "Clayton" Wheeled Escape – Merryweather & Sons
1884- ?	Horse-drawn 14 Manual Pump "Douglas" – Wm Rose & Co
1887-1920	Reel Cart
1895- ?	45ft 'Improved Kingston' wheeled escape and hose cart – Wm Rose & Co
1895-1941	36ft "Curricle" Wheeled Escape – Wm Rose & Co (assumed that this is the escape that was transferred to Peel during the Second World War).

(NB A report dated 1921 states that Douglas had five large escapes, two small escapes and a tower ladder but gives no other detail. Some of the old Wheeled Escapes were positioned near the internment camps during the Second World War but there is no record of them after the camps were disbanded.)

DOUGLAS CORPORATION

1909-1929		Horse-drawn Greenwich Gem Steam Pump "Raglan" – Merryweather & Sons (It remained in Villiers Yard until after the Second World War but was not in use after 1936.)
1921-1948	MN 1233	65hp Leyland Pump Escape and 50ft "Bayley" Wheeled Escape

APPENDICES

1929-1941	MN 6117	14hp Bean Motor Tender (sold to Castletown Commissioners)
1935- ?		'Hatfield' Trailer Pump – Merryweather
1936-1962	MAN 875	100ft Turntable Ladder – Dorman/Merryweather (sold for scrap)
1936- ?	MAN 876	Major Pump – Albion/Merryweather (sold for scrap)
1941-1965	EMN 823	Motor Tender – Fordson (transferred to LGB 1965)

The four Auxiliary Towing Vehicles allocated to Douglas in 1942 and retained for further use had light trailer pumps, which the Fire Service kept when the vehicles were sold out of service.

1942-1946	FMN 237	Austin Auxiliary Towing Vehicle (sold to J Curtis Ltd)
1942-1955	FMN 238	Austin Auxiliary Towing Vehicle (transferred to Rushen Fire Authority)
1942-1946	FMN 248	Austin Auxiliary Towing Vehicle (sold to Douglas Holiday Camp)
1942-1946	FMN 280	Austin Auxiliary Towing Vehicle (sold to IOM Dairies)
1951-1965	NMN 50	Major Pump Escape – AEC/Merryweather (transferred to Local Government Board 1965)
1955-1962	FMN 267	Austin Auxiliary Towing Vehicle (sold to Davies Garage)
1962-1965	5531 MN	Dennis F28 Pump Water Tender (transferred to LGB 1965)
1962-1965	5724 MN	100ft Turntable Ladder – AEC/Merryweather (transferred to LGB 1965)
1962-1965	6002 MN	Commer Personnel Carrier (transferred to LGB 1965)

RAMSEY - SUN FIRE OFFICE

1803-1808		Manual Pump (transferred to Douglas)

RAMSEY TOWN COMMISSIONERS

1884- ?		Hand-cart and buckets
1887- ?		Hand-cart – Wm Rose & Co
1888-1929		Manual Pump – second hand from Stourbridge
1896-		60ft Wheeled Escape – Shand Mason & Co (preserved by IOM Fire Service)
1928-1942	MN 5695	30hp Motor Pump Merryweather/Hatfield "Richdale".
1939-1954	EMN 106	24hp Morris/Merryweather Motor Tender with 45ft ladder (sold to Civil Defence Commission)
1939- ?		Merryweather Hatfield No.2 Trailer Pump
1940-1955	EMN 204	25hp Morris/Merryweather Pump Escape (sold to Laxey Commissioners)
1942-1960	FMN 284	Austin Auxiliary Towing Vehicle (transferred to LGB 1960)
1955-1960	TMN 424	Dennis F8 Pump Water Tender (transferred to LGB 1960)

CASTLETOWN BARRACKS

1845-1896		Manual Pump – J Stone & Co, Deptford (sold to Castletown Commissioners)

CASTLETOWN COMMISSIONERS

1890-1928		Hand Fire-Cart with 30ft telescopic ladder – J Morris & Co
1896-1955		Manual Pump – J Stone, Deptford (given to Manx Museum)
1928-1941		40ft "Ajax" telescopic ladder replaced 30ft ladder and added to hand-cart, which was converted to Ladder-Cart
1941-1942	MN 6117	14hp Bean Motor Tender (sold to Kirk Michael Commissioners)
1942-1953	FMN 259	Austin Auxiliary Towing Vehicle (transferred to Civil Defence Commission)
1943-1946	FMN 451	Austin Auxiliary Towing Vehicle (transferred to IOM Government)
1953-1960	PMN 72	Dennis F8 Pump Water Tender (transferred to LGB 1960)

PEEL TOWN COMMISSIONERS

1885-1941		Hand Fire Cart – Wm Rose & Co
1921-1941		Manual Pump – Shand Mason & Co
1941-1946		36ft "Curricle" Wheeled Escape – Wm Rose & Co
1941-1953	EMN 983	Motor Tender – 20hp Commer/Merryweather (sold to Civil Defence Commission)
		Hatfield Trailer Pump – Merryweather
1942-1946	FMN 404	Austin Auxiliary Towing Vehicle (transferred to Kirk Michael Commissioners)
1953-1960		PMN 71 Dennis F8 Pump Water Tender (transferred to LGB 1960)

PORT ERIN VILLAGE COMMISSIONERS
1897-1939	"Metropolitan" 60ft Wheeled Escape – Wm Rose & Co
1914-1939	45ft Extending Ladder and Implement Van – H Simmis & Co

PORT ST MARY COMMISSIONERS
1900-1939	Hose and standpipe
1922-1939	Hand-cart Implement Van

RUSHEN JOINT FIRE PROTECTION BOARD
(Rushen Fire Authority)

PORT ERIN STATION
1942-1955	FMN 267	Austin Auxiliary Towing Vehicle (sold to Douglas Corporation)
1939-1960	DMN 890	50ft Escape Carrier – Morris/Merryweather and Beresford Light Trailer Pump (transferred to LGB 1960)
1955-1956	FMN 238	Austin Auxiliary Towing Vehicle (sold to Kirk Michael Commissioners)
1959-1960	601 MN	4x4 Austin Gypsy Light Pump

PORT ST MARY SUB-STATION (CLOSED IN 1955)
1939-1955		Hand-cart Implement Van
1955-1955	FMN 238	Austin Auxiliary Towing Vehicle (sold to Kirk Michael Commissioners)

LAXEY VILLAGE COMMISSIONERS
1920-		Hand Fire=Cart – J Blakeborough & Sons Ltd (preserved by the IOM Fire Service)
1940-1941	BMN 207	Dodge Motor Tender (transferred to the IOM Harbour Board)
1942-1955	FMN 249	Austin Auxiliary Towing Vehicle (transferred to Civil Defence Commission)
1955-1960	EMN 204	25hp Merryweather Pump Escape (transferred to LGB 1960)

KIRK MICHAEL VILLAGE COMMISSIONERS
1931- ?		Hand Fire Cart
1942-1946	MN 6117	14hp Bean Motor Tender
1946-1956	FMN 404	Austin Auxiliary Towing Vehicle (transferred to Civil Defence Commission)
1956-1960	FMN 238	Austin Auxiliary Towing Vehicle (transferred to LGB 1960)

ISLE OF MAN GOVERNMENT
(Salvage Division Government Office)
1940-1946	DMN 925	12hp Morris Van
1939-1945	FMN 493	8hp Morris Saloon Car
1943-1955	FMN 451	Austin Auxiliary Towing Vehicle (transferred to Civil Defence Commission)
1942-1948	FMN 196	8hp Ford Saloon Car (Chief Fire Staff Officer)

IOM HARBOUR BOARD
1941-1947	BMN 207	Dodge Motor Tender

AUXILIARY FIRE SERVICE
1942-1945   Fourteen Standard Home Office Austin Auxiliary Towing Vehicles with 35ft extension ladders and a 500 gpm Trailer Pump were acquired by the IOM War Emergency Committee and allocated to fire-posts throughout the Island

1942-1945	FMN 237	ATV with 35ft ladder and Trailer Pump allocated to fire-post No.1
1945	FMN 237	transferred to Douglas Fire Brigade
1942-1945	FMN 280	ATV with 35ft ladder and Trailer Pump allocated to fire-post No.2
1945	FMN 280	transferred to Douglas Fire Brigade
1942-1945	FMN 238	ATV with 35ft ladder and Trailer Pump allocated to fire-post at Woodbourne Bakery
1945	FMN 238	transferred to Douglas Fire Brigade
1942-1945	FMN 248	ATV with 35ft ladder and Trailer Pump allocated to fire-post No.10
1945-		transferred to Douglas Fire Brigade
1942-1945	FMN 249	ATV with 35ft ladder and Trailer Pump allocated to Laxey and retained

APPENDICES

1942-1945		ATV with 35ft ladder and Trailer Pump allocated to Ramsey
1942-1943	FMN 284	ATV allocated to Ramsey, reallocated later to Andreas
1943-	FMN 284	ATV with 35ft ladder Trailer Pump and allocated to Andreas fire-post and retained
1942-1945	FMN 259	ATV with 35ft ladder and Trailer Pump allocated to Castletown and retained
1942-1943	FMN 451	ATV with 35ft ladder and Trailer Pump allocated to Castletown, later transferred to Ballasalla fire-post
1943-1945	FMN 451	ATV with 35ft ladder and Trailer Pump allocated to Ballasalla fire-post and retained
1943-1943	FMN 404	ATV with 35ft ladder and Trailer Pump allocated to Peel later transferred to Foxdale fire-post
1943-1946	FMN404	ATV with 35ft ladder and Trailer Pump allocated to Foxdale fire-post then to Kirk Michael and retained
1943-1945	FMN 267	ATV with 35ft ladder and Trailer Pump allocated to Rushen fire-post and retained

Information on the allocation of the ATVs is scant and they were moved from time to time but altogether the Island had fourteen but retained six after hostilities. Foxdale, Andreas and Sulby fire-posts remained active for some time after 1945. Five of the six eventually passed to the Civil Defence Commission but FMN 238 remained with the Fire Service stationed at Kirk Michael.

CIVIL DEFENCE COMMISSION

1953-1965	EMN 983	Commer Motor Tender (sold to the Manx Motor Museum)
1953- ?	FMN 259	Austin Auxiliary Towing Vehicle
1954-1967	EMN 106	Morris Motor Tender (loaned to King William's College)
1955-1967	GMN 882	Austin Major Pump
1955-1973	FMN 249	Austin Auxiliary Towing Vehicle
1955-1968	FMN 451	Austin Auxiliary Towing Vehicle
1956-1970	FMN 404	Austin Auxiliary Towing Vehicle
1967-1974	311 HMN	Bedford Green Goddess Major Pump
1968-1974	876 KMN	Bedford Green Goddess Major Pump(loaned to King William's College)
1968-1974	877 KMN	Bedford Green Goddess Major Pump
1968-1968	878 KMN	Bedford Green Goddess Major Pump (transferred to IOM Fire Service)

LOCAL GOVERNMENT BOARD
ISLE OF MAN FIRE SERVICE (Transferred in 1988 to the Department of Home Affairs and restyled)
ISLE OF MAN FIRE AND RESCUE SERVICE

DOUGLAS STATION (FOXTROT1)

1965-1968	NMN 50	Major Pump Escape – AEC/Merryweather
1965-1968	EMN 823	Fordson Motor Tender
1965-1971	5531 MN	Dennis F28 Pump Water Tender (allocated to Castletown 1971)
1965-1988	5724 MN	100ft Turntable Ladder – AEC/Merryweather
1965-1968	6002 MN	Commer Personnel Carrier
1968-1979	999 KMN	Land Rover Emergency Tender
1968-1988	999 CMN	Dennis F35 Pump Escape
1971-1992	999 WMN	Dennis F46A Pump Water Tender (Reg. No. reallocated)
1974-	311 HMN	Bedford Green Goddess Major Pump/ Command Vehicle
1975-2008	NMN 999	Hydraulic Platform – ERF/Simon re-chassised by Simon Engineering on Volvo FL617. Donated to Romania 2008
1977-1990	MAN 103T	Leyland Sherpa General-Purpose Van
1979-	HMN 999	Ford Emergency Tender (transferred to Civil Defence)
1980-1984	PMN 72	Dennis F8 Foam Tender/Hose Carrier Jetmaster trailer-mounted Foam Monitor
1980-1994	KMN 999	Dennis R61 Water Tender Ladder (Reg. No. reallocated)
1981-1990	442 LMN	4x4 Austin Gypsy Tender
1984-1988	5531 MN	Dennis F28 Foam Tender/Hose Carrier
1988-1998	MAN 999B	Foam Tender/Hose Carrier – Volvo FL10/Nova Scotia (Reg. No.

		reallocated)
1988-2004	MAN 999U	30 metre Turntable Ladder – Volvo FL6/Metz (Reg. No. reallocated)
1990-2008	BMN 999P	Water Tender Ladder – Volvo FL6//Fulton Wylie (donated to Romania)
1990-2004	BMN 999U	4x4 Water Tender Ladder – Mercedes 917AF/Carmichael (transferred to Airport Fire Service and then to Romania in 2008)
1992-2006	999 GMN	Rescue Vehicle Volvo FL614/Carmichael (Reg. No. reallocated)
1992-	999 WMN	WTL - Volvo FL 614/Carmichael
1999-	OMN 999	WTL Volvo FL614/Saxon Designated Spare Pump
2002-	999 UMN	Volvo FL6E/Saxon converted to Foam Carrier
2004-	BMN 999U	Bronto Skylift Aerial Ladder Platform – Volvo FLE18A/Angloco
2004-	XMN 999	WTL Volvo FLE15A/Saxon
2006-	999 GMN	Enhanced Rescue Vehicle - Volvo FL6H/Angloco
2007-	BMN 999L	Bronto Skylift Aerial Ladder Platform – Volvo FL6E/Angloco
2008-	NMN 999	WTL Volvo - FL280/Emergency One
1992-	HMN 695M	Volvo FL614 converted to General-Purpose Vehicle designated for crane use

APPLIANCES IN RESERVE

1989-	HMN 242V	6x6 Steyr/Pinzgauer/Saxon (DGLS PINZ 1)
1994-	WMN 999	Water Carrier-Mercedes1124AF/Carmichael
1990-	HMN 571L	6x6 Steyr/Pinzgauer/Saxon (DGLS PINZ 2)
2006-	HMN 608P	6x6 Pinzgauer/Saxon (DGLS PINZ 3)
	VMN 999	Personnel Carrier

FIRE SERVICE STAFF CARS AND GENERAL-PURPOSE VEHICLES (FOXTROT 8)

1987-	999 YMN	Vauxhall Cavalier
1988-	MAN 695G	Vauxhall Cavalier
1988-	BMN 743H	Ford Fiesta D
1988-	BMN 744H	Ford Fiesta D
1988-	BMN 745H	Ford Fiesta D
1989-	GMN 999	Rover Montego D
1989-	EMN 999	Astramax Van D
1990-2003	BMN 999W	Nissan 4x4 Van (Registration No. reallocated)
1990		Ford Sierra
2002-	GMN 141A	Ford Transit 350 – General-Purpose Van
2003-	BMN 999W	Ford Connect - General-Purpose Van
2003-	GMN 999D	Ford Transit 350 – Control Unit/Fire Safety Demo Vehicle
2003-	EMN 999	Ford Connect T230 General-Purpose Van
2006-	999NMN	Ford Focus Zetec Estate
2006-	HMN 695M	Volvo FL 614 formerly 999 GMN converted from rescue to General-Purpose.
2007-	999 LMN	Ford Transit 280S Van
2007-	HMN 299U	Ford Fiesta-style Climate Saloon
2007-	HMN 415Y	Ford Fiesta-style Climate Hatchback
2008-	999 YMN	Ford Mondeo Zetec Estate
2008-	GMN 999	Ford Mondeo Zetec Estate
2009-	FMN 999	Ford Focus Zetec Hatchback
2009-	JMN 999	Ford Focus Zetec Hatchback
2009-	999 EMN	Ford Focus Zetec Hatchback

LAXEY STATION (FOXTROT 2)

1960-1961	EMN 204	Major Pump – Merryweather (converted and allocated to Kirk Michael)
1960-1981	1817 MN	Pump Water Tender — Dennis F28
1981-1987	601 MN	Austin Gypsy Light Pump
1981-2006	OMN 999	Pump Water Tender — Dennis DS (donated to Malawi)
1987-2001	BMN 999A	4x4 Water Tender Ladder – Unimog/Fulton Wylie (sold)
1990-1998	999 LMN	4x4 Pump Water Tender – Land Rover
1998-	MAN 999B	Water Tender Ladder - MAN10.224F/Saxon
2001-	BMN 999A	6x6 WTL — Pinzgauer/Saxon
		Fire Fogger Trailer Pump

APPENDICES

RAMSEY STATION (FOXTROT 3)
1960-1962	FMN 284	Austin Auxiliary Towing Vehicle
1960-1079	TMN 424	Dennis F8 Pump Water Tender
1962-1967	DMN 890	Morris Escape Carrier
1967-1990	999 GMN	Dennis F38 Pump Escape
1978-1994	MAN 579X	Leyland Sherpa Emergency Tender
1979-1994	999 UMN	Dennis R61 Pump Water Tender (on disposal Registration No. reallocated)
1978-1990	FMN 999	4x4 Land Rover Pump Water Tender (transferred to reserve)
1990-2006	BMN 999R	6x6 Water Tender Ladder – Pinzgauer/Saxon, Registration No. reallocated (Re-registered HMN 571, now in reserve)
1994-2008	KMN 999	WTL Volvo FL614/Carmichael (donated to Romania Registration No. reallocated for second time)
1994-	HMN 999	6x6 Emergency Tender – Steyr/Pinzgauer/Bedwas
2006-	BMN 999R	6x6 WTL Pinzgauer 718K/Angloco
2008-	CMN 999D	WTL — Volvo FL280/Emergency One
2008-	KMN 999	WTL — Volvo FL280/Emergency One
		Fire Fogger Trailer Pump

KIRK MICHAEL STATION (FOXTROT 4)
1960-1961	FMN 238	Austin Auxiliary Towing Vehicle
1961-1963	EMN 204	Pump Water Tender - Merryweather
1963-1978	FMN 999	Pump Water Tender 4x4 Land Rover (transferred to Ramsey)
1968-1981	601 MN	4x4 Austin Gypsy Light Pump (transferred to Laxey)
1981-1996	NMN 999	4x4 Pump Water Tender – Land Rover/Pilcher Green (Registration No. reallocated)
1987-1995	PMN 999	Pump Water Tender — Dennis R61 (Registration No. reallocated)
1995-	PMN 999	4x4 WTL — Mercedes 1124AF/Carmichael
1996-	999 MMN	6x6 Steyr/Pinzgauer 718K/Saxon

PEEL STATION (FOXTROT 5)
1960-1975	PMN 71	Pump Water Tender - Dennis F8
1964-1989	EMN 999	Pump Water Tender - Land Rover
1975-1981	WMN 999	Pump Water Tender – ERF, converted to Pump Escape (No. reallocated)
1981- ?	WMN 999	Pump Escape - ERF
1989-2004	BMN 999L	6x6 Water Tender Ladder – Pinzgauer/Saxon (No. reallocated, now re-registered as HMN 242V and placed in reserve)
2004-2008	MAN 999U	4x4 Water Tender Ladder – MAN 12.225/Carmichael (donated to Romania after short spell with Airport Fire Service and Registration No. reallocated)
1992-2008	999 CMN	WTL - Volvo FL614/Carmichael (donated to Romania 2008 and Registration No. reallocated)
2004-	MAN 999U	WTL - MAN 12.225/Saxon
2008-	BMN 999P	WTL - Volvo FL280/Emergency One

RUSHEN STATION (FOXTROT 6)
1960-1962	DMN 890	Morris Escape Carrier (transferred to Ramsey)
1960-1968	601 MN	Austin Gypsy Light Pump (transferred to Kirk Michael)
1962-1983	5716 MN	Pump Escape — Dennis F28
1968-1990	999 LMN	4x4 Pump Water Tender (transferred to Laxey)
1983-2006	TMN 999	Dennis DS Pump Escape (donated to Malawi)
1990-1999	BMN 999A	4x4 Water Tender Ladder – Unimog/Fulton Wylie
1991-2006	CMN 999E	6x6 Pinzgauer/Saxon (re-registered HMN 608P in 2006, in reserve)
1999-	TMN 999	WTL — Volvo FL614/Saxon
2006-	CMN 999E	6x6 WTL – Pinzgauer 718K/Angloco

CASTLETOWN STATION (FOXTROT 7)
1960-1980	PMN 72	Pump Water Tender — Dennis F8 (transferred to Douglas)
1968-1977	878 KMN	Major Pump — Bedford Green Goddess (transferred to Douglas)
1977-1996	999 MMN	Pump Water Tender — ERF (on disposal Registration No. reallocated)

1980-1984	5531 MN	Pump Water Tender — Dennis F26 (transferred to Douglas)
1981-1990	441 LMN	4x4 Austin Gypsy Tender
1984-1999	999 PMN	Pump Water Ladder — Dennis DS (Registration No. reallocated)
1990-2009	BMN 999T	6x6 Water Tender Ladder — Pinzgauer/Mountain Range
1999-	999 PMN	WTL — Volvo FL614/Saxon
2008-	999 CMN	WTL — Volvo FLL280/Emergency One

RONALDSWAY AIRFIELD

1935-1940		12hp Morris Van Crash Tender

RONALDSWAY (HMS URLEY)

1940-1946	RN 40307	Austin Major Pump
1940-1946	RN 29686	Crash Tender – Fordson WOT1
1940-1946	RN 37214	Crossley Crash Tender

(These appliances were registered by the Ministry of Civil Aviation on 28th August 1946, and subsequently purchased by the Isle of Man Airports Board and registered in their ownership on 26th June 1951.)

Ronaldsway Fire Service has appeared under different styled logos as follows:

IOM AIRPORTS BOARD 1951 – 1986 as the ISLE OF MAN AIRPORTS BOARD AERODROME FIRE SERVICE and then RONALDSWAY AIRPORT FIRE SERVICE. In 1986 transferred from the Airports Board to the DEPARTMENT OF HIGHWAYS PORTS AND PROPERTIES (later to the DEPARTMENT OF TRANSPORT). A new logo was introduced and all appliances painted in yellow bearing the logo "The Airport Isle of Man".

1948-1951	MN 1233	Major Pump – Leyland (ex Douglas Corporation)
1951-1955	GMN 882	Major Pump – Austin (sold to Civil Defence Commission)
1951-1969	GMN 888	6x4 Crash Tender – Fordson WOT1
1951-1967	GMN 889	6x4 Crash Tender – Crossley
1955-1979	TMN 760	4x4 Foam Tender – Thornycroft/Pyrene
1959-1978	XMN 917	Foam Tender – Ford Thames
1959-1984	444 LMN	4x4 Austin Gypsy Personnel Rescue Vehicle
1960-1979	1819 MN	4x6 CO_2 Tender – Austin (sold to Thermo Skyships, Jurby)
1965-1990	621 BMN	Water Tender/Domestic – Bedford/Angus
1973-1996	MN 4359	6x6 Foam Tender – Thornycroft Nubian
1979-	B54 MAN	6x4 Rapid Intervention Vehicle – Range Rover/Carmichael
1979-2003	E526 MAN	4x4 Foam Tender – Jet Ranger 2000/Carmichael
1984-1987	MAN 381L	Personnel Rescue/IRB – Land Rover Series 2A
1987-1989	J119 MAN	Personnel Rescue/IRB – Toyota Hilux
1989-	BMN 36P	Personnel Rescue/IRB – Daihatsu Fourtrax
1990-2003	BMN 731W	4x4 Foam Tender – Simon Saro Defender (damaged in accident at airport)
1996-	DMN 293N	4x4 Foam Tender – Simon Protector Fire 3
2001-	FMN 263J	6x6 Foam Tender – Carmichael Cobra2 Fire 2
2004-	GMN 455X	6x6 Foam Tender – Carmichael Cobra2 Fire 1
		Land Rover Fire 5
		Angus Hose Trailer

From time to time when other vehicles have been away for refurbishment a loan Nubian has appeared on station to provide the necessary cover.

2008-2008	BMN 999U	Water Tender Ladder – Mercedes 917AF/Carmichael on loan from IOMF&RS (withdrawn and donated to Romania)
2008-	JMN 366E	Water Tender Ladder - Mercedes1120F/Carmichael on loan from IOMF&RS

APPENDICES

(v) LIST OF STATUTES

1777	High Baiiffs Act
1834	Douglas Waterworks Act
1856	Joint Stock Companies Act
1860	Douglas Town Act
1864	Douglas Town (Amendment) Act
1865	Ramsey Town Act
1874	Ramsey Town (Amendment) Act
1882	Douglas Town Act
1884	Peel Town Act
1884	Castletown Act
1885	Ramsey Town Act
1886	Local Government Act
1888	Local Government (Theatres) Act
1889	Local Government (Amendment) Act
1899	Douglas (West Baldwin) Water Act
1912	Local Government (Theatres) Amendment Act
1916	Local Government Consolidation Act
1922	Local Government Amendment Act
1939	Heath Burning Act
1940	Local Government (Fires) Act
1950	Building Byelaws Act
1950	Fire Escapes Act
1950	Local Government (Fire Services) Act
1952	Local Government (Fire Services) Act
1954	Local Government (Fire Services) Act
1974	Local Government (Fire Services) (Amendment) Act
1975	Fire Precautions Act
1975	Building Byelaws Act
1976	The Housing (Miscellaneous Provisions) Act
1976	Civil Aid Services (Planning) Act
1981	Local Government (Fire Services) Act
1981	Home Affairs Board Act
1984	Fire Services Act
1990	Fire Services (Amendment) Act
2003	Heath Burning Act

(vi) LIST OF REGULATIONS & MISCELLANEOUS ORDERS

1870	General Orders, Byelaws, Rules and Regulations
1923	Theatre Regulations
1938	Rushen Fire Protection Order
1942	Heath Burning Regulations
1950	Building Byelaws
1952	Fire Escape Regulations
1953	Fire Reinforcement Scheme
1959	Fire Authority Order
1960	Rushen Fire Authority Dissolution Order
1964	Fire Authority Order
1964	Fire Services Committee Order
1976	Building Byelaws
1976	Fire Precautions (Hotel and Boarding Houses) Order
1976	Fire Precautions (Application for Certificates) Regulations
1979	Housing (Flats) Regulations
1980	Fire Precautions (Residential Homes) Scheme
1980	Cinematograph (Safety) Regulations
1980	Cinematograph (Children) Regulations
1980	Fire Precautions (Cinemas) Order
1981	Cinematograph (Safety) (Amendment) Regulations
1996	Fire Precautions (Flats) Regulations

(vii) BIBLIOGRAPHY

The Minutes of Peel Town Commissioners
The Minutes of Douglas Town Council
The Proceedings of Tynwald
The Minutes of the War Committee of Tynwald
The Statutes of the Isle of Man
The Minutes of Laxey Village Commissioners
The Minutes of Ramsey Town Commissioners
The Minutes of Castletown Commissioners
The Minutes of Port Erin Village Commissioners
The Minutes of the Local Government Board
The Minutes of the Rushen Joint Fire Protection Board
The Annual Reports of the Boards of Tynwald
The Report of the Summerland Inquiry
The Report to the IOM Department of Agriculture, Fisheries and Forestry on the Bradda Head Fire
Manual of Firemanship (HM Stationery Office)
London's Fire Brigade (Jackson)
A History of Firefighting (Hughes)
Fire Fighting Vehicles (Warne)
ABC of Fire Engines (Rolfe)
Fire Engines and Fire Fighting (Burgess-Wise)
A History of Blackburn Fire Brigade (County Borough of Blackburn)
Inspection Report 2007 by HMFSI (Scotland)
The Manx Sun
The Mona's Herald
The Isle of Man Times

The Examiner
The Manks Mercury
The Isle of Man Courier
Isle of Man Newspapers
Manx Radio

(viii) GLOSSARY OF TERMS

ADO	Assistant Divisional Officer
AFS	Auxilliary Fire Service
ALP	Aerial Ladder Platform
ARP	Air Raid Precautions
ATV	Auxiliary Towing Vehicle
BA	Breathing Apparatus
BCF	Bromochlorodifluoromethane
bhp	brake horsepower
CAA	Civil Aviation Authority
CFO	Chief Fire officer
CFSO	Chief Fire Staff Officer
CO2	Carbon Dioxide
CV	Command Vehicle
DCFO	Deputy Chief Fire Officer
DCO	Deputy Chief Officer
DHPP	Department of Highways, Ports and Properties
DO	Divisional Officer
ERV	Enhanced Rescue Vehicle
ET	Emergency Tender
Ff	Firefighter
FPO	Fire Prevention Officer
ft	feet
FT	Foam Tender
gals	gallons
GP	General Purpose Vehicle
gpm	gallons per minute
HC	Hose Carrier
HMFSI(S)	Her Majesty's Fire Service Inspectorate (Scotland)
hp	horsepower
HP	Hydraulic Platform
IOMF&RS	Isle of Man Fire and Rescue Service
IOMFS	Isle of Man Fire Service
LFf	Leading Firefighter
LGB	Local Government Board
lpm	litres per minute
m	metres
MHK	Member of the House of Keys
MLC	Member of the Legislative Council
PE	Pump Escape
PDA	Predetermined Attendance
PWT	Pump Water Tender
RFSM	Rescue and Fire Services Manager
SAFO	Senior Airport Fire Officer
Sgt	Sergeant
StnO	Station Officer
SubO	Sub-Officer
Supt	Superintendent
TL	Turntable Ladder
WE	Wheeled Escape
WTL	Water Tender Ladder

The Sealink ferry *Earl Godwin* was on charter to Manx Line on their Douglas to Heysham route in the early part of 1981 and as the vessel was new to the Island the IOMF&RS arranged for a practice for personnel familiarization whist she was berthed at the Victoria Pier in Douglas. *(Author)*

All Island practice at Corlett's Flour Mill, Laxey - October 1962.